CURRICULUM DEVELOPMENT

CURRICULUM DEVELOPMENT

Arul Jothi
M.Sc., M.Ed.
Principal, Arcot Sri Mahalakshmi Women's Teacher Training Institute,
Villapakkam, Vellore Dist.-632521 T.N.

Dr. D.L. Balaji
B.Com., M.A., M.Phil., D.Lit.,
Correspondent, Arcot Sri Mahalakshmi Educational Institutions,
Villapakkam, Vellore Dist.-632521 T.N.

Pratiksha Jugran
Lecturer, Deptt. of Education,
Drona College of Management and Technical Education,
Dehradun

CENTRUM PRESS
NEW DELHI-110002 (INDIA)

CENTRUM PRESS
H.O.: 4360/4, Ansari Road, Daryaganj,
New Delhi-110 002 (India)
Ph.: 23278000, 23261597

B.O.: No. 1015, Ist Main Road, BSK IIIrd Stage
IIIrd Phase, IIIrd Block,
Bangalore - 560 085 (India)
Tel.: 080-41723429
Visit us at: www.centrumpress.com

Curriculum Development

First Edition, 2009

PRINTED IN INDIA

Printed at Balaji Offset, Delhi

Contents

Preface (*vii*)

UNIT-I : Concepts and Definitions **1**

Concept of Curriculum • Classification of Curriculum Concepts • Definitions—Curriculum and Syllabus • Relationship and Differences • Needs for Curriculum Development • Curriculum Determinants • National Aspirations & Needs • Culture, Social Change, Value System, Philosophical, Sociological and Psychological Foundations

UNIT-II : Types of Curriculum **43**

Curriculum Organisation—Educational Objectives and Curriculum Organisation • Subject Matter and Curriculum Organisation • ABC'S Curriculum Organisation • Learning & Curriculum Organisation • Types of Curricula—Subject Centered, Co-related, Fused, Core, Student-Centered—Their Relative Values and Weaknesses

UNIT-III : Curriculum Designing **86**

Assessing Needs • Formulating Objectives • Selection of Content • Organisation of Content • Selection of Learning Experiences • Organisation of Learning Experiences • Model of Curriculum Development—Ralph E. Taylor, D. K. Wheeler and Hilda Taba

UNIT-IV : Curriculum Transaction **129**

Strategies for Curriculum Transaction • Organisation of Instruction • Models of Teaching • Team Teaching • Individualizing the Curriculum • Distance Learning

Models • Resources for Curriculum Transaction—Computer and the Internet

UNIT-V : Evaluation of Curriculum **177**

The Curriculum Cycle—Evaluation as Comparing Objectives and Outcomes • Focus of Curricular Evaluation: Subject Content—Organisation and Mode of Transaction • Outcome of Curriculum Evaluation : Change/Refinement of Content, Organisation and Mode of Transaction

UNIT-VI : Models of Curriculum Evaluation **220**

Taylor's Model • Stane's Model • The CIPP Model • Goal-free Evaluation

Bibliography 256

Index 261

Preface

Curriculum Development can be defined as the systematic planning of what is taught and learned in schools as reflected in courses of study and school programs. These curricula are embodied in official documents (typically curriculum "guides" for teachers) and made mandatory by provincial and territorial departments of education.

The primary focus of a curriculum is on what is to be taught and when, leaving to the teaching profession decisions as to how this should be done. In practice, however, there is no clear distinction between curriculum content and methodology - how a topic is taught often determines what is taught. For this reason, and for others, there is need to distinguish the official or planned curriculum - the formally approved program of study - from the *de facto* or lived (sometimes called hidden) curriculum - the "lessons" that are actually learned.

Many attempts to change education by revising the authorized curriculum have not been successful - mandated innovations are not always implemented extensively or effectively in classrooms. In fact, because of widespread reliance on textbooks as a basic teaching resource, textbooks often constitute the *de facto* content of the curriculum, thus giving publishers a powerful role in curriculum development. A comprehensive, ongoing, cyclical process "to determine the needs of a group of learners; to develop aims or objectives for a program to address those needs; to determine an appropriate syllabus, course structure, teaching methods, and materials; and to carry out an evaluation of the language program that results from these processes". The curriculum development process should reflect needs analyses and ideologies about language, language teaching and language learning.

There are four factors which go to determine the development of curriculum. They are the students, teachers, the community and the subject matter. It is, therefore, necessary that all these four elements are actively associated with the process of curriculum development. This book aims to equip educators and curriculum-makers with a highly efficient and resourceful guide on all that entails an enriching educational experience through a wide-ranging, fulfilling educational curriculum. It provides the framework for building a curriculum which strives to incorporate the best of all aims of education, and endeavours to make students more complete human beings and achievers.

— ***Pratiksha Jugran***

UNIT-I

Concepts and Definitions

Concept of Curriculum

Introduction

A university should answer the needs of its belonging society. That affirmative seems an expense common place, for the fact of it being emptied along the practice of the planning of the education in Brazil. In spite of the profits, he/she has to be repeated for the truth level that contains. In the measure in that we thought about a reform curricular, this relationship between teaching and society should be protected. Actually, a proposal of curricular change stays besides the restricted extent of a course, because it doesn't quit being a change proposal, also, for the society.

A **curriculum** that assures the commitment and the necessary credit for the transformation of the current reality of the binomial inseparable: teaching and research plus extension, so that the success of the medical course of the Federal University of Alagoas (UFAL) can contribute, in a more appropriate way, with the improvement of health conditions and life styles of community. It turns the curricular **development** a complex process because it needs the involvement of all (academy, service and society).

The Construction Process

UFAL nominated a team to run the tasks of curricular reform. The commission began the collective construction of the new **curriculum** for the medicine course two years ago using, mainly, the technique of strategic planning and, involving about 40% of the faculty of the course, student union, teaching monitors, technicians of the General offices of Health of the State and Municipal district. The results of these activities were edited in a sequential and textual way, and introduced the academic community to subsidize a new stage of the construction. The text had the intention of answering questions as:

Why changing?

What is there to change?

How to change?

Is it possible to change?

Where is my place in the proposal?

What are objectives of our course?

What modules and contents do these objectives contemplate?

What is the manager's role in the conduction of this ***curriculum****?*

What administrative structures are planned?

What the necessary infrastructure?

What infrastructure is necessary?

What are the necessary partnerships?

The textual presentation format of the proposal didn't impact strongly as previously expected. One of the largest difficulties found by our reform commission is in the visualization, for the teachers, technician, students, managers and partners (services and community) of the role of each one of the elements, in the **development** of the **curriculum**, when this has been introduced in a sequential and textual way.

There are few publications, made available by the literature, that contemplate the academic community's inquietude in the construction of the **curriculum**, facing the difficulty of seeing inside its text and context. This hinders the suggestions and the planning of the necessary actions above to answer the mentioned questions.

There is urgency, therefore, in rethinking the drawing of presentation of the proposed new curricular. This is obtained through the use of tools that allow the actors of the process an including vision of the necessary interactions to the course and, consequently, it can aid the **development** of a larger meaning learning. Inside of the possibilities of a better vision of this **curriculum** the linkage appears with the technique of conceptual mapping. This technique is an approach created by Novak (1977), based on constructivist theory (Cognitive Psychology of Ausubel). He understands that the individual builds his knowledge and meanings starting from his predisposition to accomplish this construction.

Conceptual Map and Curricular Development

The significant learning theory (Ausubel et al, 1978), which has been influencing the education enormously, follows a constructivist model of the human cognitive processes. In matter, the principle of assimilation describes how the student acquires **concepts**, and how his cognitive structure is organized. The fundamental premise of Ausubel is illusory simple: "The significant learning happens when new information is acquired by a deliberate effort on the part of the apprentice in tying the new information with **concepts** or preexistent relevant propositions in his/her cognitive structure. (Ausubel et al., 1978)"

Ausubel (1978) proposes that the cognitive structure can be described as a series of organized **concepts** in a hierarchical way, which would represent the knowledge and a person's experiences then (Novak, 1977). In this context, the **concepts** would be defined as "registrations of events or objects" to which a "label or name" were associated (Ford et al, 1991). This is the origin of the representation of the knowledge through "Maps" of **concepts** and their connections.

The Conceptual Maps, developed by John Novak (Novak, 1977) are instruments used as a language for description and communication of **concepts** of the theory described by Ausubel previously. Such a structure involves from the including **concepts** to the least inclusive ones. They are used to aid the ordination and the nested sequencing of the teaching contents, in way to offer appropriate incentives to the student. The conceptual maps have been used a lot as an important teaching instrument, learning and evaluation in the area of the health, mainly for the nursing (Rooda, 1994; Irvine, 1995; Beitz, 1998; Weiss & Levison, 2000), but some authors have been suggesting that the conceptual maps are a powerful instrument in the **development** of a **curriculum** (Starr, 1990; Van Neste-Kenny et al, 1998; Harden, 2001; Prideaux, 2003). However, there are papers on this subject, which leads us to argue if the use of the technique of Conceptual Map can promote better visualization of the actors' role and their actions in the construction of a new **curriculum**.

This work aims to show how to elaborate a "curricular map" to represent the main **concepts** of the new proposal, allowing to the actors of the process a wide vision of the interactions and of the needs of changes demanded by a new **curriculum**.

Methodology

Formation: Initially, the commission of curricular, teachers' group that is captaining the construction of the new proposal, participated in a course of 8 hours about map construction. Hierarchization of the **Concepts**: After the training, the key **concepts** for the new proposal were nested and classified in:

"Changing propeller factors: Social, Institutional, Individual

"Objectives of the Medical Course of UFAL

"Steering principles of the reform curricular

"Necessary changes in the ***curriculum*** *to follow the new curricular guidelines*

"Presentation structure of the new general pedagogic proposal

Construction of the First Map Curricular: The first curricular map was built by members of the reform commission tends as document base the text edited with the results of the several workshops happened in 2002/2003. It intends to build new maps starting from the demands generated by the initial map that contemplates the general structure of the new **curriculum**. For larger visibility and socialization of the elaborated map, this was put on a cork board, attached on a wall. When visualizing the map it can be observed the **concepts** that were already treated, the gaps and demands still existent, as well as the necessary changing actions, the coherence and the interconnection among the defined principles.

Results

An important result of the construction of the map of the reform of our **curriculum** was the actors' active involvement in the identification of the steering principles, and of the changing needs in the **curriculum**. This way we can achieve the objectives of the medical course of UFAL. During the elaboration period the information were synthesized for the construction of the visual representation of the first map curricular contemplating the inquiries: Why changing? What for changing?

What are the objectives of the course of medicine of UFAL? What will be the steering principles of the new **curriculum**? What are the necessary changes? What strategies are necessary to render them? How much did the group already walk in this direction? What are the next steps? What type of curricular organization should be proposed to contemplate the social demands of the State, the new national guidelines for the medical course and the objectives of the course?

The necessary negotiations for the construction were developed naturally; because these **concepts** were discussed during the workshops previously happened.

Conclusion

For the reform team, teachers' group that have been participating actively of the elaboration of the new **curriculum**, the construction of the map appeared as a powerful tool in the visualization of the demands originated from of the curricular reform, in the identification of the relationship among the **concepts** and of the gaps still existent for the consolidation of the curricular proposal curricular.

Classification of Curriculum Concepts

The **Classification of Concepts in Consumer Education** was authored by Rosella Bannister and Charles Monsma in 1980 at Eastern Michigan University. Research was conducted at the National Institute for Consumer Education (Michigan Consumer Education Center) with funding provided by the United States Department of Education.

The **classification** has become an accepted framework, used by classroom teachers, programme planners and **curriculum** designers in the United States and other nations. A copy of the complete taxonomy is available from NICE, 207 Rackham Building, Eastern Michigan University, Ypsilanti, MI 48197.

Decision Making

Definition: The act or process of choosing.

Application to Consumer Education

The broad category of decision making, including both the act of choosing and the conditions of choice, serves as a foundation for the entire field of consumer education.

Consumer educators have long recognized that the decisions which consumers make are influenced by a wide range of factors. Two levels of influence can be identified: those which are personal to individuals and those which are a part of the broader external environment within which consumers live. While the personal factors, such as values, are often major elements in consumer education courses and textbooks, the external factors such as economic, political, and societal influences, are seldom covered thoroughly.

The influence which flows between the factors affecting consumer decisions and the actual decisions which consumers make is reciprocal; those decisions also have an impact upon the context in which future decisions will be made.

External Factors Affecting Consumer Decisions

Definition: Those elements in the outside environment of consumers which influence their choices; includes the economic, political, and social systems as well as ecological and technological influences.

Application to Consumer Education

Consumer educators should consider the economic, political, social, and physical environments of the marketplace, as well as technological influences on it. Whereas most consumer education programmes and materials focus on the individual level of values, decision-making and wise use of resources, the changing economic setting and a commitment to democratic processes demand an enlargement of the scope of consumer education. Consumer educators should examine public and private sector political and economic decisions which directly affect the marketplace and should educate the public about their ramifications. Students should learn how to evaluate the social and economic impact of their decisions. New technological realities must be recognized and anticipated.

The context of analysis for these problems must be global, recognizing the increasing interdependence of all nations and their peoples. Future possibilities as well as present realities must be considered when making individual and collective consumer decisions.

Many broad social and economic changes have been underemphasized in consumer education programmes and materials. If consumers are to deal realistically with the context of their decisions, these changes must be addressed.

Economic System

Definition : The organization or structure of the production, distribution, and consumption of goods and services in a society.

Application to Consumer Education

Consumer education focuses on the consumer decisions which result from interactions between consumers and producers in the economic system. This is why the discipline of economics has often been accepted as the dominant analytical contributor to consumer education. While not wishing to de-emphasize the importance of other external systems and influences on consumer decisions, some knowledge of the economic system within which consumer transactions take place is necessary to understanding both the causes and implications of consumer decisions. Many basic economic **concepts** are vital to effective consumer education.

Particularly as the economy changes, the effects of these changes must be anticipated and understood by consumer educators. If consumers are to cope with these changes, and especially if they hope to influence the operation of the economic system of which they are an integral part, a strong base of economic understanding is a necessity.

While the relationship between economics and consumer education is strong, it would be inaccurate to imply that either field subsumes the other. Parts of each field can best be seen as subsets of the other, each field having a different scope and focus, but with many areas of overlap between them. Listed below are those economic **concepts** which seem most directly related to consumer decisions, although a much longer elaboration would be possible if all areas of overlap were included.

Unemployment

***Inflation*:** Additional economic **concepts** which are closely related to important consumer education concerns include: Economic Concentration, Monetary Policy, Fiscal Policy, Productivity, Economic Growth, International Trade, Interdependence, Income Distribution.

Political System

Definition: The organization or structure of government and those forces which influence public policy in a society.

Application of Consumer Education

Most consumer education materials now recognize that much legislation has been passed which relates to the transactions made by consumers in areas such as credit and product safety. Less often recognized is the impact of public policy and political power relationships on the overall environment within which consumers operate. Government monetary and fiscal policies affect the overall state of the economy. The rigor of anti-monopoly policies or enforcement of competitive rules affects the price and availability of goods and services, and government itself has become a major supplier of the services which consumers receive.

While there has been a long term trend of tremendous growth of the public sector, the recent movement toward challenging taxation and regulation levels of government has attempted to swing the pendulum back in the other direction. Consumer educators must be conscious of the implications for consumers both of government action and the challenges to it. The costs and benefits to consumers of increasing or decreasing the governmental role must be carefully measured.

This is an important research perspective of consumer education, which has too often been neglected in favour of marketing studies related to buyer behavior and the effects of marketing strategies. Consumer perspectives must take their place along with aggregate economic effects and impact on business, as inputs to the public policy process.

Social System

Definition: The structure of relationships among human beings in a society.

Application to Consumer Education

Our consumer choices are affected by the roles we play, the status we hold or desire, and the cultural values or standard of living we seek to maintain. These elements of our social milieu are often reinforced and sometimes challenged through advertising, which attempts to turn socially attractive appeals into specific buying decisions. The values and goals of the society around us work, even when we are not conscious of their action, to influence consumer behavior. Not only does the operation of the social system affect individual behavior; it also provides a mechanism through which resources can be shared among individuals, groups, and nations.

Many of the changes presently occurring in the social structure have a direct impact on individual and collective consumer decisions. Changing sex roles, changes in the work force, variations in lifestyle, and the variety of demands emanating from a pluralistic culture — all these things affect the nature and quantity of goods and services which are used by consumers. Social pressures for or against change may create tensions which find their outlet in the way resources are earned or spent. While seldom given direct focus in consumer education materials, the impact of the social system rivals that of economic and political concerns in overall influence on consumer decisions.

Ecological Influence

Definition: The affect of factors in the physical or ecological environment on decisions made by consumers.

Application to Consumer Education

Throughout the decades of unrestrained economic and seemingly inexhaustable resources, consumer educators paid little attention to the interrelationship between the physical environment and individual consumer decisions. The question of possible restraints was one which related to personal values and resources rather than to aggregate availability of resources or societal needs Although various scenarios of the future are being put forward, ranging from total pessimism to complete optimism, all points of view now recognize the necessity to take into account ecological realities. Conservation, pollution, alternative sources of energy, new modes of transportation — these and other considerations related to the physical environment have become a part of consumer education as they affect a wide range of consumer decisions.

Technological Influence

Definition: The practical application of scientific or mechanical advances in ways which affect consumer decisions.

Application to Consumer Education

Numerous sources in the literature of many fields point to the increasing impact of technology on the lives of all people. Technological advances are an everyday part of consumer transactions at many levels. New consumer products such as transistorized calculators and in-home computers become available on a regular basis. New developments in the use of nuclear power or new medical techniques make additional services available to consumers and confront them with decisions about individual or collective use of these resources. New techniques for the carrying out of consumer transactions, such as electronic funds transfer and universal product code, must be mastered and evaluated by consumers in order to function effectively and exercise appropriate control measures in marketplace transactions. Consumers need to develop individual and collective competence in technical matters so that technology can retain its proper role as servant rather than master in the human decision-making process.

Personal Factors Affecting Consumer Decisions

Definition: Those elements related to the individual characteristics or backgrounds of consumers which influence their choices.

Application to Consumer Education

Consumer education courses and **curriculum** materials have often used the personal characteristics of individual consumers as a starting point, particularly questions of individual values and goals. The field must continue to emphasize this area, recognizing that the integration of societal factors with personal influences on behavior is a vital area of concern. Social changes in family and sex roles affect individual lifecycle patterns. Lifestyle possibilities may be affected by resource constraints on the entire society.

Individual values and needs should be assessed in terms of societal values and needs, and the goal setting process should be based on more than individual considerations. Gaps between individual goals and societal needs or conflicts between values may cause tensions which should be addressed by consumer education. Most consumer decisions will still be the result of individual factors affected by direct and personal concerns. It is the task of consumer education to aid consumers in understanding, integrating, and molding the full range of factors which affect their decisions.

Resources

Definition: The human and material assets which are used by consumers in implementing their decisions.

Application to Consumer Education

Consumers must be familiar with the wide range of resources available for their use. The personal wealth gained through employment or from other sources is most universally considered, but many kinds of resources, both individual and communal, can be substituted for financial resources. An individual has time, energy, and ability to contribute in obtaining goods or services, as parents do in cooperative day care centers. Public forms of entertainment, such as parks, can be substituted for private forms which may be more expensive. Wise use of available resources has always been and will continue to be a primary function of consumer education.

Lifecycle

Definition: A series of stages through which an individual or group passes during its lifetime.

Application to Consumer Education

The concept of lifecycle is an extremely useful one for consumer educators as it can provide a framework for discussing the changes in the lives of consumers which affect the kinds of decisions which must be made. Differences in age, source and level of income, and the composition of the household of which the consumer is a part will affect both the nature and the outcome of consumer choices. Consumers must understand and prepare for lifecycle changes, sometimes planned but often unexpected, which will occur to everyone. Consumer educators must be careful to keep lifecycle descriptions flexible and not assume that all consumers will follow one lifecycle pattern. Changes in the social structure make it apparent that many patterns of employment and household arrangements are widespread throughout the society.

Values and Goals

Definition: Values are the ideas and principles which an individual, group, or society consider correct, desirable, or important. Goals are those specific aims or objectives which reflect a set of values.

Definitions—Curriculum and Syllabus

The concept of curriculum can be perceived as a connective link between teacher and student, organized in such a way to achieve goals previously set by the teacher, the learning organization or by the curriculum specialists.

The above definition, of course, does not cover all the meanings of curriculum, especialy when we think of them in a variety of contexts and situations where different goals and objectives need to be persued.

Then, in some situations the curriculum is used to correctly diagnose learning problems and restore connections between the teacher and the learner, while in other situations it can be conceived as a framework that provides external settings for the learning process.

However, the definitions above do not translate all the aspects involving curriculum and its interaction with the teaching and learning community.

I advocate the definition of curriculum that suports a complex network of physical, social and intellectual conditions that shape and reinforce the behavior of individuals, and takes in consideration the individual's perceptions and interpretations of the environment in order to reinforce the learning objectives and to facilitate the evaluation procedures.

Considering this point of view, the process of decision-making in updating the curriculum will be supported by a platform of shared values, images and beliefs, that will be crutial in the organization process of the intended and planned learning.

The expressed, implied, and emergent dimensions of curriculum need to work together in order to provide the curriculum specialists with the unstated and unplanned activities, unintended learning occured in class, learner's perceptions of certain conditions, positive and negative effects on the learner, gaps between learners, uniqueness of individual learners, and so many other clues, in order to incorporate changes in the curriculum that will reduce failures.

Relationship and Differences

Many people still equate a curriculum with a syllabus. Syllabus, naturally, originates from the Greek (although there was some confusion in its usage due to early misprints). Basically it means a concise statement or table of the heads of a discourse, the contents of a treatise, the subjects of a series of lectures.

In the form that many of us will have been familiar with it is connected with courses leading to examinations-teachers talk of the syllabus associated with, say, the Cambridge Board French GSCE exam. What we can see in such documents is a series of headings with some additional notes which set out the areas that may be examined.

A syllabus will not generally indicate the relative importance of its topics or the order in which they are to be studied. In some cases as Curzon (1985) points out, those who compile a syllabus tend to follow the traditional textbook approach of an 'order of contents', or a pattern prescribed by a 'logical' approach to the subject, or consciously or unconsciously—a the shape of a university course in which they may have participated.

Thus, an approach to curriculum theory and practice which focuses on syllabus is only really concerned with content. Curriculum is a body of knowledge-content and/or subjects. Education in this sense, is the process by which these are transmitted or 'delivered' to students by the most effective methods that can be devised (Blenkin et al 1992: 23).

Where people still equate curriculum with a syllabus they are likely to limit their planning to a consideration of the content or the body of knowledge that they wish to transmit. 'It is also because this view of curriculum has been adopted that many teachers in primary schools', Kelly (1985: 7) claims, 'have regarded issues of curriculum as of no concern to them, since they have not regarded their task as being to transmit bodies of knowledge in this manner'.

Concepts & Relationships

Concepts of layers are our favorite things to think about and how it relates to God. The concept, an idea that keeps turning and growing and the layer, one over shadowing the other, bleeding downward and floating upward into adjacent layers, no doubt more than a small fascination on our part. We used to watch the maple leaves float quietly from the top of the tree, having disjointed themselves at the nubby root of the stem and flutter down to our level, taking with them a sparkle and shine and gleaming ray of sunlight filtering through the forest. Each leaf another adventure, while we lay with our back warm against the earth before the killing frosts came. We dreamt and spent our time contemplating nothing more than the leaf, the tree and the sun and who made such a beautiful thing for me to see.

Now we study other layers and relationships and enjoy everything we learn. We was recently fascinated with the luminescence of certain species of squid and jellyfish deep under the sea that talk to one another in pulsing light generated from their own bodies in a sightless world. This we learned from a television documentary, having rarely placed more than a big toe into the ocean and never having gone under except to swim! God sees in these same layers of light and sound and radiant warmth. Not pretending to know what he sees or how he manages it, we love to contemplate on the magnitude of what he has placed here and how it is organize.

How about the things we all learn from space exploration and telescopes that measure the thinnest layer of light? God is the universe, he created it and moved on to be a part of everything that remains in it. When we see the constellations and clusters and get the explanations of black holes and solar systems, what starts with physics and ends with the concepts so vast and complicated that only one God could have dreamt such a deep dream of life and promise and relationships so unique and intricate! Layers swirling and twirling and binding and tugging on each other matter most to me. The family unit, the church and spirit, lost love and sorrow, all necessary in our personal layers one with each other. We can perceive the variations of colour of a single leaf in the fall and see the ray of sunshine upon a baby's face. We learn and grow and sleep and dream about each other and about our concept of ourselves and God. What matters most is how we act in our beliefs, how we show our compassion for the people and creatures around us. If we share our dreams and count our blessings, we can be happy with God.

Take the time to contemplate the layers around us both in the physical world and the spiritual needs we have with each other. Doesn't God have a sure fixed vision of everything that is placed upon this earth? Can't he feel and hear our prayers and thanks even when we don't want the emotion to come out? He is deep inside our souls and in every living creature. He is the connection, the fusion, the stuff of life that binds us.

We like to think sometimes of templates, each of a different thing. We think of these templates as a score or count or picture of that item, having been extracted from the other things around it. These templates are each a slate of nature that God has created in an instant to see the status of the earth and the conditions we have maintained for ourselves. For instance, in our mind, we see the template for a physical item as electrical wires and the wooden poles to support them. Knowing God discerns the difference in the metal threads within the rubber wrapped wire and the wooden pole having been a living tree at one time. He knows in an instant the cure and temperature and grade of the rubber, he knows the exact count of wires used in the line and the age of the tree before it was felled for the project. He could look upon any landscape and extract a template or snapshot of just these wires and poles and the netted complications of their path and tell you in an instant if a single line were bare or broken, a pole off balance or tethered too tightly, leaning in an incorrect position.

A master planner and ultimate engineer, God has learned from every thought we have given him and the ones we try to hide. He knows and accepts all things.

The template grows a layer and, in our mind's eye, God has picked every leaf and taken stock of the level of chlorophyll left in the rare and striking colors of fall. Each leaf has started to emit the presence of the deeper shades of red, golden browns and rust, having been hidden for the summer thus far. He can name and change any one of the leaves, he moves the breezes to make them fall and takes the bugs to scour their surface and names them too! God takes stock of the land and knows the strength of every branch, the tiny turns of the roots underground and moisture left in the stems. He takes this snapshot along with others and the count of our lives and balances everything so perfectly.

He watches the child climb the low branches of an apple tree, sees the insects inside the fruit and watches the bird perch upon the topmost cluster of leaves.

He only knows what happiness the child will have and what tragedy in their lives will make them stronger. He knows and he sees. We can only dream and lie wanting for it never to end while all the time pursuing our deeper relationship with the masterful engineer who brought us all together on this green earth. We are waiting everyday to come closer to meeting our needs and the needs of others in the layers we perceive around us.

Let us enjoy the concepts of layers and take stock in our lives for God, improve what we can and give enough to others to bring happiness where shadows lie, a smile where there was none and food to the hungry.

Managing Differences in Relationships

Each one of us has our own way to cope with stress in our relationships. When couples disagree, the goal is to be able to listen and respond to each other so that you can work together to resolve the problem. At times, though, couples can get caught up in stress styles that aren't helpful.

For example, when one partner tends to avoid conflict and the other is more aggressive the relationship may become unbalanced. The quieter, conflict-avoidant partner will soon find that their needs are being neglected and will begin to feel dissatisfied while the more aggressive partner may not even suspect the depth of unhappiness that their partner is experiencing.

This is what happened to Jack and Mary. Mary was very comfortable asking Jack for what she needed in the relationship. In fact, because she grew up the oldest of three children, she sometimes felt entitled to insisting on having things her way. Jack sometimes wasn't sure what he needed and had trouble expressing what he wanted from Mary. In addition, Jack had learned growing up that his "job" in a relationship was to "take care" of his partner even at the expense of his own needs. As a result, when Jack finally realized that his needs weren't being considered, he was resentful and angry. Mary was surprised because she had assumed that the relationship was fine since Jack wasn't asking for anything and when he did occasionally ask he would quickly acquiesce to Mary.

Recognizing your own style of managing relationship stress and becoming empathetic toward your partner's style can help you as a couple approach each other with more open hearts. we have even offered a "money back guarantee" to couples that when they practice managing their stress styles, the relationship will improve.

The first step is identifying your own style. When you sense a disagreement in the air do you:

- Become aggressive, believing that the "best defense is a good offense"?
- Move quickly to a "win-lose" perspective?
- Blame your partner?
- Avoid the conflict at all costs?
- Agree with your partner to avoid conflict?
- Change the subject?

Using any one of these negative stress styles can quickly either escalate your conversation or end it prematurely, blocking any meaningful communication between you. The good news is that you are in charge of your own stress style. You can choose to respond to your partner instead of reacting. Next time you sense that you and your partner are heading into an old pattern of negative communication try these steps:

1. Remind yourself that you are in charge of your own stress style. Resolve to keep a respectful tone.

2. Be resilient in listening by focusing your energy on understanding what your partner is feeling. Ask your partner to share their concerns. You will have time to share your own concerns and feelings. Now is the time to listen deeply to your partner's thoughts.
3. When your partner feels that you have understood him/her then take your turn to share your feelings and concerns as well.

Listening, feeling understood and knowing that you care about each other's thoughts and feelings will build good will between you and help you to move onto solving the problem. Managing the negative stress style cycle is a good first step toward helping you feel that you and your partner are on the same team, not on opposing sides. When you can move on to solving the problem, your relationship wins.

Needs for Curriculum Development

After reviewing the procedures in this step, curriculum team members will understand how to conduct a needs assessment and use the results to formulate intended outcomes.

Curriculum development was described as the process of determining **who** will be taught **what** and **how.** The **needs assessment and analysis** step in curriculum development systematically focuses on learning about an issue or problem and the people who are directly effected by it. A needs assessment provides the information to determine outcomes (educational objectives) based on a factual foundation and learners needs. A needs assessment also provides baseline data to evaluate the achievement of intended outcomes. The goal is to have those who are most directly affected by issues and problems define them, isolate the contributing factors, and suggest solutions.

Wentling, (FAO, 1993) defines a problem (issue) as the gap between **desired behavior** (what should be known and/or done) and actual performance (behavior).

A NEED OR GAP IS:

DesiredPerformance	-	Actual	=	NEED
(What Should Be)	-	(What Is)	=	GAP

The needs assessment process identifies the nature and scope of the gap. An underlying principle is to "start with what people already know and build on what they already have." The first task then is to establish what the target audience knows, their attitudes about the issues and contributing factors, and their practices. Without this information, intended outcomes and content are unlikely to address the needs of the target audience.

This step is subdivided into two parts: (1) procedures for conducting a **needs assessment** and (2) **needs analysis.** The results of the assessment are used to state intended outcomes and form evaluation strategies. After reviewing the procedures in this step. curriculum team members will understand how to conduct a needs assessment and use the results to formulate intended outcomes.

Needs Assessment Procedures

Needs assessment procedures include surveys and interviews conducted with members of the targeted audience and members in their communities. Members of the curriculum design team should be directly involved with gathering data. It is helpful to have a team member experienced in survey design and evaluation.

Team involvement in the assessment process produces content and methods relevant to the needs of the target audience. Similarly, if members from the target audience and potential facilitators are involved, the curriculum will be meaningful and relevant.

KAP (*i.e.*, Knowledge, Attitudes, and Practices) is a needs assessment method developed by R. Adhikarya (FAO, 1994). It focuses on specific and critical elements of an issue and the knowledge, attitude, and practice levels of target audiences. The process gathers qualitative information about the target audience and the issues effecting them. The reasons for attitudes and practices are discussed through focus groups, interviews and surveys. Information provided by a KAP survey is useful to formulate intended outcomes, to select content, and to design methods to meet the needs of the targeted audience.

The KAP survey generates information for four major steps in the curriculum development process:

1. Members of the targeted audience are consulted and provide information regarding their needs in relation to a specific problem;
2. Intended outcomes can be stated to relate to the specific needs of the targeted audience;
3. Baseline data can be used in formative evaluations to test the appropriateness of content and methods; and
4. A summative evaluation can compare baseline data to the outcomes from implemented curriculum.

A needs assessment identifies the target audience and the knowledge, attitude, and practice gaps. A needs assessment is conducted in five basic steps:

1. Conduct focus group discussions with key informants (leaders in the community) and with target audience groups (*i.e.*, rural out-of-school youth). The goals are to identify the key audience and their characteristics (*i.e.*, the predetermined audience does not apply to all cases); identify major problems areas (*e.g.*, overpopulation issues); determine the causes of the problems; and generate possible solutions.

   Sample Population Education Questions:

   1. What do you feel are the major issues or problems confronting rural out-of-school youth?
   2. What are the causes of these problems?
   3. How do they relate to overpopulation issues?
   4. What gaps (the difference between desired performance and actual practice) do you think exist in population related knowledge, attitudes, and practices among rural out-of-school youth?
   5. What are some possible solutions?
   6. Are there other major areas of concern or problems?

2. Identify major topics related to rural out-of-school youth from focus group discussions.

A Sample of Population Education Issue Topics:

- *Agricultural Production:* Large family farms are divided equally among many children resulting in small farms with insufficient income to support a family.
- *Environment:* Forests art destroyed to provide additional land for agricultural production.

3. Develop a survey on the topics of concern generated that focus on target audience levels of knowledge, attitudes, and practices. The survey could be used in focus groups or in one-on-one interviews. Before you use the survey, test it to make sure the questions are valid (*i.e.*, they ask what they are intended to ask) and the responses are meaningful. For example, a common survey mistake is to ask more than one question in a question (*e.g.*, Do you know and practice eating balanced nutritional meals?). This makes no sense. What am I trying to find out? Do I want to know if you know what constitutes a balanced meal or if you eat balanced nutritional meals? Sample questions in each area (knowledge, attitudes, and practices) might include:

Sample KAP Population Education Survey Questions:

Knowledge Question:

o In planning for your future, what employment opportunities do you have in this community?

Attitude Question:

o What is your idea of the ideal family size?

What are the major reasons you would like that size family?

Practices Question:

o Do you use some method of family planning (contraception) ?

If yes, which method? Why or Why not?

4. Conduct additional focus groups and interviews with members of the target group and community leaders. It is important to train interviewers how to ask questions

and record responses. It is probably best to avoid pen and pencil surveys because the audience in our example is out-of-school youth. In cases where surveys are appropriate (*i.e.*, the target audience could adequately complete the survey), they provide a quick and relatively inexpensive way to get information about the characteristics of the audience (demographic data) and identify trends in issues. But surveys cannot probe deeper or ask additional questions as an interviewer might. The value in conducting focus groups and interviews is that the respondents will often mention issues and concerns omitted from survey questions. Remember the goal is to learn more about the target audience and the factors contributing to the issue or problem. Start with the end in mind. This information will be used to develop intended outcomes and to establish baseline data for a summative evaluation.

5. Tabulate the results of the survey and interviews. Look for the factors or causes for the problem in terms of Knowledge, Attitudes, and Practices. According to Wentling,

"There are three broad reasons why people don't behave as expected or desired:

Lack of:

- o Knowledge or skills;
- o Motivation;
- o Organization and Environment" (FAO, 1993).

If a reason for not following certain practices is organizational or environmental (including cultural and/or moral values), it would be inappropriate to develop curriculum materials to change behavior when education and training will not make a difference. For example, if an area is overpopulated and the dominant religious belief forbids the use of contraceptives, it is a misuse of resources to develop curriculum to teach about contraceptives and family planning techniques.

One can not expect the intended outcomes to occur (*i.e.*, to reduce population through the use of contraceptives) by educational programmes when the barrier is organizational policy. A correctly conducted needs assessment would identify such problems long before intended outcomes are formulated.

Another method to assess needs is the **Delphi** technique. A representative panel of experts or leaders in the community (including members of the target audience) are asked to list the factors or aspects of an issue (*e.g.*, overpopulation). A composite list is compiled from all the lists and each panel member votes on their top priority items.

The results are tabulated and panel members are asked to vote again on their top priorities. This process is repeated until the prioritized list is agreed upon by the panel members. The advantage of this technique is that many aspects of the issue are explored and a number of people have been involved in identi-fying and prioritizing aspects of the issue. It provides a prioritized list of factors involved in the issue from the perspective of a number of people (both community and experts).

Town or village meetings can be conducted to obtain input on major issues and problems within the community. A recorder or objective observer takes notes of the discussion to be analyzed later. The advantages of using this technique is its inclusiveness and community involvement through a public forum. The major disadvantage is that people who feel comfortable speaking in public and have strong opinions are heard while others who may be intimidated by numbers or by stronger opinions are not.

Curriculum Determinants

The curriculum determinants used in formulating the conceptual framework for this proposed programme are as follows: 1) The Learner, 2) Society and Culture (including organizational theory and leadership), 3) Knowledge (theories and structure), and 4) Theories, Research, and Practice in Curriculum and Instruction, and 5) Qualitative and quantitative research. The emphasis in this programme is on the use of the determinants in planning, implementing, and evaluating programmes in elementary/secondary schools. The programme is field-oriented and focuses upon providing graduates with expertise to provide creative leadership in a variety of settings. Students in the B. Ed. Programme are expected to complete professional internships in educational institutions prior to the completion of the degree. The internships are intended to allow students to apply concepts and principles of curriculum within institutional settings. The B. Ed. Programme fulfills the certification requirements for curriculum-instructional specialists at the doctoral level.

National Aspirations & Needs

A school's curriculum consists of everything that promotes learners' intellectual, personal, social and physical development. As well as lessons and extracurricular activities, it includes approaches to teaching, learning and assessment, the quality of relationships within school, and the values embodied in the way the school operates.

In partnership with practitioners and curriculum experts, a school should develop an approach to curriculum design based upon three key questions:

- what are we trying to achieve?
- how do we organise learning?
- how well are we achieving our aims?

A well-designed curriculum is built on a clear vision of what it is trying to achieve. It:

- has clear aims that reflect the national aims for education and learners' needs as individuals and citizens
- promotes the intellectual, personal, social and physical development of all learners
- establishes high expectations for all, extending horizons and raising aspirations
- identifies outcomes relating to knowledge, skills, and personal attitudes and attributes
- is underpinned by clear values.

Culture, Social Change, Value System, Philosophical, Sociological and Psychological Foundations

Cultural awareness:

- Before venturing on a global assignment, it is probably necessary to identify the cultural differences that may exist between one's home country and the country of business operation. Where the differences exist, one must decide whether and to what extent the home-country practices may be adapted to the foreign environment. Most of the times the differences are not very apparent or tangible. Certain aspects of a culture may be learned consciously (*e.g.* methods of greeting people), some other differences are learned subconsciously (*e.g.* methods of problem solving). The building of cultural awareness may not be an easy task, but once accomplished, it definitely helps a job done efficiently in a foreign environment.
- Discussions and reading about other cultures definitely helps build cultural awareness, but opinions presented must be carefully measured. Sometimes they may represent unwarranted stereotypes, an assessment of only a subgroup of a particular group of people, or a situation that has since undergone drastic changes. It is always a good idea to get varied viewpoints about the same culture.

Clustering cultures:

- Some countries may share many attributes that help mold their cultures (the modifiers may be language, religion, geographical location, etc.). Based on this data obtained from past cross-cultural studies, countries may be grouped by similarities in values and attitudes. Fewer differences may be expected when moving within a cluster than when moving from one cluster to another.

Determining the extent of global involvement:

- All enterprises operating globally need not have the same degree of cultural awareness. Figure 2 illustrates extent to which a company needs to understand global cultures at different levels of involvement. The further a company moves out from the sole role of doing domestic business, the more it needs to understand cultural differences. Moving outward on more than one axis simultaneously makes the need for building cultural awareness even more essential.

Social Change

Social change is a general term which refers to:

- change in social structure: the nature, the social institutions, the social behaviour or the social relations of a society, community of people, and so on.
- When behaviour pattern changes, in large numbers and is visible and sustained it results in a social change. Once there is a deviance from culturally inherited values, it may result in a rebellion against the established system, causing a change in the social order.
- any event or action that affects a group of individuals that have shared values or characteristics.
- acts of advocacy for the cause of changing society in a normative way (subjective).

The term is used in the study of history,sociology,economies, and politics, and includes topics such as the success or failure of different political systems, globalization, democratization, development and economic growth. The term can encompass concepts as broad as revolution and paradigm shift, to narrow changes such as a particular cause within small town government.

The concept of social change imply measurement of some characteristics of this group of individuals. While the term is usually applied to changes that are beneficial to society, it may result in negative side-effects or consequences that undermine or eliminate existing ways of life that are considered positive.

Social change is a topic in sociology and social work, but also involves political science, economics, history, anthropology, and many other social sciences.

Among many forms of creating social change are theater for social change, direct action, protesting, advocacy, community organizing, community practice, revolution, and political activism.

Models of Change

- *Hegelian:* The classic Hegelian dialectic model of change is based on the interaction of opposing forces. Starting from a point of momentary stasis, Thesis countered by Antithesis first yields conflict but subsequently results in a new Synthesis.
- *Kuhnian:* Thomas Kuhn in *The Structure of Scientific Revolutions* argued with respect to the Copernican Revolution that people are unlikey to jettison an unworkable paradigm, despite many indications that the paradigm is not functioning properly, until a better paradigm can be presented.
- *Heraclitan:* The Greek philosopher Heraclitus used the metaphor of a river to speak of change thus, "On those stepping into rivers staying the same other and other waters flow." (DK22B12) What Heraclitus seems to be suggesting here, later interpretations notwithstanding, is that in order for the river to remain the river change must constantly be taking place. Thus one may think of the Heraclitan model as parallel to that of a living organism, which, in order to remain alive must constantly be changing.
- *Daoist:* The Chinese philosophical work Dao De Jing, I.8 and II.78 uses the metaphor of water as the ideal agent of change. Water, though soft and yielding, will eventually wear away stone. Change in this model is to be natural, harmonius, and steady, though imperceptible.

Value System

A **value system** is a set of consistent ethic values (more specifically the personal and cultural values) and measures used for the purpose of ethical or ideological integrity. A well defined *value system* is a moral code.

Personal and Communal

One or more people can hold a value system. Likewise, a value system can apply to either one person or many.

- A **personal** value system is held by and applied to one individual only.
- A **communal** or **cultural** value system is held by and applied to a community/group/society. Some communal value systems are reflected in the form of legal codes or law.

Corporate Value Systems

Fred Wenstøp and Arild Myrmel have proposed a structure for corporate value systems that consists of three value categories. These are considered complementary and juxtaposed on the same level if illustrated graphically on for instance an organization's web page. The first value category is Core Values, which prescribe the attitude and character of an organization, and are often found in sections on Code of conduct on its web page. The philosophical antecedents of these values are Virtue ethics, which is often attributed to Aristotle. Protected Values are protected through rules, standards and certifications. They are often concerned with areas such as health, environment and safety. The third category, Created Values, is the values that stakeholders, including the shareholders expect in return for their contributions to the firm. These values are subject to trade-off by decision-makers or bargaining processes. This process is explained further in Stakeholder theory.

Consistency

As a member of a society, group or community, an individual can hold both a personal value system and a communal value system at the same time. In this case, the two value systems (one personal and one communal) are **externally consistent** provided they bear no contradictions or situational exceptions between them. A value system in its own right is **internally consistent** when:

- its values *do not contradict* each other and
- its exceptions are

  - o *abstract* enough to be used in all situations and
  - o *consistently* applied.

Conversely, a value system by itself is **internally inconsistent** if:

- its values *contradict* each other and
- its exceptions are
  - o highly *situational* and
  - o *inconsistently* applied.

One of the conditions required for consistency in any (?) logical (*i.e.* value-conserving) system of statements is their transitivity. (See: *Intransitivity. Occurrences.*) Without it, it might eventually happen that *A* is of greater value than *B*, yet *B* is of greater value than *A*—which is a case of mutual contradiction in certain statements that determine values of *A* and *B* in the system. Value system consistency can be a value in and of itself.

Value Exceptions

Abstract exceptions serve to reinforce the ranking of values. Their definitions are generalized enough to be relevant to any and all situations. **Situational** exceptions, on the other hand, are ad hoc and pertain only to specific situations. The presence of a type of exception determines one of two more kinds of value systems:

- An **idealized** value system is a listing of values that lacks exceptions. It is, therefore, absolute and can be codified as a strict set of proscriptions on behavior. Those who hold to their idealized value system and claim no exceptions (other than the default) are called *absolutists*.
- A **realized** value system contains exceptions to resolve contradictions between values in practical circumstances. This type is what people tend to use in daily life.

The difference between these two types of systems can be seen when people state that they hold one value system yet in practice deviate from it, thus holding a different value system.

For example, a religion lists an absolute set of values while the practice of that religion may include exceptions.

Implicit exceptions bring about a third type of value system called a **formal** value system. Whether idealized or realized, this type contains an implicit exception associated with each value: "as long as no higher-priority value is violated". For instance, a person might feel that lying is wrong. Since preserving a life is probably more highly valued than adhering to the principle that lying is wrong, lying to save someone's life is acceptable. Perhaps too simplistic in practice, such a hierarchical structure may warrant explicit exceptions.

A Model System

First appearing in Runaround, *part of a science fiction novel by Isaac Asimov, this value system exemplifies a* realized *value system that is* internally consistent *and has* abstract *exceptions*

Three Laws of Robotics:

1. A robot may not harm a human being, or, through inaction, allow a human being to come to harm.
2. A robot must obey the orders given to it by human beings, except where such orders would conflict with the First Law.
3. A robot must protect its own existence, as long as such protection does not conflict with the First or Second Law.

Conflict

Although sharing a set of common values, like hockey is better than baseball or ice cream is better than fruit, two different parties might not rank those values equally. Also, two parties might disagree as to certain actions are right or wrong, both in theory and in practice, and find themselves in an ideological or physical conflict. Ethonomics, the discipline of rigorously examining and comparing value systems, enables us to understand politics and motivations more fully in order to resolve conflicts.

An example conflict would be a value system based on individualism pitted against a value system based on collectivism. A rational value system organized to resolve the conflict between two such value systems might take the form below. Note that added exceptions can become recursive and often convoluted.

- Individuals may act freely unless their actions harm others or interfere with others' freedom or with functions of society that individuals need, provided those functions do not themselves interfere with these proscribed individual rights and were agreed to by a majority of the individuals.
- A society (or more specifically the system of order that enables the workings of a society) exists for the purpose of benefiting the lives of the individuals who are members of that society. The functions of a society in providing such benefits would be those agreed to by the majority of individuals in the society.
- A society may require contributions from its members in order for them to benefit from the services provided by the society. The failure of individuals to make such required contributions could be considered a reason to deny those benefits to them, although a society could elect to consider hardship situations in determining how much should be contributed.
- A society may restrict behavior of individuals who are members of the society only for the purpose of performing its designated functions agreed to by the majority of individuals in the society, only insofar as they violate the aforementioned values. This means that a society may abrogate the rights of any of its members who fails to uphold the aforementioned values.

Philosophical Foundations of Scientific Ethics

A philosophical foundation, like an architectural one, provides an underpinning for a larger structure. Its bricks and cinder blocks are basic concepts and assumptions that support a system of beliefs and practices. The support provided by a philosophical foundation is logical and conceptual, not physical: a foundation justifies the structure it supports. If we view scientific ethics as a system of rules, concepts, beliefs, and practices, then its foundation consists of basic principles and concepts that justify this system. My aim in this chapter is to explore the basic principles and concepts that underlie scientific ethics. I will argue that scientific ethics is founded both on concerns and goals internal to science and on societal norms. This two-tiered foundation supports six basic principles of research as well as other ethical principles that apply to science. I will also develop some policy implications based on this philosophical analysis.

Ethics: A System of Moral Rules

In approaching the topic of scientific ethics, it will be useful to first make a few remarks about ethics. A simple definition of ethics (or morality) might be as follows:

Ethics is a system of public, general rules for guiding human conduct (Gert, 1988).

The rules are general in that they are supposed to apply to all people at all times and they are public in that they are not secret codes or practices. The rules guide conduct by forbidding, permitting, or requiring particular actions in various circumstances (Fox and DeMarco, 1990). Philosophers have offered a wide variety of moral theories to justify moral rules, ranging from utilitarianism to Kantianism to social contract theory (Fox and DeMarco, 1990). Although there are some fundamental differences among various ethical theories, most of them support (or can be interpreted to support) roughly the same set of general principles (Beauchamp and Childress, 1979). Some of these are as follows:

The nonmalificence principle: Do not act in ways that cause needless injury or harm to others.

The beneficence principle: Act in ways that promote the welfare of other people.

The principle of autonomy: rational individuals should be permitted to be self-determining.

The formal principle of justice: treat equals equally and unequals unequally.

Material principles of justice: Punish on the basis of desert. Distribute goods on the basis of need, merit, social contribution, effort, or equality.

From these general principles we can derive a variety of other rules, such as:

> *Do not kill, Do not torture or maim, Do not steal, Do not lie or deceive, Keep your promises, Don't cheat, Be fair, Do not deny people freedom, Respect privacy.*

And of course many more principles can be derived from the ones mentioned here.

Sometimes the same action will be supported by a variety of rules but sometimes the rules will endorse different actions, *i.e.* they will conflict. For instance, if someone asks you if you like the new dish they have prepared and you do not, you may have to choose between telling them the truth and (possibly) hurting their feelings. You have a duty not to lie but you also have a duty not to harm, and in this case you cannot fulfill both duties at one. You must resolve this conflict. Since moral rules can conflict, they are what W.D. Ross (1930) refers to as prima facie rules (or duties). When conflicts arise, we have to decide which rule(s) to follow. Some of the ethical theories discussed by philosophers may recommend different ways to settle these conflicts, even though they agree on most of the basic rules.

Justifying Moral Rules: Reflective Equilibrium

Earlier I said that a philosophical foundation provides a justification. So what's the foundation of moral rules (or theories)? This is not an easy question to answer, in part, because our method of justifying moral rules, as many writers have noted, does not resemble our method of justifying scientific theories or hypotheses (Harman, 1977). Science uses the experimental method to justify its claims: in science we can conduct tests and experiments that provide empirical evidence or data to justify theories or hypotheses. But we cannot use this method in ethics.

Since the experimental method cannot be used in ethics, many writers have urged that we use the method of reflective equilibrium to justify ethical principles and theories (Rawls, 1971). According to this method, we use our considered (*i.e.* unbiased, reflective) judgments (or intuitions) about what is (or would be) right or wrong, good or bad in particular situations as a data base.

We can then propose theories and principles intended to provide a coherent account of these judgments. The reflective part of the method comes in when we use these principles and theories to revise our original data, and modify our principles in light of the revised database, and so forth and so on. Reflective equilibrium is an ideal state in which we have carried out this process to the point where we are no longer revising our database or principles.

Although this method is accepted by many ethicists, some have objected to it on the grounds that it leads (or could lead) to moral relativism (Gert, 1988). It could be the case that two different societies reach equilibrium points characterized by radically different principles and databases. Hence, what is "right" or "wrong" would vary from society to society. Of course, other writers might use its relativistic implications as a reason for accepting the method (Herskovits, 1972). Although I have no intention of entering this thorny debate here, I'll return to the relativism problem later in the context of scientific ethics.

Scientific Ethics

The general ethical code discussed above can be applied to many different practical contexts, such as law, medicine, sports, business, personal relationships, and of course, science. When the general code is applied to a particular area of human life, the resulting code is an institutional code. Institutional codes are not simply miniature versions of the general ethical code, otherwise they would be superfluous. An institutional code differs from a general ethical code in that it reflects the practical concerns and goals of members of a community, discipline, or profession. For instance, medicine is chiefly concerned with promoting the health of patients and safeguarding their welfare

(Beauchamp and Childress, 1979). If a conflict arises between telling the truth and preventing harm, many physicians will decide to lie. In medicine, at least, truth is sometimes sacrificed for health (Beauchamp and Childress, 1979). Although institutional codes are sometimes represented by explicitly formulated professional or communal codes, such as the Hippocratic Oath or a university's code of conduct, they cannot be identified with these explicitly formulated codes. The reason for this is that people may accept parts of an institutional code that are not found in explicitly formulated codes and people may pay little heed to many of the rules that are explicitly formulated (Gibbard, 1990). We can now arrive at a definition of scientific ethics:

Scientific ethics is an institutional code of conduct that reflects the chief concerns and goals of science.

In this definition, 'conduct' refers to all aspects of scientific activity, including experimentation, testing, education, data analysis, data storage, data sharing, peer review, government funding, the staffing of research teams, etc.... It does not include conduct that does not have a direct bearing on science. 'Science' refers to academic science, not military or business science. Although academic science, military science, and business science share some common principles, they have different goals and concerns. These different goals and concerns give rise to different ethics.

In the military, national security is the primary goal, and secrecy is essential to achieving this aim. Secrecy is also important in business science in order to promote its main goal, the maximization of profit. There has been much debate among philosophers about the aims of academic science, but clearly two of its chief concerns include the search for explanatory knowledge and true beliefs about the world (NAS, 1989). Since ethical rules in science should promote these goals, several of science's most important principles emerge. My list is not original, since some of these principles have been identified by other authors, including Jacob Bronowski (1956), Nicholas Rescher (1965), Sanford Lakoff (1980), David Hull (1988), and the National Academy of Science's Panel on Scientific

Responsibility and the Conduct of Research (1992). However, my compilation provides a useful synthesis:

Definition of Sociology

i. *Sociology:* Sociology (in the sense in which this highly ambiguous word is used here) is a science which attempts to understand social action through a causal explanation of its course and effects. "Action" is the human behavior to which the acting individual (or individuals) attaches a subjective **meaning**. Action in this sense may be either external or internal behavior, failure or refrain. Action is "social" if the acting individual takes account of the behavior of **others** and is thereby oriented in its course.

ii. *Meaning:* "Meaning" may be of two kinds. The term may refer first to the subjective meaning of the factual or historical case of a particular actor, or to the average or approximate subjective meaning attributable to a mass of actors; or secondly to the subjective **meaning** of conceptually constructed **pure type** of **thought** action. In no case does it refer to an objectively "correct" meaning or one which is "true" in some metaphysical sense. This distinguishes the empirical sciences of action, such as sociology and history, from the normative disciplines, such as jurisprudence, logic, ethics, and esthetics, which seek the "correct" and "valid" meanings of the objects.

iii. *Action:* The line between meaningful action and merely reactive behavior to which no subjective meaning is attached, cannot be sharply drawn empirically. A very considerable part of all sociologically relevant action, especially purely traditional action, is marginal between the two. In the case of many psycho-physical processes, meaningful, *i.e.* understandable, action is not to be found at all; in others it is observable only by the expert psychologist. Many mystical experiences which cannot be adequately communicated in words are, for a person who is unfamiliar to such experiences, not fully understandable. On the other hand, the ability to perform the same kind of action is not a necessary prerequisite to understanding; "one need not to be Caesar in order to understand Caesar." The full "imaginary experience" of the same kind of action is helpful for the clarity of understanding, but not an necessary condition for meaningful interpretation. Understandable and non-understandable components of a process are often intermingled and bound up together.

iv. *Interpretation:* All interpretation of meaning, like all scientific works, strives for "clarity." The clarity of interpretation can be either rational (logical or mathematical) or empathic (emotionally or artistically appreciative) character. Rational clarity is attained by **intellectually** clear and consistent understanding of its meaning-context of action. Empathic clarity is attained by empathic participation to imaginary experience of **emotional-**context of action. The highest degree of rational understanding, *i.e.*, intellectually immediate and clear comprehension, is attained in cases involving the meanings of logically or mathematically related propositions. We have a perfectly clear understanding of what it means when somebody employs the proposition 2 x 2 = 4 or the Pythagorean theorem in reasoning or argument, or when someone "correctly" carries out a logical train of reasoning according to our accustomed modes of thinking. In the same way we also understand what a person is doing when he or she tries to achieve certain ends by choosing appropriate "means" on the basis of the valid type of "experienced-situation" that is "familiar" to us. Such an interpretation of rationally end-oriented action has, for the understanding of the selected **means**, the highest degree of clarity. With a lower degree of clarity, which is, however, adequate for most purposes of explanation, we are able to understand "errors," including "confusion of problems" of the sort that we ourselves are liable to, or the origin of which we can detect by empathic participation.

On the other hand, many ultimate "ends" or "values" toward which human action may be oriented, often **cannot** be understood completely, though sometimes we are able to grasp them intellectually. The more radically they differ from our own ultimate values, however, the more difficult it is for us to make them understandable by imaginary **participation** in them. In this case, depending upon the circumstances, either we must be content with a purely **intellectual** interpretation of such values, or when even that fails, sometimes we must simply accept them as given facts. Then we can try to understand the action motivated by them on the basis of whatever opportunities for approximate emotional and intellectual interpretation seem to be available at different points in its course. These difficulties apply, for instance, for people not susceptible to the relevant values, to many virtuous acts of religious and charitable zeal; also certain kinds of extreme rationalistic fanaticism of the type involved in some forms of the ideology of the "human rights" are in a similar position for people who totally repudiate such values. The more we ourselves are susceptible to them, the more readily can we emotionally participate in such reactions as anxiety, anger, ambition, envy, jealousy, love, enthusiasm, pride, vengefulness, loyalty, devotion, and appetites of all sorts, and thereby understand the irrational conduct which grows out of them. Such conduct is "irrational," that is, from the point of view of the rational pursuit of a given end. Even when such emotions are completely unexperienced to the observer, he or she can still have a significant degree of empathic understanding of their meaning and can interpret intellectually their effects on the course of action and the selection of means.

v. *Type-Construction:* For the purposes of **type-**construction it is convenient to treat all irrational, affectually influenced elements of action as factors of "deviation" from a conceptually pure type of rational action. For example a "panic" on the stock exchange can be most conveniently analyzed by attempting to determine first what the course of action would have been if it **had not** been influenced by irrational affects; it is then possible to introduce the irrational components as accounting for the observed deviations from this hypothetical course. Similarly, in analyzing a political or military campaign it is convenient to determine in the first place what **would** have been a rational course, given the ends of the participants and adequate knowledge of all the circumstances. Only in this way is it possible to assess the causal significance of irrational factors as accounting for the deviations from this type. The construction of a purely end-rational action as a **type** ("ideal type") serves for the clarity of understanding and interpretation. By comparison with this it is possible to understand the ways in which actual action is influenced by irrational factors of all sorts, such as affects and errors, in that they account for the "deviation" from the purely rational behavior which would be expected to take place.

vi. *Rationalistic Method:* **In so far** and only in these reasons of methodological convenience, is the method of "understanding" sociology "rationalistic." This procedure should not be understood as a "rationalistic preconception" of sociology, but only as a methodological means. It certainly does not involve a belief in the actual predominance of rational elements in human life. For, on the question of how far in reality the **direct** action is or is not conditioned by the rational end-expectation, nothing whatever can be said. That there is, however, a danger of rationalistic interpretations where they are out of place naturally cannot be denied. All experience unfortunately confirms the existence of this danger.

Social and Psychological Foundations

The outcomes that follow address social and **psychological foundations** of education. In constructing the outcomes, indicators, and assessments proposed here, material from the following documents was incorporated:

- NCATE Programme Standards for Elementary Teacher Preparation
- ACEI Elementary Education Programme Standards
- Council of Learned Societies in Education-Standards for Academic and Professional Instruction in **Foundations** in Education, Educational Studies, and Educational Policy Studies
- Maryland Essential Dimensions of Teaching

Knowledge, skills, and dispositions that are **foundations** of the profession of teaching are infused throughout the documents named above. NCATE standards are the organizing framework, and ACEI Programme standards are the outcomes. The indicators, assessment types, and sample assessment tasks have been constructed to be foundational.

In constructing the material contained here, the following assumptions were made:

1. Knowledge and understanding of ALL **concepts** related to the **foundations** of teaching must be introduced during the first two years of a four-year programme leading to teacher certification. Though in many cases students= ability to work with these **concepts** will be rudimentary, it is incumbent on faculty to introduce foundation material early and to provide opportunities for students to demonstrate proficiency before they enter formal candidacy for teacher certification. The level of knowledge and understanding required and the demand for application of that knowledge and understanding will distinguish pre-professional from professional courses.
2. Many knowledge bases and foundational skills are prerequisites for competent demonstration of the knowledge and understanding identified as foundational

to the profession of teaching. While these prerequisites will be fulfilled in students= general education curricula, teacher educators shall demonstrate to the education community and to the public that prerequisite performance standards are met by persons recommended for candidacy for teacher education programmes.

3. Knowledge and understanding foundational to the profession of teaching will be addressed in students= general education curricula and appropriate introductory teacher education courses. Teacher education programmes may find a variety of academic and experiential configurations that convey and test the outcomes delineated here.
4. Though many modes of instruction are possible, one is essential. Teacher candidates must be given early, sequential exposure to the practice of teaching. Fieldwork shall begin as early as involvement in education courses begins and will be an ongoing and progressively demanding part of aspiring teachers= course of study.

UNIT-II

Types of Curriculum

Curriculum Organisation—Educational Objectives and Curriculum Organisation

1national Curricular Framework

The national curricular framework for elementary and secondary education is envisaged in the context of the National System of Education as elaborated earlier. The basic features and the main thrusts of the curricular framework are as follows:

(i) Emphasis on the development of human resources for the realisation of the national goals of development.

(ii) Broad-based general education to all learners at the elementary (primary and upper primary) secondary stages.

(iii) A common scheme of studies for elementary and secondary stages.

(iv) The common core components comprising the following:

The history of India's freedom movement;

The constitutional obligations; Content essential to nurture national identity;

India's common cultural heritage; Egalitarianism, democracy, and secularism;

Equality of the sexes;

Protection of the environment;

Removal of social barriers;

Observance of the small family norm;and Inculcation of the scientific temper.

(v) Emphasis on defining Minimum Learning Outcomes (MLOs) for each area of learning at all stages of education.

(vi) Provision for flexibility in terms of selection of content/ components and learning experiences which would facilitate the attainment of minimum learning outcomes laid down for each stage of school education.

(vii) Emphasis on child-centred and activity-based processes rather than the teacher-centred approach during the transaction of curriculum.

(viii) Recasting of the examination system and introduction of continuous and comprehensive evaluation that incorporates both scholastic and non-scholastic aspects of education spread over the total span of instructional time.

(ix) Establishment of an appropriate machinery, such as a National Testing Service (NTS) for the selection, and the development of norms of comparable competence across the nation.

(x) Applicability of the curriculum to all learners, irrespective of their modes/channels of learning in order to ensure comparability of attainment and to facilitate horizontal and vertical mobility of the learners.

(xi) Provision of essential facilities for effective transaction of curriculum in all schools/non-formal learning centres.

Minimum Levels of Learning

In order to bring about a broad commonality in the standards of education throughout the country, emphasis has been laid on the introduction of the norms of minimum levels of learning for each stage of school education indicated in terms of minimum learning outcomes to be attained by all the pupils in respect of each curricular area at each stage of school education. The minimum learning outcomes for each curricular area will have to be specified keeping in view the research findings regarding the mental ability of pupils at different stages of their development and the academic and physical resources that could be made available in the school for effective transaction of the curriculum.

The emphasis on defining the Minimum Levels of Learning highlights the importance of the integrative nature of learning-evaluation. Put differently, learning (development) and evaluation (assessment) have been construed as two inseparable aspects of the same phenomenon. It is futile to evaluate the progress of the learners towards the stated objectives unless It is ensured that conscious efforts have been made to provide adequate and appropriate learning experiences for growth and development. Thus a major shift from evaluation (passing judgement) to learning (development in terms of desired objectives) has been advocated.

While emphasis has been laid on the introduction of the norms of minimum levels of learning and adoption of a common scheme of studies at different stages of school education, flexibilty is envisaged in the selection of comer it and learning experiences as well as in the selection of strategy for curriculum transaction in order to make leaning more relevant to the needs and environmental contexts of the pupils and to allow scope for initiatives and experimentation on the part of the teacher, the school and the local educational authorities. A high degree of flexibility and local initiatives are envisaged in designing and introducing remedial and enrichment programmes and materials not only by the State educational authorities but also by the individual schools and teachers to cater to the needs to slow and fast learners studying in the same class/grade in a school. However, the scope for flexibility in the methodology and approach to transaction of curriculum is not expected to be used for introducing differential courses or similar measures which would accentuate desparities in standards of education in different parts of the country.

Common Core Components

While the rationale underlying the school curriculum of a country reflects its socio-cultural and political ethos, its faithful transaction reflects the genius of its people. The search for national identity has been on since the resistence to colonisation of the country began. This search has not ended yet.

As a matter of fact it is more acutely felt now than ever before. Therefore it is but natural that there is a strong plea for centering the curricular efforts for promotion of national integration and social fusion and cultivation of values as enshrined in the Constitution. Thus an important aspect of the common core components is the emphasis on instilling a nationally shared perception and values and creation of an ethos and value system in which a common Indian identity could be strengthened.

The ways and means have to be found out to introduce the common core components at all levels of school education. Some suggestions are offered to initiate action on the subject.

After the minimum learning outcomes and related general content are identified for each area of learning and for each grade, further scrutiny may be made to explore the possibility of infusing the specific core component with the theme.

Where such natural infusion is not possible, an attempt can be made to select new content for each of the ten components to be added as topics/units to each relevant subject. One can envisage cyclic development of a new course of study pertaining to each of the components. For example, a set of courses on the history of India's struggle for freedom can be developed for grades I to X, independent of other subjects.

On the other hand, it is also possible to integrate such content appropriately in the regular subjects included in the present scheme of studies.

An eclectic organisation is possible by, way of integrating clusters of components such as social science components or science components or moral value components and designing syllabi for different grades.

At the primary stage, core components could be integrated with language and environmental studies so as to make them a medium to develop appreciation of culture and perception of the individual, social and national identity through activities, songs, stories, reading material, plays, skits, etc.

At the upper primary stage, both infusion and unit approach could be adopted.

At the secondary stage, the elements of civics, economics and sociology may be identified in an integrated manner. In addition to the common core components, the integrated course could cover the content which would reflect the contribution of India in the field of science, astronomy, metallurgy, medicine, creative arts, etc. in the ancient, medieval and contemporary periods. The core components could be made more interesting through visuals and biographical notes of scientists and eminent Indians in different fields. However, while introducing the core components, it is necessary to ensure that the depth and coverage of information is kept at the appropriate level and does not increase the total information load beyond the existing level in different subjects. This could be done by reducing the content in some of the existing subject areas and properly blending the core components in the total scheme of studies as far as possible.

Formulation of Objectives

In curriculum organisation, formulation of objectives has a significant place because of the fundamental role they play in determining the content, strategies and evaluation as components of curriculum cycle. While identifying objectives, it is necessary to proceed towards various degrees of specificity, from very general objectives of curriculum, through somewhat specific objectives for each stage of education, to precisely stated specific objectives of each subject area in the form of expected learning outcomes indicating what exact behaviour would a learner be able to demonstrate after the curriculum transaction.

Thus, the curriculum organisers are required at the outset to indicate overall objectives of curriculum which would coincide with the overall aim of school education. It is necessary to further formulate carefully the stage-wise objectives keeping in view the developmental characteristics and level associated with different stages of education. Each subject area would have its own specific objectives clearly defined in terms of behavioural outcomes. Put differently, efforts should be directed at the achievement of a particular set of objectives for which specific learning experiences are provided under a particular subject area. However, it should not be forgotten that human learning makes one unified whole and that separate subject areas have been created only for the sake of convenience.

For education to help our country to express and promote its unique socio-cultural identity, to meet the challenges of the times and to develop appropriately its human resources, the objectives will have to be formulated with utmost care keeping in view the national priorities and values enshrined in our constitution, socioeconomic and cultural considerations, position of physical resources, global inter-relationships, pedagogical concerns and nature and level of learners. Needless to mention, objectives related to Common Core Components should be given a central place.

General Objectives of Education

School curriculum, on the whole, should aim at enabling the learners to acquire knowledge, develop concepts, and inculcate skills, attitudes, values and habits conducive to the all-round development of their personality and commensurate with the social, cultural, economic and environmental realities at national and international levels.

School curriculum should, therefore, help to promote development in the learner of:

Language abilities and communication skills needed for social living and further learning;

Competencies that facilitate mathematical operations and their applications in day-to-day life and learning;

Knowledge, attitudes and habits necessary for keeping physically fit and strong in conformity with normal developmental pattern;

A proper understanding about the role and importance of sex in human life, and healthy attitude towards sex and members of opposite sex;

Qualities that make a man socially effective and happy in various social settings such as friendliness, coopera-

tiveness, compassion, self-descipline, self-criticism, self-control, humour, courage, love for social justice, self-control, etc.;

Moral and character values such as honesty, truthfulness, dependability, courtesy, fearlessness, compassion, etc.

Pre-vocational / vocational skills, willingness to work hard, entrepreneurship and dignity of manual work necessary for increased productivity and job satisfaction;

Ability to appreciate and discover beauty in various life situations and integrate it into one's own personality,

Understanding of the environment and its limited resources and the need for conservation of natural resources and energy;

Appreciation of various consequences of large families and over population and need of checking population growth;

Understanding of the diverse cultural and social systems of people living in different parts of the country and the country's composite cultural heritage;

Appreciation for the need of a balanced synthesis between the change-oriented technologies and the continuity of country's cultural heritage;

Knowledge of national symbols and desire and determination to uphold the ideals of national identity and unity;

Capability of appreciating and tolerating differences and diversities of various sons and the capacity to choose between alternative value systems;

An awareness of the inherent equality of all and need of global fraternity with a strong commitment to humane values and to social justice;

Scientific temper characterised by spirit of inquiry, courage to question and objectivity leading to elimination of obscurantism, superstition and fatalism;

Knowledge of scientific methods of inquiry and its use in solving problems;

Appreciation of sacrifices and contributions made by the freedom fighters and social workers in the country's freedom struggle and social regeneration, and readiness to follow their ideals;

Appreciation of and readiness to practice in life the national goals of socialism, secularism, democracy and non-violence.

Divergent and independent thinking and ability to discover new relationships and combinations;

Qualities and characteristics necessary for self-learning and for life-long learning leading to creation of a learning society

Objectives at Various Levels of Education

The emphasis on the 'child-centred approach' to education necessarily implies that objectives of education to be achieved at a particular stage/class level should be determined carefully, keeping in view the norms of development-physical, mental, social, emotional and moral of children of relevant age group. Exact expected learning outcomes related to each objective for a particular class should be precisely worked out.

Most of the objectives indicated above will continue through various classes. However, the level of achievement with regard to a particular objective will be rising from one class to another class in a spiral fashion. Thus there will be a sort of learning continuum so far as targets of achievement with regard to a particular objectives are concerned and it will reach its terminal point at a particular class level depending on the nature of the concerned objectives.

Characteristics of a Learner

At the pre-primary stage, a child is at the pre-operational stage in terms of his mental processes. At this stage, the child's thinking remains pre-logical and is greatly influenced by perception and sensory experience. Intuitive thought begins at this stage and he/she can distinguish between different appearances of the same objects. However, there is no fully developed conceptualization of objects.

As compared to the kind of thought that involves true logical operations, intuitive thinking is rigid and irreversible. A child at pre-primary stage finds difficulty in putting sticks of different lengths together to form a series from shortest to longest. But he/she finds no difficulty in putting them in pairs and indicating which one of them is shorter. The difficulty arises in making a longer series. The same difficulty arises with respect to space.

The child enters the primary stage with the mental processes largely in the concrete operational stage. During this stage the child begins to think logically about the real world but is very much tied to concrete situations. There occur operations both of the logical and the arithmetical kind and also in the regions of space and time. These operations, however, are still carried out only on objects involving concrete situations. He/she still finds difficulty in generalising from one situation to another. But the intuitive structures, which have been more or less rigid and irreversible during the pre-operational stage, gradually lead to processes of higher thinking.

At the upper primary stage, the learner gradually moves on to the formal operational stage which starts from the age of about 12 onwards and goes on through adolescence. At this stage he/she will gradually be able to think logically in terms of all the hypothetical situations relevant to a particular problem. The operations previously performed only on what is closely related to concrete experiences can now be applied to propositions, either verbal or numerical. At earlier stages, formal logic and mathematical deductions have been difficult for the learner. At the stage of formal operations, he/she will be able to think logically and perform mathematical deductions.

Since the intellectual development varies from age to age, it is essential that the curriculum is designed in consonance with these stages. New ideas and knowledge should be presented at a level consistent with the child's stage of mental development.

Taxonomy of Educational Objectives

The **Taxonomy of Educational Objectives**, often called **Bloom's Taxonomy**, is a classification of the different objectives that educators set for students (learning objectives). The taxonomy was proposed in 1956 by Benjamin Bloom, an educational psychologist at the University of Chicago. Bloom's Taxonomy divides educational objectives into three "domains:" Affective, Psychomotor, and Cognitive. Like other taxonomies, Bloom's is hierarchical; meaning that learning at the higher levels is dependent on having attained prerequisite knowledge and skills at lower levels (Orlich, et al. 2004). A goal of Bloom's Taxonomy is to motivate educators to focus on all three domains, creating a more holistic form of education.

Most references to the Bloom's Taxonomy only notice the Cognitive domain. There is also a so far less referred, revised version of the Taxonomy, published in 2001 under the name of "A Taxonomy for Learning, Teaching, and Assessing."

Affective

Skills in the **affective domain** describe the way people react emotionally and their ability to feel another living thing's pain or joy. Affective objectives typically target the awareness and growth in attitudes, emotion, and feelings. There are five levels in the affective domain moving through the lowest order processes to the highest:

Receiving

The lowest level; the student passively pays attention. Without this level no learning can occur.

Responding

The student actively participates in the learning process, not only attends to a stimulus; the student also reacts in some way.

Valuing

The student attaches a value to an object, phenomenon, or piece of information.

Organizing

The student can put together different values, information, and ideas and accommodate them within his/her own schema; comparing, relating and elaborating on what has been learned.

Characterizing

The student holds a particular value or belief that now exerts influence on his/her behaviour so that it becomes a characteristic.

Psychomotor

Skills in the **psychomotor domain** describe the ability to physically manipulate a tool or instrument like a hand or a hammer. Psychomotor objectives usually focus on change and/ or development in behavior and/or skills.

Bloom and his colleagues never created subcategories for skills in the psychomotor domain, but since then other educators have created their own psychomotor taxonomies.

Cognitive

Skills in the **cognitive domain** revolve around knowledge, comprehension, and "thinking through" a particular topic. Traditional education tends to emphasize the skills in this domain, particularly the lower-order objectives.

There are six levels in the taxonomy, moving through the lowest order processes to the highest:

Knowledge

Exhibit memory of previously-learned materials by recalling facts, terms, basic concepts and answers

- Knowledge of specifics-terminology, specific facts
- Knowledge of ways and means of dealing with specifics-conventions, trends and sequences, classifications and categories, criteria, methodology
- Knowledge of the universals and abstractions in a field-principles and generalizations, theories and structures

Questions Like: What are the health benefits of eating apples?

Comprehension

Demonstrative understanding of facts and ideas by organizing, comparing, translating, interpreting, giving descriptions, and stating main ideas:

- Translation
- Interpretation
- Extrapolation

Questions Like: Compare the health benefits of eating apples vs. oranges.

Application

Using new knowledge. Solve problems to new situations by applying acquired knowledge, facts, techniques and rules in a different way

Questions Like: Which kinds of apples are best for baking a pie, and why?

Analysis

Examine and break information into parts by identifying motives or causes. Make inferences and find evidence to support generalizations

- Analysis of elements
- Analysis of relationships
- Analysis of organizational principles

Questions Like: List four ways of serving foods made with apples and explain which ones have the highest health benefits. Provide references to support your statements.

Synthesis

Compile information together in a different way by combining elements in a new pattern or proposing alternative solutions

- Production of a unique communication
- Production of a plan, or proposed set of operations
- Derivation of a set of abstract relations

Questions Like: Convert an "unhealthy" recipe for apple pie to a "healthy" recipe by replacing your choice of ingredients. Explain the health benefits of using the ingredients you chose vs. the original ones.

Evaluation

Present and defend opinions by making judgments about information, validity of ideas or quality of work based on a set of criteria

- Judgments in terms of internal evidence
- Judgments in terms of external criteria

Questions Like: Do you feel that serving apple pie for an after school snack for children is healthy? Why or why not?

Some critiques of Bloom's Taxonomy's (cognitive domain) admit the existence of these six categories, but question the existence of a sequential, hierarchical link. Also the revised edition of Bloom's taxonomy has moved Synthesis in higher order than Evaluation. Some consider the three lowest levels as hierarchically ordered, but the three higher levels as parallel. Others say that it is sometimes better to move to Application before introducing concepts. This thinking would seem to relate to the method of problem-based learning.

Curriculum Organisation

A well-designed curriculum is organised to achieve its aims. It:

- helps every learner to make progress, building on their experiences both within and outside of school
- is based on a clear and shared understanding of how learners learn
- recognises the dynamic interplay between content, pedagogy and assessment
- provides a coherent and relevant set of learning experiences, both in and out of lesson time
- provides for the full range of capabilities and aspirations
- uses expertise from outside the teaching staff to enrich learning
- uses time flexibly to meet learning needs
- provides opportunities for learners to experience the benefits of different learning approaches, including learning through subject disciplines, thematic

approaches, areas of study of their own choice and problem identification

- provides opportunities for learners to learn on their own, in a team, in a large group and with virtual collaborators
- provides opportunities for learners to learn in a range of places and to benefit from resources in the local community
- includes global, national, local and personal dimensions
- reflects and makes use of current technology
- meets statutory requirements.

The curriculum includes 48 courses units (UV) (24 per year, approximately 800 contact hours) including 32 UV (16 per year) are specific to this pre-strand. In relation to the objectives previously described, the specific curriculum includes theorotical and applied courses (lectures, seminars, practicals, tutored project...) in the following scientific areas:

1. Mathematics (general grounding in mathematics, differential equations, integrals, Fourier series, statistics and probability, optimisation...),
2. Informatics (algorithms and programming, architecture of operating systems, logical systems, networks...),
3. Physics (electromagnetism, waves and propagation, nanophysics, materials...),
4. Numerical and computer analysis (linear and non linear systems, simple differential equations and partial differential equations programming in C, introduction to Matlab,...),
5. electronics and automatic control (analog and numerical electronics, signal measurement and treatment, linear systems, control...),
6. Telecommunications (systems, components, information theory...),

After three core semesters, students can choose further courses in the fourth semester in:

1. Mathematics (numerical modelling, functional analysis, mechanics...). This choice leads to specializing as engineers in Mathematics and Modeling engineering,
2. Software and material computer science (computer structure and functioning, date structures, C language and networks,...). This choice leads to specializing in Computer engineering,
3. Networks and Telecommunications (data structure, assembly language, Internet...). This choice leads to specializing in Networks and Telecommunications engineering.

During the four pre-strand semesters, students will be working on projects, meeting professionals (specific week), visiting factories, attending lectures. The aim is for them to discover the industrial context in which they will be working as engineers. An industrial placement, after the fourth semester, contributes to their understanding of the industrial world.

Besides courses specific to the MIC pre-strand, Human Sciences are part of the curriculum (4 or 5 UV). Students develop skills in social interaction, oral and written expression in French, in English and in another language (Communication, English L1, L2 and Sports). At the end of the last semester, students'level in English is assessed by a TOEIC, with a required minimum score of 750.

A general economics and company management course (1 UV per year) helps engineering students grasp the economic context in which they will be working as engineers.

Every year, 1 UV corresponds to the Individualised professional Project (PPI). Students study a variety of aspects of engineers'work and benefit from individual coaching to define their professional project in keeping with their own ability and ambition

Finally, 2 UV (elective modules) correspond to courses which are chosen by the students outside their scientific field of their pre-strand. These can be scientific or non scientific. They can also choose to work on a community of humanitarian project.

Subject Matter and Curriculum Organisation

Definition: Subject matter is what something is about.

In artwork, the subject matter would be what the artist has chosen to paint, draw or sculpt. In patent law, the subject matter would be the technical content of a patent or patent application found in the description, claims and drawings.

In other words, subject matter is what the inventor has choosen to invent, and in a patent application the inventor must reveal the subject matter (invention) in a way dictated by law.

Examples

Example 1: The specification must conclude with a claim particularly pointing out and distinctly claiming the subject matter which the applicant regards as his invention or discovery.

Example 2: The distinction between patentable and unpatentable subject matter continues to be a topic of debate among software developers, academics, lawyers, and USPTO examiners.

Example 3: The patented subject matter, and additional subject matter still pending in the US and foreign patent offices, includes claims to methods and devices for delivering medicinal substances to the interior of cells in various body tissues.

Curriculum Organisation

The new secondary curriculum offers schools a real opportunity to innovate, building on existing good practice.

To make the most of the opportunities offered by the new secondary curriculum, schools will need to reflect on their current curriculum.

- What are its strengths and what needs to be developed?
- How well does it meet the wider aims of the curriculum?
- Does it reflect local contexts and meet the needs, interests and aspirations of all learners?
- How might you develop your curriculum to improve motivation and engagement and raise standards?

- Are there assumptions about how you use time, resources and approaches to planning that could helpfully be challenged or improved?

The activities in this section are designed to support thinking and discussion. The schools that piloted these materials found them useful in providing an evaluation of the strengths of their existing curriculum, and in identifying priorities for future development.

To help schools implement and develop the new curriculum, a programme of support is available for headteachers, curriculum planners and subject leaders.

ABC'S Curriculum Organisation

The Institute began by recruiting 18 accomplished practitioners to serve on the Core Faculty. Their initial training period was on process consultation. The training was a combination of presentations, reflection (both within the group and in journals), and role plays, facilitated by specialists, consultants, and scholars from Michigan State University, The University of Michigan, Alliance members, and other organizations, in a number of relevant topic areas. The training was self-directed and sustained over a three month period. It was modeled on the best practices of adult learning style – a framework endorsed by the National Staff Development Council.

With the help of expert university scholars, the Core Faculty further refined the curriculum for the next wave of 75 coaching candidates who would be selected and trained. In addition to its original base in research and effective practice, the curriculum now incorporates needs identified by focus groups conducted with principals of high priority schools. Within teams, the Core Faculty identified and prioritized all the topics that were covered in their training, and how they would be covered in the training for the next group of coaching candidates.

The Institute then recruited and selected 75 coaching candidates according to high standards of knowledge, skills, dispositions and experience. The Core Faculty implemented the curriculum in an iterative process of day-long sessions, practice, and reflection-on-practice, which allowed the coaches' learning to be enriched and reinforced by dialogue with colleagues and the Core Faculty.

Coaching candidates also have access to a password-protected online environment where they are able to review over 300 articles, Web sites, books, and other resources, and to communicate among themselves using email and threaded discussions.

Learning & Curriculum Organisation

The **Learning Curriculum** is a comprehensive learning plan that focuses on individual and organizational advancement. This plan is for all library staff to develop the skills needed to become members of teams and to improve the way we operate as an organization. The Learning Curriculum is comprised of ten components which in turn include a number of modules. The learning plan covers approximately 150 contact hours.

Components of the Learning Curriculum:

- Introduction: Development of the Organization
- Defining Customer Service
- Measurement, Evaluation and Continuous Improvement for Planning and Decision-Making
- Development of Self, Teams and Workgroups
- Exploring Leadership and Followership
- Individual Improvement
- Computer Skills
- Library Basic Skills
- Leadership Development
- Train-the-Trainer

Introduction: Development of the Organization

1. *Principles and Practices of the Learning Organization*
   Participants will be introduced to the five disciplines of the learning organization (Systems Thinking, Shared Visioning, Mental Models, Personal Mastery and Team Learning) and will explore how these apply to the UM

Libraries. Participants will also examine how learning occurs in organizations today. By considering real work scenarios, they will identify ways to apply principles and practices in their own work.

Length: Six hours

2. *Shared Visioning: The UM Libraries as a Learning Organization*

   In this module, staff will help create a shared vision of the UM Libraries' future. A chief focus of the process will be to think and plan from the perspective of primary users —faculty and students.

   Length: Three hours

3. *Learning to Thrive in an Ever-Changing Workplace*

   This module will cover the change process in organizations, strategies for dealing with extensive change and managing one self effectively. Participants will complete an inventory that is designed to promote greater understanding of personal change style.

   Length: Three hours

4. *Creating a Workplace in Which Diversity is Valued*

   Building on the results of the Libraries' Culture and Diversity Audit 2000, this workshop examines the larger organizational context to establish the importance of valuing diversity in the workplace. Participants will learn how to effectively create a work environment where serving diverse groups of internal and external customers is key and individual differences are respected. In the workshop, the dimensions of diversity are explored and participants work together to clarify a vision for respecting, managing and leading diversity within the Libraries.

   Length: Six hours

5. *Working and Learning Together*

   Communication and dialogue are key elements of working and learning together. This module will focus on fostering collaboration and supporting one another in an environment of change. Participants will learn tools for effective dialogue. The importance of workshops, meetings and other types of learning events will be discussed. This module follows-up on the Learning to Thrive in an Ever-Changing Workplace.

Length: Three hours

Defining Customer Service

1. *The UM Libraries' Customer Service Philosophy*

   What does quality service mean in the UM Libraries? The value of shaping effective customer service and the role staff plays in the delivery of service will be presented in this module. The importance of good measures for evaluating the quality of service such as LIBQUAL+ will be discussed.

   Length: Three hours

2. *Working with Each Other: The Internal Customer Relationship*

   Participants will engage in an in-depth look at the internal customers-who they are and how they work together. Key skills for developing effective interpersonal relationships will be practiced.

   Length: Three hours

3. *Learning From Each Other: Achieving Service Excellence in Dealing With External Customers*

   External customer service requires the ability to listen to customer queries and negotiate for a successful outcome. These skills in addition to the skills useful in dealing with difficult behaviors and resolving conflicts will be discussed and practiced.

   Length: Four hours

Measurement, Evaluation, and Continuous Improvement for Planning and Decision-Making

1. *Creating a Culture of Assessment*

   This module will investigate the main forces influencing current library goals and work environments and how these forces demand the adoption of new attitudes and thinking and support for structures integral to assessment and evaluation. Participants will practice customer-focused data gathering, and integrating assessment into organizational systems and work activities.

Length: Six hours

2. *The Basics of Measurement and Evaluation*

   Participants will examine the systems thinking approach to evaluation. This workshop will define the purposes of evaluation, provide tools and techniques to design the optimum evaluation strategy, and compare and select the most effective and efficient data-collection methods. Standards and guidelines for achieving results will be explored.

   Length: Six hours

3. *Measuring and Evaluating Series:*
   - Programmes and Services
   - Projects and Work Processes
   - Team Performance

   A series of hands-on workshops where participants will learn how to apply the tools and techniques of measurement and evaluation to a programme, service, project, team performance or work process. In each workshop, participants will identify a specific case and will follow the steps to: design an evaluation strategy, establish an effective data-collection method, set benchmarks, determine reporting mechanisms, define results, and recognize important steps to take upon completion of the process.

   Length: Three hours each

4. *Grant Proposal Writing*

   What makes a good proposal? Good proposals stem from good concepts and must be written in sufficient detail to allow reviewers to understand the following: what the project hopes to accomplish, if the project personnel have the necessary expertise to accomplish the goals and objectives, the potential of the project and its cost effectiveness, and the evaluation and dissemination plans. Participants will learn what to do before they write the proposal, and understand the steps in writing the proposal, the review process, and other details that can make a difference. Discussion will include the grant award process and what to do if the proposal is not funded

Length: Three hours

5. *Evaluating Individual Performance*

   Participants will review the Performance Review and Development process and understand their role in it. They will also learn to write clear, goal-oriented performance objectives. Staff and faculty evaluation measures will be discussed.

   Length: Two hours

Development of Self, Teams and Workgroups

1. *Becoming a Self-Managing Team*

   This module will focus on understanding the development of a self-managing team and the roles and responsibilities of team leaders and members. Discussion of the stages of team development will be included. Helping teams get their work done through a better understanding of group dynamics will round out the session.

   Length: Six hours

2. *Communication in Groups and Teams*

   How to conduct skillful discussion and dialogue to ensure effective group work will be covered. Participants will practice their interpersonal communication skills and techniques for managing conflict and disagreement.

   Length: Six hours

3. *Facilitation Skills*

   Participants will learn basic skills and tools to assist in the management of group process. The role and responsibilities of the facilitator in managing group dynamics will be discussed. Helping groups and teams get results through tools such as brainstorming, multi-voting, nominal group technique and force field analysis will be included in this module.

Length: Six hours

4. *Decision-Making and Consensus Building*

   This module will cover different decision-making processes and when to use them in group work. Participants will practice tools for divergent and convergent thinking and building consensus.

   Length: Three and one half hours

5. *Making Meetings Work: Skills and Techniques*

   What makes a meeting effective? There are a number of roles that people play and techniques they can use that will result in better meetings. This module will also include defining consensus and tools for reaching it.

   Length: Three hours

6. *Tapping Creativity: Tools for Problem Solving and Decision Making*

   Participants will explore creativity and how to effectively tap into it for problem solving and decision making. An understanding of how to nurture creativity and what can block it will be discussed. This module will also focus on tools such as brain-writing, mind mapping, and metaphorical thinking that can stimulate the flow of creativity.

   Length: Three hours

7. *Becoming an Effective Coach*

   The importance of being a good coach is the focus of this module. Participants will understand the coaching process and have an opportunity to practice the skills critical for this role.

   Length: Three hours

8. *Mentoring Others*

   Guiding and supporting others through their work and life choices can build an enduring relationship that develops both members. Learn how to start, maintain and evaluate a mentoring relationship. Participants will learn the key principles and the specific techniques and tools associated with effective and successful mentoring. Participants will also explore different mentoring styles and the key behaviors necessary for an effective mentoring experience.

Length: Three Hours

9. *Increasing Self-Awareness of Behavioral Style and Preferences*

   Understanding yourself and how you relate to others is the basis of this module. The Myers-Briggs Type Indicator is one tool that can be used to increase this understanding. Participants will create a plan for personal development.

   Length: Three hours

10. *Managing Stress and Burn-Out*

    What is stress and what causes it? This workshop will help participants identify signs and symptoms of stress, learn a variety of mental and physical techniques to better manage stress, and develop an action plan to improve stress management skills. Also covered is Wellness-what it is and how it can be achieved.

    Length: Two hours

11. *Planning, Setting Priorities, and Effective Time Management*

    There are only so many hours in one day! How do you balance all of your priorities? Participants will discuss tools and techniques for setting and balancing priorities and planning the effective use of time

    Length: Four hours

Exploring Leadership and Followership

1. *Understanding Leadership*

   To be an effective leader in today's world, you must be one who leads others to lead themselves. In this workshop, participants will learn to succeed as a leader by examining the intrinsic leadership potential that lies within. Discussions will focus on qualities that make a self-leader, effective leadership practices, and understanding a preferred leadership style. What is a leader's role and work in a Learning Organization? What are the differences and similarities between leadership and management? Participants will also discuss various organizational structures that support self-leadership such as self-managing teams and distance working.

Length: Two three hour sessions

2. *Effective Followership*

   Effective leadership requires effective followership. Participants will understand the range of followership styles, practices of self-leadership and how to influence without authority.

   Length: Three Hours

3. *Shared Leadership*

   Everyone is a leader and a follower in this organization. Staff will explore what this means. How will this be achieved? Learn how leaders turn followers into self-leaders by providing opportunities for followers to express and develop their own leadership skills. Participants will also examine power and influence in organizations and how leaders effectively use both.

   Length: Two three hour sessions

Individual Improvement

1. *Understanding Your Learning Style and Preferences*

   The Learning Style Inventory will be administered to participants to determine individual learning styles. The test is a statistically reliable and valid, twelve-item assessment tool based on Experiential Learning Theory. It identifies preferred learning styles and explores the opportunities different styles present for problem solving, working in teams, resolving conflict, and communicating at work and home. The Four Learning

Styles and their impact on career choices will also be discussed.

Length: Two hours

2. *Improve Your Project Management Skills: Managing For Success*

   This one-day seminar provides the practical knowledge needed for completing a project successfully. Participants will understand the principles and process of project management and knowledge areas as they are typically applied to the project life cycle. Participants will understand why it is crucial to focus on managing uncertainty and will be introduced to the nine principles "simultaneous managers" use to be more effective in decision-making.

   Length: Six hours

3. *Presentation Skills*

   Campus theatre director and actor leads a workshop focusing on stage presence, movement, expression, voice and improvisation. The goal is to expand your communication skills, increase comfort level when speaking to an audience, and to help people become more interactive with your audience when making presentations or providing instruction.

   Length: Three hours

4. *Safety and Security Measures*

   In this two-part workshop, you will meet University of Maryland Police Department Officers who will (1) discuss steps to identify problem situations as defined by the UMPD, (2) suggest strategies to institute within each library department to facilitate safety and security, (3) advise how to practice personal safety, and (4) describe limits for enforcing library policy, including knowledge of when to ask for additional assistance. In the second half of the workshop you will interact with library trainers to discuss important safety information outlined in the Libraries' Safety and Security Guidelines.

   Length: Three hours

5. *Sexual Harassment Prevention*

   This is a required workshop for all library staff, Graduate Assistants and student workers. A workshop where you will learn to recognize sexual harassment, document incidents, and define quid pro quo and hostile environment harassment as stated by EEOC. Included are issues related to employer liability and resolution procedures available at the University.

   Length: Three hours

6. *Professional Writing Series*

   A series of writing workshops is designed to sharpen professional writing skills. Individual classes focus on writing concisely, writing clearly and writing cohesively and avoiding grammar and punctuation errors. Participants will also learn to use an assortment of writing resources such as Strunk and White's The Elements of Style and Hacker's A Pocket Style Manual. A guide to online and print resources is located on the Libraries' Staff Training and Development web page.

   The Staff Training Library, located in McKeldin Room XX, contains over 40 books and reference guides on topics ranging from Web Development and office applications to public speaking and professional writing. Staff members may borrow any of these materials for quick trouble-shooting or more extensive self-directed training.

   Length: Two Hours

Computer Skills

Staff Training and Development provides computer training forstaff.

1. *Understanding Windows*

   Participants who are new to computers or who would like to understand more about the about the operating system, hardware, and software should take this workshop. The workshop will help participants become comfortable with the mouse and keyboard, the desktop and start menu taskbar, windows, and managing files and folders. Skill exercises follow each new topic and a self-assessment concludes the workshop.

Length: Two Hours

2. *Microsoft Office 97 and 2000*

The following individual workshops comprise sessions devoted to Microsoft Office Suites: **Basic and Intermediate Word, Basic and Intermediate Excel, Basic and Intermediate PowerPoint, and Basic and Intermediate Access**. Basic classes are open to people who have never used the programme before as well as self-taught users who want to fill gaps in their knowledge. Before participants advance to intermediate sessions, a self-test provided by trainers should be taken.

Length: Individual workshops vary in length.

3. *Electronic Mail*

Instruction is available for **Netscape** electronic mail package.

Length: Two Hours

4. *Using Netscape and Forms on the Web*

Participants will learn about the features of the Web browser Netscape and become skilled in "surfing the web". They will also learn about using the web forms that the University uses to conduct administrative business processes and web forms.

Length: Two Hours

5. *Website Tutorials and Guides*

Tutorials and guides currently available on the Staff Training website include: **Excel Basics, Internet Clockworks, PowerPoint 97 for Beginners, Intermediate PowerPoint 97, Simeon for Everyone, Word 97 for Beginners, and Intermediate Word.** More tutotials will be added to supplement training workshops. A guide to resources for Web Development is also available.

6. *Web Design: HTML*

Introduction to HTML teaches the basics of hypertext markup language: what its components are and how to use them to create a Web page. This class is for beginners and for people who are self-taught and want to fill gaps in their knowledge. Participants use HTML tags to create a simple Web page with headers, lists, paragraphs, and hyperlinks.

Intermediate HTML I classes are offered for people who already understand basic HTML and want to expand their skills. Intermediate classes focus on topics such as images, tables, nested lists, and named anchors. Participants in the HTML classes receive several informative handouts, including the O'Reilly HTML Pocket Reference. WebSpinner training is incorporated into HTML workshops on an individual basis.

Length: Two Hours

7. *Web Design: Graphics*

Introduction to Adobe Photoshop teaches the basics of preparing a digital image for the Web: cropping, resizing, improving colour balance, increasing contrast, adding text to an image, and removing flaws. **Intermediate Adobe Photoshop** increases participants' flexibility by teaching new options for image enhancement techniques. Participants also learn how to work with multiple images, create image files that appear non-rectangular, and create original graphic designs.

Length: Two Hours

Library Skills

Workshops and modules in this component will cover the variety of basic skills necessary for library staff to do their jobs. A wide range of topics is currently presented on an on-going basis in the area of database training. Tours of library facilities are also given. Workshops dealing with preservation issues will be offered. Future workshops will be offered as needs are identified.

Length: Individual time of sessions will vary.

Leadership Development

This component will prepare managers to support organizational change by providing them with the opportunity to learn leadership skills in a collaborative context. Those managers who have direct responsibility to implement organizational change initiatives will come together to learn how to be more effective leaders, individually and together. Creating a statement of a collective philosophy of leadership for the UM Libraries, clarifying individual values, beliefs and assumptions about effective leadership, and examining the new roles and expectations of leadership will be several outcomes of this workshop. Managers will identify ways in which they can be consistent in their leadership approach and allow for their individual styles and approaches.

Train-the-Trainer

A group of staff will be trained in the basics of training design and deliver in a five-day programme. Tom Goad's five-step process will be used as the basis for the programme. As each of the five steps (analyzing, designing, developing, conducting and evaluating) is introduced, participants will work in a small design team to apply the key concepts and practices of that step. This will lead to the design of learning events that can be presented to library staff and will provide participants an immediate opportunity to apply the learning in the programme itself. Participants must attend all five days.

Programme Outline:

- Principles and Practices of Adult Learning
- A Five-Step Model for Training
- Understanding Your Training and Learning Style Preferences
- Determining Learning Needs
  - o Sources of information
  - o Designing a training needs assessment tool
  - o Analyzing results
- Defining Learning Objectives and Outcomes
- Designing the Training Workshop or Programme
- Selecting Methods and Approaches for Optimal Learning
  - o The range of approaches to consider

- o Assessing resistance
- o Determining complexity of the material
- o Choosing effective methods and approaches

- Conducting Training
  - o Preparing the learner
  - o Preparing yourself
  - o Presentation skills
  - o Staging a learning experience
  - o Facilitating the learning process
- Evaluating Training
  - o Kirkpatrick's Model
  - o Designing Surveys
  - o Analyzing and Using the Results

Length: Five days (30 hours)

For additional information about the Learning Curriculum, contact Sue Baughman, Assistant Dean for Organizational Development.

Types of Curricula—Subject Centered, Co-related, Fused, Core, Student-Centered—Their Relative Values and Weaknesses

Type of Curriculum	Key Characteristics of the Type
Explicit Curriculum	• also known as the "official" or the "formal" curriculum • consists of the experiences related to content, instructional procedures, and materials for teaching specified subject areas • usually formally outlined by a designated government agency
Extra-curriculum	• consists of formally recognized and sanctioned activities outside the formal classroom setting • designed to extend, enrich, and/or supplement the explicit curriculum • designed also toward the "whole" student or enriching the affective component
Hidden Curriculum	• also known as the implicit curriculum or the covert curriculum • consists of the accidental or undersigned aspects of education; considered by-products by many educators • consists of the informal interactions of teacher and student; is often viewed as a product of the school ethos or culture
Null Curriculum	• also known as the "non-curriculum" • consists of the missing components of educational life; in other words, students often learn as much from what is NOT taught as what IS taught

Subject-Centered Curricula	Student-Centered Curricula
Separate-Subjects Curricula • emphasis on cognition over affect • emphasis on basics and the acquisition of information • designed to build mental discipline	**Core Curriculum** • the most subject-centered of this category • organized like the broad-fields curricula but based on student needs and problems • organized around questions or themes
Broad-Fields Curriculum • also called a *fused* curriculum • retains emphasis on acquisition of knowledge but arranges content into more general fields of study (language arts instead of separate literature and grammar)	**Social-Problems Curriculum** • also called the social-functions model • places less emphasis on the content to be learned than the core curriculum • examples of social problems might be successful family life or personal health
Spiral Curriculum • also called *structure of knowledge* (Jerome Bruner's model) • content organized around the knowledge to be taught and knowledge is broken down into hierarchical components • curricular materials are emphasized for their power of prosthetic learning	**Activity-Centered Curriculum** • determined by the needs and interests of the students • less formally planned than other curricula • emphasis on learning by doing and individual problem solving • a problem task might be local pollution

Subject-centered

Many learning activities in schools emphasize subject-matter or academic disciplines. Either a particular subject-area, the broader themes of a discipline, interdisciplinary concepts or themes, the correlations among two or more subject areas, or particular processes can serve as this organizing center. In each case, the characteristics of the subject-matter, and the procedures, conceptual structures or relationships which are found within or among the subject-matter, dictate the kinds of activities that will be selected.

In centering activities on subject-matter, designers have to avoid the possibility that activities will not "fit" with a given learner or set of learners. This possibility results from the fact that subject-matter, at least as formulated my subject-matter or discipline experts, is often highly abstract. Experts tend to utilize schemas and categorizations (taxonomies) which have little apparent relationship to the experiences of the uninitiated. Trying to teach 10 year olds about insects utilizing the schemas utilized by entomologists may be counterproductive. Therefore, curriculum designers need to look for ways of linking subject-matter to students own experience, and concentrate on the developmental structure of the subject-matter (that is, the sequence in which the subject-matter is most easily and naturally learned).

Designers who are developing a curriculum organized around a given **subject-area** (for example, World War II) will look at the facts, concepts, and skills related to, or encompassed by, that subject area, and plan activities that will lead students from their prior experiences into mastery of the elements of the subject area.

A variant of the subject-area-centered curriculum is one that is focused on a **discipline**. In this case, the center of the curriculum is the conceptual structures and processes that define the discipline and inform the work of people within the discipline. Students engage in activities that imitate the activities of scholars in the field. For example, history or sociology students may write research papers that utilize primary source materials; chemistry students will perform key experiments from the history of chemistry; or literature students will write, edit, and perform their own plays.

The problem with discipline-centered curriculums is that they are likely to ignore the knowledges and skills that lie between and among the various disciplines but which may be central in the lives or futures of the students. For example, students need to learn the relationship between science, technology, and culture; these relationships are usually ignored by the sciences themselves. One way around this problem is to center activities not on a given discipline but on a **broad field** including several disciplines. Obvious examples are "social studies," general science, and integrated mathematics, which merge several separate "fields" into an interdisciplinary subject area. These broad fields, or interdisciplinary subject areas, allow for more correlation, integration, and holism than strict disciplinary studies.

Broad fields can also be defined around **conceptual clusters**, such as "Science, Technology, and Society,"

Darwinism, The Renaissance, Ancient Greece, or Political Economy, or overarching themes, such as "Colonialism" or "Rituals." The various concepts, skills, and attitudes related to these clusters of concepts can be "mapped" utilizing a concept map or "web" (O+H p 248) which can then serve as the template for the development of a web site. The inter-relationships among the subject areas and topics involved in the broad field or in the specific implications of an overarching theme can be the basis for activities in which students compare and contrast related areas, developing interdisciplinary understandings and metacognitions which can serve to organize the complexity of real-world knowledge.

Web sites designed to support interdisciplinary or thematic units might include a wide selection of resources, along with a menu of activities or essential questions designed to foster student inquiry into relationships the exist among these resources.

A final way that subject-matter can be the organizing center of a curriculum is to focus on certain **processes**, such a "problem-solving," "decision-making," "computer programming," or "questioning." Each of these processes can involve a wide variety of subject-matters or specific problems and issues. A variety of activities can guide students toward increasingly sophisticated models of the process—models that include the ways in which the process is varied to meet differing goals.

Core Curriculum

In 1983, the National Commission on Excellence in Education asserted that high school students should complete a core curriculum that includes 4 years of English, 3 years of social studies, 3 years of science, 3 years of mathematics, 2 years of a foreign language, and 1/2 year of computer science. Legislatures and state education agencies quickly responded to this call for action, and over 40 states increased their graduation requirements by the turn of the decade (Coley, 1994). The new regulations posed special challenges to some small high schools, requiring them to expand course offerings.

Researchers have found, however, that core curricular offerings in small high school settings overall are well aligned with national goals (Barker, 1985). Moreover, Haller, Monk, Spotted Bear, Griffith, and Moss (1990) found that high schools enrolling as few as 100 to 200 students offer base courses in core curricular areas such as mathematics and science at rates comparable to high schools enrolling between 1,200 and 1,600 students. Another common concern regarding the core curriculum in small high schools is the availability of advanced courses, such as calculus and advanced placement English. While researchers have found that there is less incidence of advanced courses in the smallest high schools (Haller et al., 1990), large size is no guarantee that such courses will be offered or that student enrollments in these courses will be high (Monk, 1986).

Vocational Offerings, Special Services, and Extracurricular Opportunities

Another alleged benefit of large-scale high schools is their ability to support a breadth of vocational offerings, specialized services, and extracurricular opportunities. Research on the relationship between school size and these areas of the curriculum has produced mixed results. Although larger high schools do tend to offer a broader array of courses in occupational and technical education, smaller high schools appear to offer more favorable proportions of vocational offerings per student (Ramirez, 1989). Economies of scale are likely to allow larger high schools to offer more specialized services to students with disabilities and special needs. Many smaller school systems seem able to combat this potential problem through shared programmes and well-focused curricula (Webb, 1989).

Extracurricular opportunities in small high schools are less extensive than in large high schools. Small high schools have fewer clubs and athletic teams and may not support full orchestras or marching bands. Nevertheless, student participation rates are greater in smaller high schools than in larger high schools and individual students in smaller settings are involved in a greater diversity of activities (Schoggen & Schoggen, 1988).

Enhancing Curriculum Opportunities in Small High Schools

While this evidence of high participation rates is encouraging to proponents of small high schools, the pressure to expand educational opportunities for students in low enrollment settings remains. There are several "in-house" options for expanding educational opportunities in small schools, such as integrated curricula and innovative scheduling. An integrated or fused curriculum attempts to reduce the number of separate subjects through interdisciplinary courses. This "less is more" philosophy is consistent with the curriculum reform espoused by Ted Sizer and the Coalition of Essential Schools, and often involves scheduling students in longer blocks of time than the traditional 45-to 50-minute periods (Sizer, 1993).

Although difficult to develop and maintain, interdistrict pooling of instructional resources and the use of distance education and other technologies can serve to broaden educational opportunities for students in small schools. Collaboration and sharing among schools and school districts is particularly common in efforts to expand vocational and special services curricula. Advances in computer and video technologies have permitted many rural school districts to electronically import courses otherwise unavailable in the school system at a cost of one third to one half of a resident teacher's salary (Smith, 1990). Computerized learning programmes, interactive television, and Internet access are additional resources that can enhance the curriculum of small high schools. Success has been reported in using these technologies to provide advanced placement and college credit courses as well as instructional services for students with special needs (Regional Laboratory for Educational Improvement of the Northeast and Islands, 1994).

Curriculum Adequacy Through High School Restructuring

While certainly a laudable goal and an important measure of curriculum quality, curriculum breadth says little about the actual delivery of educational services to students and does not assess the extent to which students are actively participating in a high school's instructional programme. This discrepancy between the presence of curricular opportunities and the willingness or ability of students to take advantage of these opportunities is important to consider when gauging overall curriculum quality. High schools, large and small, face the challenge of designing, organizing, and implementing curricula that engage students in the learning process and motivate them to meet high standards of academic achievement. Lee and colleagues (1995) provide guidance in this area, as they have found three curricular components common to high schools that have successfully restructured their instructional programmes.

1. A common academic curriculum. Student achievement gains were found in schools with a common academic curriculum, where course offerings are narrow and academic content is strong.
2. High levels of academic press. This curriculum expectation centers on the notion that all students will meet high academic standards and devote considerable effort to academic endeavors.
3. Authentic instruction. Students are engaged in sustained, disciplined, and critical thought through a variety of instructional approaches, such as independent study, project-based learning, and real-world problem solving.

Small High Schools: Promising Sites for Curriculum Change

Proponents of small high schools have claimed for many years that lower enrollments allow for the engaging and meaningful kind of instructional programme described above. Small schools, for example, are often credited with stimulating innovations such as multiage classrooms, peer tutoring, and individualized instruction. Support for small-scale schooling has been derived largely from rural communities, where the vast majority of small public high schools exist. Recent reform efforts in urban areas, however, have sparked a great deal of interest in understanding how reducing the size and scope of schooling operations might facilitate constructive curriculum change within large city school systems. For example, Deborah Meier, director of the innovative Central Park East Secondary School in East Harlem, has identified six central service delivery benefits associated with small-scale schooling (Meier, 1995): (1) feasibility of democratic practices; (2) collective accountability of faculty performance; (3) personal and individualized attention to student needs; (4) safe, orderly learning environments; (5) parental access to school leadership; and (6) connections between adult and student cultures. These features promote the development of a curriculum that is attentive and responsive to community and student needs. Others have argued that it is exactly these features that make small schools the ideal site for curriculum reform efforts (Unks, 1989).

Small high school size does not, in and of itself, guarantee a high quality curriculum; it does appear to facilitate its development. Proponents of reducing the size and scope of schooling operations are careful to point out that structural change (*e.g.*, creating smaller schools, schools-within-schools, house plans, etc.) will not succeed in improving curricular opportunities for students without a committed group of teachers, a supportive (and perhaps independent) administration, a more flexible central authority, and adequate resources (Lee et al., 1995; Meier, 1995; Raywid, 1996).

Practitioners, researchers, and policy makers continue to struggle with the question, "How big does a high school have to be to offer a comprehensive curriculum?" A seemingly more relevant question may be, "What are the conditions that facilitate curricular adequacy and quality within all high schools?" It seems clear that as the educational community attempts to answer this question, the structural feature of school size will be central to the discussion.

What is Student-centred Learning?

Kember (1997) described two broad orientations in teaching: the teacher centred/content oriented conception and the student centred/learning oriented conceptions. In a very useful breakdown of these orientations he supports many other authors views in relation to student-centred view including: that knowledge is constructed by students and that the lecturer is a facilitator of learning rather than a presenter of information. Rogers (1983b:188) identified the important precondition for student-centred learning as the need for: '... a leader or person who is perceived as an authority figure in the situation, is sufficiently secure within herself (himself) and in her (his) relationship to others that she (he) experiences an essential trust in the capacity of others to think for themselves, to learn for themselves'.

Choice in the area of the learning is emphasised by Burnard, as he interprets Rogers' ideas of student-centredness as 'students might not only choose what to study, but how and why that topic might be an interesting one to study' (1999:244). He also emphasises Rogers' belief that students' perceptions of the world were important, that they were relevant and appropriate. This definition therefore emphasises the concept of students having 'choice' in their learning.

Harden and Crosby (2000:335) describe teacher-centred learning strategies as the focus on the teacher transmitting knowledge, from the expert to the novice. In contrast, they describe student-centred learning as focusing on the students' learning and 'what students do to achieve this, rather than what the teacher does'. This definition emphasises the concept of the student 'doing'. Other authors articulate broader, more comprehensive definitions. Lea et al. (2003:322) summarises some of the literature on student-centred learning to include the followings tenets:

1. 'the reliance on active rather than passive learning,
2. an emphasis on deep learning and understanding,
3. increased responsibility and accountability on the part of the student,
4. an increased sense of autonomy in the learner
5. an interdependence between teacher and learner,
6. mutual respect within the learner teacher relationship,
7. and a reflexive approach to the teaching and learning process on the part of both teacher and learner.'

Gibbs (1995) draws on similar concepts when he describes student-centred courses as those that emphasise: learner activity rather than passivity; students' experience on the course outside the institution and prior to the course; process and competence, rather than content; where the key decisions about learning are made by the student through negotiation with the teacher. Gibbs elaborates in more detail on these key decisions to include: 'What is to be learnt, how and when it is to be learnt, with what outcome, what criteria and standards are to be used, how the judgements are made and by whom these judgements are made' (1995:1).

In a similar vein in earlier literature, the student-teacher relationship is particularly elaborated upon by Brandes and Ginnis (1986). In their book for use in second level education (post-primary), entitled 'A Guide to Student-Centred Learning', they present the main principles of student-centred learning as:

- The learner has full responsibility for her/his learning
- Involvement and participation are necessary for learning
- The relationship between learners is more equal, promoting growth, development
- The teacher becomes a facilitator and resource person
- The learner experiences confluence in his education (affective and cognitive domains flow together)
- The learner sees himself differently as a result of the learning experience.

The theoretical standing of student-centred learning is often surprisingly absent in the literature. However, it appears to relate primarily to the constructivist view of learning in the importance it places on activity, discovery and independent learning (Carlile and Jordan 2005). Cognitive theory also highlights activity but in a different form than that supported by the constructivists (Cobb 1999). The cognitive view supports the idea that the activity of learning is computed in the head, or as often described 'in the mind'. The constructivist view of activity is related more to performing physical activities, for example, projects, practicals. Student-centred learning has some connections with the social constructivist view, which emphasises activity and the importance of communities of practice/others in the learning process. However, the definitions of SCL do not necessarily highlight the importance of peers in learning (Cobb 1999; Bredo 1999).

The Effectiveness and Critiques of Student-centred Learning

The use of student-centred learning appears to be reflective of today's society where choice and democracy are important concepts, however is it an effective approach to learning? Lea et al. (2003) reviewed several studies on student-centred learning and found that overall it was an effective approach. A six-year study in Helsinki, which compared traditional and activating instruction, found that the activating group developed better study skills and understanding, but were slower in their study initially (Lonka and Ahola 1995). Equally, Hall and Saunders found that students had increased participation, motivation and grades in a first year information technology course (1997). In addition, 94% of the students would recommend it to others over the more conventional approach (Hall and Saunders 1997). Students in a UK University elaborated on the impact of student-centred learning on them, *i.e.* they felt there was more respect for the student in this approach, that it was more interesting, exciting, and it boosted their confidence (Lea et al. 2003).

Student-centred learning, despite its popularity, is not without its critics. The main critique of student-centred learning is its focus on the individual learner. In addition, there are some difficulties in its implementation, *i.e.* the resources needed to implement it, the belief system of the students and staff, and students' lack of familiarity with the term.

Simon (1999) describes that student-centred learning, in the School system, can be in danger of focusing completely on the individual learner and taken to its extreme does not take into account the needs of the whole class. Simon highlights the point that 'if each child is unique, and each requires a specific pedagogical approach appropriate to him or her and to no other, the construction of an all embracing pedagogy or general principles of teaching become an impossibility' (Simon 1999:42). Edwards (2001:42) also highlights the dangers associated with student-centredness in adult education where in empowering an individual there is a potential danger of 'a person's physical isolation from other learners'.

The importance of the social context of learning and the value of interaction with peers is emphasised in the socio-cultural view of learning (Bredo 1999). The concept of being an independent learner choosing his/her own route of learning, may in fact drive some of the sociability out of the learning process if care is not taken to emphasise the importance of peers. In relation to this individuality, Lea et al.'s study on psychology students highlighted their concern over being abandoned or isolated from other supports in a student-centred learning approach (2003).

O'Sullivan (2003) described student-centred learning as a Western approach to learning and may not necessarily transfer to the developing countries, such as Namibia, where there are limited resources and different learning cultures. It can be equally hard at times to see how the approach can be economical in the large classes associated with many current University undergraduate courses. A comprehensive study was conducted in 2004, by the University of Glasgow, on the use of student-centred learning with full-time undergraduate students (2004). In this study they found that student-centred learning (SCL) was more prevalent in the later years of the student degrees, and this they believe is often down to class sizes.

Another concern regarding student centred learning is the belief that students hold in relation to their learning. Students who value or have experienced more teacher-focused approaches, may reject the student-centred approach as frightening or indeed not within their remit. Prosser and Trigwell's work in higher education emphasises the different belief systems held by staff and students (2002). They found that lecturers with a teacher-centred approach to teaching held views that students should accommodate information rather than developing and changing their conceptions and understanding. The reverse was true for those with more student-centred approaches to their teaching. Perry's work on the development of University students highlights how students move from a dualistic view that knowledge is right or wrong to a relativist view that all answers are equally valid (Perry 1970). This study highlights that even during the University years, students can change their view on learning and as they move through the years so to may their views on student-centred learning change. In support of Perry's work, Stevenson and Sander (2002) highlighted that 1st year medical students were suspicious of the value of student-centred learning methods.

Finally, students' familiarity with the term can be poor. Lea et al. (2003) conducted a study on 48 psychology students in the University of Plymouth on students' attitudes to student-centred learning. They found that, despite a University student-centred policy, 60% of the students had not heard of the term.

UNIT-III

Curriculum Designing

Assessing Needs

Deciding what should be included in a curriculum has long been a topic of controversy. The struggle to identify what should be taught in schools has been evident throughout the development of American schools (Kliebard, 1995) and continues today. Curriculum debate has endured at least since Plato (360 BCE) first stated his vision that education should produce a balanced, smoothly functioning, and just society. More than a thousand years later, Rousseau (1762) countered with his declaration that the purpose of education was to develop the unique worth and freedom of the individual. John Dewey (1938), taking a more pragmatic position, did not believe that education needed to be an either-or situation. Instead he held that the schools could serve both Rousseau's and Plato's purposes without compromising individual development or sacrificing social balance.

Despite these philosophical debates, career and technical education has been viewed by some as benefiting industry at the expense of the self-development needs of its students. Nobel asserts that private corporations are placing political pressure on the educational system to produce a "cadre of adaptable 'problem solvers' and technicians" (Noble, 1998. He notes that this pressure is reminiscent of the political pressure placed on the schools of Dewey's era by the National Association of Manufacturers coalition to force schools to focus on vocational education. The controversy is not limited to curricular theoreticians and political players. In A Study of Schooling, Sirotnik (1998) found that parents, teachers, and students could not reach a consensus of what the goal of education should be, even when asked to select only between intellectual development, social development, personal development, and vocational development

Given the controversy, it seems unlikely that state or national standards can provide the information required to develop effective curricula. And, if left to educators, how do they develop a career or technical education curriculum that keeps the students from becoming technically adept pawns of corporations? The answer lies in needs assessment. Needs assessment is a powerful tool that can help clarify and validate true needs (Selvadurai & Krashinski, 1989). Since a needs analysis collects information that can be used in making educational decisions (Selvadurai & Krashinski), integrating needs assessment throughout the curriculum development process can help to assure that career and technical programmes do not create an either-or situation but rather, as Dewey proposed, benefit both the learners and society.

Practitioners often cringe when they are presented with the prospect of justifying a programme with a needs analysis. Why must the assessments be performed? After all, should not the practitioners already know from their own schooling, community contacts, student interactions, and their own critical perspective what is required? In order to address this concern, and before attempting to integrate needs assessment with curriculum development, a basic understanding of the curriculum development process is required.

Developing Curriculum

Posner (1998) suggested that the curriculum development process has "two necessary and complimentary elements: curriculum development technique and curriculum conscience". Curriculum development techniques are the "nuts and bolts" processes used to arrive at the curriculum. Models that describe procedures to develop curriculum abound and include Ralph Tyler's "Tyler Rationale", Hilda Taba's "Seven Steps",

Decker Walker's "naturalistic mode" (Posner, 1998) and Wiggins and McTighe's "Backward Design" (1998) as just a few frequently cited examples. A curriculum conscience is the ability to understand the implications and consequences of curricular decisions. Paulo Freire has been referenced as an example of someone bringing a "critical consciousness" to curriculum development (Posner, 1998).

Needs analysis is important for both of these elements of curriculum development. Information about actual needs is required for the procedural development of the programme and can also help identify some of the implications and consequences that assist the curriculum designer in making the required value judgments that are part and parcel of the critical consciousness.

The Tyler Rationale is a technique used for curriculum development that identifies fundamental questions that must be answered during the development process (Tyler, 1949). Since the technique is based on answering questions, and needs analysis helps answer questions, incorporating needs analysis into the process is a natural extension.

The Tyler Rationale is relatively pragmatic and straightforward, and it can be readily applied to career and technical programme development. It closes the loop between curriculum development and assessment. Though not necessarily a linear process (Tyler, 1949), this non-linearity allows the developer to adjust the information in each stage of development based on information and decisions made in other stages. This adjustment is important as the information gathered at various stages is used to triangulate the data. It is, however easier to describe the process if it is explained one step at a time.

The curriculum questions Tyler (1949) proposed are:

1. What are the purposes or objectives of the programme?
2. What experiences are likely to attain these objectives?
3. How can these experiences be effectively organized?
4. How can the effectiveness of learning be evaluated?

The four questions of the Tyler Rationale are still used by curriculum designers and scholars. However, while Tyler proposes pertinent questions, he does not suggest how to obtain the necessary answers. The following case study illustrates one method used to acquire this information. In this example, a needs analysis answered Tyler's four questions and made it possible to develop a curriculum customized to address a local manufacturer's need for skilled workers.

Formulating Objectives

Vision

In health promotion and prevention a vision is a relatively vague and usually ambitious representation of a desired state of conditions and behaviours. The time frame for this vision usually goes far beyond that of the planned project. The anticipation of a future and somewhat idealistic situation to be achieved can have a motivating effect and be a guiding principle throughout the project.

Objectives

Effect-oriented Objectives: Project objectives in health promotion and prevention describe a state (an effect) that would ideally be seen on different levels by the time the project ends:

- individual level (key-persons)
- group level
- organization level
- in settings
- society/politics

Interventions in health promotion should therefore not just aim at the individual level (behavioural changes) but should always aim at structural changes on the level of organizations, settings, society or politics. Thus, a good project objective will not describe actions but effects that one would like to see by the end of the project. It will not describe by what means and actions these effects will be obtained nor will it explain the factual planning and implementation of the project.

The 'Model for Results Classification' can help to identify results that can realistically be expected. It distinguisnes three categories of effects:

1. direct effects on health (*e.g.* fewer illnesses, better quality of life)
2. intermediate effects on health (*e.g.* healthy life style, health-promoting social and physical environments
3. health promotion effects (*e.g.* health-related life skills, motivation for health, health-promoting attitudes and behaviours)

It is usually not realistic to expect or demonstrate direct effects on health (in the sense of Nutbeam's outcomes) from health promotion or prevention projects. Such effects can usually only be achieved in the long-term and not within the time frame of a project.

Once the objectives are formulated in an effect-oriented way they can then be made operational and concrete with the help of the SMART criteria (see 'SMART objectives'); this usually requires the definition of indicators for the achievement of objectives (see 'Indicators').

Why Would You Disregard these Aspects? +

Why Would You Disregard these Aspects? –

- There is often confusion between measures (actions to be taken in order to reach an objective) and goals (desired state) and the implementation of a measure is taken to be the achievement of the objective.
- a vague description of objectives will avoid the difficulty of having to describe desired effects in a detailed way.
- if the formulation of objectives remains vague (*e.g.* to raise awareness in a target group) the attainment of the objective cannot be evaluated and you will not be accountable for disappointing results.

What You have to Gain +

What You have to Gain –

- if your objectives are formulated in a effect-oriented way they will be more motivating

- if you do not yet include strategies and measures in your objectives you will have more room to manoeuvre

What You can Practically Do +

What You can Practically Do –

- describe the desired state of the systems in which you want to intervene-try to visualize the anticipated change (see 'Visualisation'-try to assess realistically the structural and behavioural changes that can possibly be achieved in the given time frame-try to put yourself in the place of the target-group

Some Guiding Principles in Structuring the Curriculum and Selecting the Curriculum Content

With the implementation of compulsory education, every school-age child is entitled school education. For the maladjusted children who cannot benefit from the ordinary school environment, a specially designed curriculum geared to their needs is a necessity towards the actualization of equal chances in education for all.

Since the majority of maladjusted children requiring special education are of normal intelligence and their problems are largely transient, the main function of the special schools for this category of children is to help them mainstream in ordinary schools and integrate into their society. Therefore, the arrangement of their curriculum should basically follow that of ordinary primary and junior secondary schools. Also, the general principles of curriculum management in the mainstream, by and large, are applicable in these schools as well. What is required is to adapt the mainstream curriculum in the light of facilitating the personal and social development of these children, and overcoming their learning difficulties. Curriculum for these children may be modified along the following principles :

Development of a Balanced Curriculum

The existing curriculum is academically-oriented with more emphasis on cognitive development and less consideration on pupils' individual needs, abilities, interests, potentials and developmental history. Apart from this, personal and social development, self-understanding and various levels of life skills training have never been explicitly included in the curriculum as a unique subject. Therefore, when planning the curriculum for maladjusted children, their special needs should be taken into consideration. Besides the basic academic and cultural subjects, there should be appropriate weighting of learning areas in personal and social development. On top of this, a balanced weighting of subjects should be worked out according to the available resources to meet the interest and ability of individual pupils, and givie them chances to gain success and pleasure in their school life.

Development of Multiple Intelligences

It has been the practice in the field of education to differentiate children into ability groups through intelligence tests. However, these tests are biased towards assessing abilities in languages and mathematical or logical thinking. Pupils who are slow in developing these two aspects may risk having other potentials left untapped.

Howard Gardner (1983), a psychologist of Harvard University, has suggested that human beings possess multiple intelligences. At least the following seven have been detected:

linguistic,
logical-mathematical,
spatial,
bodily-kinaesthetic,
musical,
inter-personal and
intra-personal.

Gardner's theory has great implications to education since the developmental milestones of each intelligence vary with individuals and every child has his or her unique intellectual profile. Curriculum integration is a good way to nurture children's multiple intelligences through integrated and daily life learning activities. In addition, children can also figure out their own ways to develop different intelligences.

Tailoring with Consideration of Curriculum Continuity and Internal Coherence

Special schools should appropriately adapt the mainstream curriculum by means of simplification, abridgement, reorganisation, extension and selection. Teachers should be given a free hand in this process.

At the beginning of each term, schools should call cross-subject curriculum meeting to ensure continuity and coherence of the whole curriculum. The actual curriculum tailoring should then be systematically conducted as designed by the well-experienced personnel.

Incorporation of Communicationand Interpersonal Skills Training

Maladjusted children can establish effective relationship with their immediate environment be it their families, schools or communities only if their communication and interpersonal skills improve significantly. Therefore these skills should be included in the curriculum as a subject, and widely incorporated into other subjects and their school life whenever appropriate. In selection of teaching content and learning activities, teachers should provide children with opportunities to practise the skills of conveying ideas and expressing feelings, so as to promote interpersonal skills and co-operation. Apart from it, teachers can also observe and assess children's progress.

Relevance to Daily Living

The vast majority of maladjusted children incline to crave for immediate gratification and short term interest. Therefore, the content of their curriculum needs to be relevant in order to be meaningful. Generally speaking, the existing mainstream curriculum fails to motivate them to learn since it is too academic to include sufficient consideration in its practical value in day to day living. In selecting and delivering their curriculum, it is essential to include daily life materials to ensure that learning is meaningful for them.

For pupils with more severe problems, the difficulties in selecting suitable curriculum for them are aggravated by their unfavourable experiences which give them a distorted view of life. So they need a more specially designed curriculum.

Content Comparable to Their Developmental Stage and Attainment Level

In comparison with peer of the same age, maladjusted children are generally backward in attainment. This complicates the selection of teaching materials. Standard teaching materials appropriate to their attainment level may be too childish for them while those comparable to their life experience would be too advanced academically. Hence, teachers have to re-write or revise the standard teaching materials according to the developmental stages and attainment levels of their pupils.

Integration of Theoretical Studies and Practical Work

Owing to their short attention span, pupils cannot stand passive learning for long. This will easily lead to discipline and management problems. So blending the theoretical study with practical work and ensuring pupils' participation during the course can help to sustain their interest and sense of achievement. It in turn motivates their further learning.

Attention to Individual Differences

Although there are problems common to these pupils, there is a large discrepancy among them in learning and emotional difficulties. So without depriving pupils of appropriate group interaction, rooms and flexibility in the curriculum design should be allowed in order to cater for their individual needs.

Realistic Review of Achievement through Timely and Continuous Formative and Summative Assessment

The traditional norm reference assessment can only increase their sense of failure. Besides, these children are easily disturbed by their emotions and thus may affect their performance during the assessment. Therefore, continuous formative assessment at appropriate stages of learning can be more accurate in revealing the effectiveness of their learning. Besides, the assessment should be target-oriented and the means need to be diversified. Through this process, teachers can get feedback on the effectiveness of their teaching and also pupils can be immediately informed of teachers' comment on their performance, thus reducing their anxiety and gradually establishing confidence in school work.

Multi-disciplinaryApproach in Curriculum Design and Delivery

Since enhancing personal and social development is important in achieving the aims of education for maladjusted pupils, professionals concerned can render educational and counseling services. So, their participation in curriculum design and delivery should be encouraged.

As a conclusion for this section, maladjusted children require a curriculum which lays heavier emphasis on personal social development. As for the effectiveness of any curriculum, it relies on appropriate means of delivery other than a good structure and content.

Selection of Content

The curriculum for maladjusted children suggests learning areas and experience at the primary and junior secondary level. Since the ultimate aim of education for these children is integration, it may mean mainstream junior secondary education for all primary pupils; mainstream senior secondary education or technical education for those junior secondary pupils who show aptitude towards furthering their studies; or open employment for others who need jobs. So in general, the areas of learning and experience recommended to ordinary primary and junior secondary schools are also appropriate for them. However, priority must be given to the learning element related to personal and social development.

Curriculum Content for Primary Section of Schools for Social Development

Schools with residential service can provide children with whole day care in education and daily living. There must be close co-operation among teaching, residential and other non-teaching staff to ensure a consistent and coherent continuum of services.

Curriculum Content for Secondary Section of Schools for Social Development

Since these children may pass or near the age limit of compulsory education by the time they complete junior secondary education, they have a choice of vocational training or direct employment besides furthering their formal studies. So the curriculum should be flexible enough to cater for the needs of pupils of different abilities and aptitudes. However, it does not mean that pupils who opt for employment are shut out from academic pursuit since the core curriculum has already provided them a good subject knowledge foundation upon which further study through adult education or other channels of open learning is feasible.

Curriculum Organisation

To implement the above discussed curriculum orientation, the following ways of curriculum organisation are suggested for reference.

Curriculum Tailoring

Curriculum tailoring is the adaptation of a curriculum according to the academic standard and stage of maturation of the pupils. With learning content more appropriate to their levels of attainment, pupils may be better motivated to learn. Curriculum tailoring may be an extension or a cutting-down of the core learning area of a subject. Therefore it is essential to demarcate the core learning area for each stage of learning before any tailoring can be conducted.

For primary level pupils, the specific aim of education is to prepare them to integrate into mainstream schools. So core areas of learning and experience for ordinary primary schools should be covered, but priority should be given to basic knowledge and skills in each area.

As for curriculum tailoring for junior secondary pupils, more consideration should be given to learning aptitude and attainment of pupils. According to individual needs of the development of multiple intelligences, pupils must be given the appropriate options from a diversified curriculum, so that they can acquire the abilities to meet the basic requirements for further study or employment.

After selection of learning content, there should be effective ways to organise the content for delivery to pupils :

(1) In-depth understanding of the aims, content and sequence of learning of the curriculum

(2) Right choice of the starting point for remedial teaching

(3) Immediate compensation for what has not been fully grasped by pupils in learning

(4) Diversity in teaching methods

(5) Low level point of entry, correct pace, plenty of activities and timely feedback

(6) Provide experience of success to break the vicious cycle between failure and low confidence

(7) Reinforce the motivation of learning which comes from the sense of achievement

(8) Integration of similar teaching content from different subjects to avoid redundancy

Mastery Learning

Mastery learning is one of the means of gearing teaching to the needs of children of different abilities and interests.

In a mastery learning process, the concepts and materials to be learned are first divided into sequential learning units, each with clearly stated learning objectives. The units are then listed in order of increasing complexity. After finishing each unit, a formative assessment is administered to diagnose whether the pupils have attained the targets or not and to give feedback on their learning. The pupils who have not mastered a particular unit will be engaged in remedial activities aiming at providing extra and alternative learning experiences to overcome their difficulties. Then a second parallel formative assessment will be given. For those who demonstrate mastery on the first formative assessment, enrichment activities on the same unit are provided in order to broaden and expand their learning. Having mastered a unit, pupils can proceed to the next unit. In view of its characteristics, mastery learning is especially effective for those subjects with clear and orderly arranged knowledge structure. The method of instruction is group-based and teacher-paced. It can be applied in typical classroom situations where instructional time is fixed. So this suits the mode of operation in most of the schools for social development.

Research findings on mastery learning show that it is effective in promoting pupils' cognitive and affective development. It just meets the aim of education for the maladjusted.

Modular Curriculum

A modularised curriculum is made up of learning units called modules. A module is a well structured or self-contained learning unit which is complete with specific objectives, contents, teaching / learning strategies and some forms of assessment.

A module may be free standing, or a building block to provide the means for grouping and re-grouping, insertion or deletion within a larger curriculum framework. The aim of introducing a module is to facilitate choice, flexibility and reducing labelling effects.

There are many models for designing a modular curriculum. The following two are suggested for consideration:

(1) *Within a Subject Area :* Topic core and topic elective modules

The topics or domains of learning within a subject area are grouped under Core Modules and Elective Modules. Core modules consist of essential learning areas which are to be learned by all pupils. For example, in Social Studies, the following five modular or thematic units may be included : Knowing oneself, one's family, peers, society and country. Remedial and Extension modules cater for pupils with different learning abilities. Remedial modules refer to tailored materials on core modules to help weaker pupils to consolidate their learning. Extension modules are additional materials for more able pupils to deepen their understanding of the core modules. Elective modules broaden the content of the subject and provide options for the pupils with different interest and need. Some suggested elective modulars or thematic units in Social Studies are modules on adolescence, Hong Kong, China and the world.

(2) *Within the Whole Curriculum* : Subject core and Subject elective modules

Subject areas are pooled under Core Subjects and groups of Elective Subject modules. Core subjects are to be taken by all pupils within a year band. Elective subjects may be selected from a group of modules depending on the available resources at school and the needs of pupils. The elective modules may be subject-specific, inter-disciplinary or trans-disciplinary. A diagrammatic representation of the modular structure in a curriculum.

The advantages of adopting modularised curriculum for maladjusted pupils are:

(1) It is well structured to avoid redundancy in curriculum content. This structure facilitates flexible arrangement in time-tabling, grouping and staffing deployment.

(2) Each module clearly states its specific objectives in terms of concepts, skills and attitudes to be achieved, facilitating more successful experience in learning for the pupils.

(3) Modularised curriculum provides flexibility and choice. This can enhance curriculum tailoring and cater for individual differences among pupils. Moreover, its structure expedites the insertion or deletion of teaching content when necessary. This is helpful in taking care of pupils who are admitted at different times of the school year. In spite of all these advantages, attention must be paid to cohere the modules so that the curriculum is comprehensive without being fragmented or the important contents being missed out.

Curriculum Integration

The rationale behind curriculum integration is multi-functional. Two are emphasized here:

(1) To develop life-long learning abilities and habits as well as fundamental concepts and principles which is required by every learner in a fast-changing world.

(2) To arouse interest in learning by using authentic scenarios and through activities perceived as meaningful by the pupils.

Through close collaboration of teachers of various disciplines, rigid subject boundaries can be diminished, thus allowing the creation of authentic scenarios and purposeful activities.

All these are conducive to long-term learning. The initial steps to integrate the school curriculum are:

(1) setting up an interdisciplinary teacher team to design, and, later, implement the integrated curriculum for a certain level.

(2) matching the topics to be taught in each subjects every month so as to create inter-topic links which usually appears in the form of themes.

(3) aligning those related topics to be taught at the same time.

The essential step is to design some real-life learning activities in which pupils can see the meaning and aims in learning.

The sense of purpose is mainly induced by the following two ways:

(1) a few fundamental open-ended questions for pupils to investigate

(2) some authentic tasks for pupils to complete

These pupil activities are often made interesting by involving multiple intelligences.

The final steps (often carried out in the subsequent couple of years), include arranging the above-mentioned activities to cover a large number of life long learning abilities which can be conveniently assessed. These abilities include information processing, higher-order thinking, communication, and collaboration, etc. They can be conveniently assessed through shared responsibilities among subject teachers.

Organisation of Content

Once you have decided on the content of your site, you need to work out how it will be organised.

A clear logical structure helps users to understand the site, which means they can more easily work out where they are and where the content they want is likely to be found.

Simple Structure

The simplest structures involve dividing the content into a few different sections. Small sections may end up as a single page of the site; larger sections may end up as multiple pages.

For example, the cake recipe site could be organised into the following sections:

- Recipes
- Glossary
- About the author

Hierarchies

For larger sites, it may be useful to have more than one level of sections. For example, if there are a lot of recipes in the site, you might want to divide the Recipes section into several subsections:

- Sponge cakes
- Fruit cakes
- Chocolate cakes
- Other

Other Structures

There are other ways to structure sites. For example, a site with a daily comic strip might have a structure based purely on date. Some sites might even use a customisable or AI-based organisation, where content is actually reordered by the computer to best serve each user. But structured hierarchies are most useful for simple sites.

Selection of Learning Experiences

1. Can the experience bring optimum benefit to the learners? Take and second look in your exercises and

ask yourself if these exercises or activities can be replicated by the learners when they go outside in the school. Would this activities serve as the mirror on what is happening in their surrounding or just a house work and duties so the same conclusion can be applied in the situation that recall the learning experiences?

2. Does the experience help meet the evident needs of the learner? Many students will be self motivated if they discover that the activities are timely to their needs. The learner might have a term paper project and it is very timely that your subject matter is about word processor software. You will notice the aggressiveness of the student to learn the PowerPoint presentation because they have classroom report or oral examination from other subjects and they like to deliver it with the help of ICT. The learner might be task to create or design a classroom newsletter and it timely that you demonstrate the use of MS publisher application software.
3. Are the learners likely to be interested in the experience? As the teachers, it is your task to device an activities that will arouse the interest of the learner. Let said you are Social Studies teacher your topic is about historical account in the landing of the Allied Soldiers in the beach of Normandy. For the high school student, this event might not be relevant to them yet once presented with the motion pictures together the possible scenarios if this famous event did not happen what will be the future of the countries involve including the learners country and their fore fathers. Bringing the topics or discussion into the personal level of the learner is a great method to attain the appreciation objective.
4. Does the experience encourage the learners to inquire further? This is the best opportunity of a good subject matter, a well delivered lesson complement by lively exercises and by a dramatic generalization. Have you noticed your student leaving the classroom characterized by silent and thinking mode? Inferring on the previous

situation and organizing thoughts from the lesson. Have you experienced by a situation whereby the student approach you and said "Sir I have answered all the exercises in Chapter 5". So you will say, very good you advance already. You might have a situation in which the student said Sir teaches me to how do create a form using excel programme please. Then your answer is "that would be the next topic young man". You could experience the situation where the student approached you and show her work which not included in the assignment. That would be a great application of learning experience and an evident of transfer of learning.

Lastly, you might experience this as a teacher. Dong, ni unsa nimo pag buhat ana, tudlo I ako bi? (James how did you do that? Demonstrate it to me right away). Then I call the attention of the entire class to watch the demonstration as part of strategy of praise and motivation as well as collaborative learning's.

I have lost time and ideas to discuss those pointer below so I hope our visitors can share their knowledge and experiences.

5. Does the experience stimulate the learners to engage in higher levels of thinking and reasoning?
6. Does the experience involve the use of different senses and sense perceptions?
7. Does the experience approximate real life situations?
8. Is the experience in accord with the life patterns of the learners?
9. How contemporary is the experience? Is it timely and relevant?
10. Do the experiences provide for the attainment of a range of instructional objectives?

Towards a Truly Learning Organisation

There is a great deal of talk these days about the so-called "learning organisation." However, it is not always clear what is meant by the term or how it can be turned into reality. The goal of the learning organisation is to enhance the management and leadership abilities of people in an integrated, global, and results-oriented fashion. This philosophy allows business goals to be accomplished in a holistic and sustainable manner. The learning organisation must implement innovative methods for creating, acquiring, and transferring knowledge. These knowledge-processing skills can be effectively implemented through three important modes of learning: traditional, distance and action learning.

Traditional Learning

We are all familiar with the classroom setting, and the traditional mode of learning continues to be important for the modern learning organisation. Traditional learning can be described as:

Active, in that it requires the active participation of the students Constructive, with knowledge acquired becoming embedded in the learner's knowledge base.

Cumulative, with new information becoming integrated into the learner's ever-expanding knowledge base Goal-oriented, with learning activities being specifically designed to help the learner meet his or her needs.

Traditional learning will always be important. It is particularly valuable for reviewing difficult concepts, joining study groups, asking clarifying questions, face-to-face interaction and grasping visual materials. Distance Learning.

The term "distance learning" refers to a situation in which the teacher/trainer and his or her student are separated by physical distance and in which traditional one-on-one, face-to-face interaction does not occur. Today's technology (voice, video, multimedia, data transmitted over the web) bridges such gaps and allows learning to occur even if there is never any physical contact between teacher and student. Distance learning, when properly implemented, has significant benefits. Students learn when and where they want Students learn at their own pace The use of multimedia tools allows different learning styles to be accommodated. Learning is individualised, autonomous, and spontaneous. Ultimately, we are moving towards a global virtual classroom. Distance learning allows instructional materials and an amazing amount of reference material to be placed online for real time, fingertip access by the student. Students can access the teaching milieu as needed and wanted, and can acquire information and exchange knowledge with colleagues from around the globe. The result: The acquisition and exchange of knowledge is facilitated, contributing to the ongoing evolution of the learning organisation.

Action Learning

"Action learning" means quite literally "learning by doing." Teams of executives work together to address real, non-trivial organisational problems. Originally conceptualised by British Professor Reginald Revans, action-learning forces managers to confront real situations rather than passively acquiring information in a classroom setting. Members of the team constructively share concerns and experiences, with the group dynamics reinforcing the learning experience. As executives reflect on their experiences and accomplish objectives together, the depth of learning increases accordingly.

At the individual level, we can describe this as a learning wheel, during which individuals experience, reflect, connect with others and implement actions to address the problem. At the group level, we can effectively use the metaphor of the Team Learning Wheel. More specifically, Action Learning has four primary elements.

The Action Learning Team: This group of five or six highly motivated managers works together as a team to confront real organisation challenges. They should focus on what we refer to as "Quick HIPs" or "Quick High Impact Projects." The emphasis in this approach is on achieving concrete, specific and measurable operational improvements FAST.

As they work on their HIPs, team members receive support and advice from senior management or outside consultants (Facilitators). They also interact with the Project Coach, including receiving real time coaching and presenting their findings (including initial assessment, intermediate analysis, and final recommendations). The Facilitator and Project Coach, of course, work closely together to optimally support the Action Learning Team. Objectives of the Action Learning team include: Learning to solve real business issues by addressing them directly as a group Learning to be proactive and to "get things done." Applying the knowledge acquired through distance learning, workshops, or other traditional modes of learning in a hands-on setting. Improving their ability to work as a team with managers from other departments or even other countries.

Bringing about Organisational Change: Action learning teams provide a safe and supportive, yet challenging, environment for learning and skills enhancement. Teams are driven by feelings of mutual trust and confidentiality, attributes that empower team members to take chances and explore the boundaries of creative problem solving. These are real "learning communities." Individuals benefit both by sharing their knowledge and experience with others and by learning from their peers.

The projects to be addressed should be actual business challenges faced by the company; examples might include reducing product development cycle time, cutting inventory levels, implementing faster delivery, or revising a performance management system. Projects should be of manageable scope, and the team should have realistic prospects of achieving concrete, specific, and measurable impact within a few months (typically 3-4 months). It is absolutely essential that the objective of the intervention is clearly stated and that outcomes be measurable so that effectiveness can be assessed, acknowledged, and rewarded.

Project Coach

This senior executive provides ongoing encouragement and coaching, focusing in particular on the team learning experience. The Coach, who functions as the chief client for the team, takes on the following responsibilities: Defining expectations of the team, helping the team accomplish its objectives, reviewing progress from startup through midstream through completion and evaluating results of the project.

The facilitator is a highly experienced executive or consultant serves as a resource for the Action Learning Team, providing support, information, or advice as needed. The Facilitator ensures that the Team works closely together and provides advice regarding the most appropriate tools and strategies. However, the Facilitator does not give the Team pre-formulated solutions or tell them what approaches to take; that is part of the Team's Action Learning experience.

Organisation of Learning Experiences

Over time, the learning organisation modifies its own behaviours in ways consistent with newly acquired knowledge and insights. The learning organisation has a number of important strengths that can translate into sustainable competitive advantage:

Systematic problem solving. Employees learn to thoroughly explore all aspects of problems, identify viable alternatives, systematically evaluate options, and implement well-calculated strategies. Experimentation with new approaches. The learning organisation is never afraid to try new possible solutions, as long as they are thoroughly analysed and probable outcomes are critically discussed before "jumping off the diving board."

Learning from organisational experiences and past outcomes. It is essential that knowledge about previous experience be accessed and analysed, with specific attention to applying the lessons learned in new problem-solving situations.

The learning organisation is willing to learn from other companies, even direct competitors, if dong so enhances organisational outcomes.

Transferring knowledge quickly and efficiently throughout the company: The learning organisation is characterised by porous boundaries for information flow, with the knowledge acquired in one setting or division being shared throughout the organisation. This process is substantially facilitated by modern information technology (especially Intranet implementations and Knowledge Management software).

In short, this process can be described as involving dynamic, real time knowledge creation, knowledge acquisition, and knowledge transfer. At Watson Wyatt India, we work closely with our clients to help them transform their companies into truly learning organisations, in the process enriching the professional lives of their employees and improving bottom line performance.

Using a Translation Model for Curriculum

Development and Classroom Instruction: Other chapters in this book emphasize a variety of ways that representational fluency is an important component of students' models and modeling abilities-and an important part of what it means to understand basic mathematical costructs in topic areas ranging from early number concepts, to rational number concepts, to concepts in algebra, geometry, probability, statistics, or calculus. The purpose of this chapter is to report some ways that the National Science Foundation supported Rational Number Project (RNP) has used the following translation model (Lesh, 1979) to develop curriculum materials and classroom activities that are aimed at helping both students and teachers develop deeper and higher order understandings of some of the most important ideas in the school mathematics curriculum.

The Lesh translation model suggests that elementary mathematical ideas can be represented in five different modes: manipulatives, pictures, real-life contexts, verbal symbols, and written symbols. It stresses that understanding is reflected in the ability to represent mathematical ideas in multiple ways, plus the ability to make connections among the different embodiments; and, it emphasizes that translations within and between various modes of representation make ideas meaningful for students. Thus, the Lesh translation model extends Bruner's theory by adding to his three modes of representation real-life context and verbal symbols. The Lesh Model emphasizes interactions within and among representations. For example, the arrows connecting the different modes depict translations between modes; and, the internal arrows depict translations within modes. The model suggests that the development of deep understanding of mathematical ideas requires experience in different modes, and eperience making connections between and within these modes of representation. A translation requires a reinterpretation of an idea from one mode of representation to another. This movement and its associated intellectual activity reflect a dynamic view of instruction and learning.

Model of Curriculum Development—Ralph E. Taylor, D. K. Wheeler and Hilda Taba

Ralph is a General Partner of Battelle Ventures L.P. and Innovation Valley Partners L.P. and he manages the Washington DC regional office located at Battelle's Crystal City site. He covers all aspects of the venture business, including deal sourcing, due-diligence, deal negotiation and transaction closing, Board of Director duties, and start-up company development. Ralph has led or co-led various venture investments for the firm including BioVigilant, Hi-G-Tek, Nistica, Rajant, RemoteReality, Sypherlink, and he serves on the Board of Directors for each of these Companies. Prior to entering the venture capital industry, Ralph gained significant experience in technology R&D, business development and investment banking. He worked previously as a Senior Research Scientist at Bell Labs, in Business Development at Lucent Technologies, and as an Investment Banker on Wall Street at GoldmanSachs and JPMorgan.

At Bell Labs (originally the R&D unit of AT&T Corporation and Lucent), Ralph worked almost ten years as a Research Scientist, Engineer and Technology Manager, focused on semiconductor microelectronics processing, photonics components and fiber-optics devices, advanced materials and nanotechnology. He authored over 40 scientific publications and technical conference presentations, had his research work featured in *BusinessWeek* and *Fortune Magazine* and was cited by *MIT Technology Review Magazine* as one of the top 100 technology innovators in the USA for 1999-2000. In addition to R&D, Ralph worked on business development/strategy teams supporting Lucent Microelectronics (which became corporate spinout named Agere Systems Inc. subsequently merged into LSI Corporation), the Lucent Optical Network Communications group (now merged into Alcatel) and the Lucent Corporate Ventures group. After Lucent, Ralph made a transition to Wall Street investment banking, working at GoldmanSachs and then at JPMorgan, on mergers/acquisitions, equity offerings and convertible-debt transactions. At GoldmanSachs, Ralph covered the Technology Media & Telecommunications (TMT) industry sector, focusing on semiconductor microelectronics, photonics, communications infrastructure hardware and software. At JPMorgan, Ralph covered the Chemical Technologies industry sector, focusing on Specialty Chemicals, BioPharmaceuticals, Oil & Gas, and Energy/Power. He then joined the investment team at Battelle Ventures.

Ralph gained his academic training from Princeton University and the Massachusetts Institute of Technology (MIT), receiving a PhD in Engineering (Chemical & Biomolecular Engineering focus) and an MBA in Finance (Corporate Finance & Strategic Planning focus). He holds twelve patents issued to Bell Labs, OFS Optics and Agere Systems for innovations in semiconductor microelectronic devices, optical-fiber & photonics, fuel cells, flat panel displays, and nanotechnology systems. Ralph was selected as a Kauffman Fellow by the Center for Venture Capital Education & Entrepreneurial Leadership, affiliated with the Ewing Marion Kauffman Foundation. He was also appointed a Robert Toigo Foundation Fellow in Finance & Technology Entrepreneurship at MIT Sloan School of Business Management and appointed a Price-Babson SEE Fellow in Entrepreneurship Education & University Curriculum Development at Babson College Center for Entrepreneurship. Ralph remains active in higher education as a University adjunct professor and senior lecturer in Engineering Innovation Management, Entrepreneurship and Science/Technology Commercialization. In addition to his several for-profit Corporate Board Directorships, Ralph serves various non-profit educational organizations, academic colleges and universities as Advisory Board Member or Board of Trustees Member; he also works regularly with the National Science Foundation (NSF) on SBIR

(Small Business Innovation Research) and STTR (Small Business Technology Transfer) programmes.

D.K. Wheeler

A perceived nexus between research and teaching outcomes supports the sponsorship of research by universities and the designation of research as part of academic job descriptions. In fact, this belief has consequences that pervade academic life. It is strange, therefore, that an academic community that is trained to question and challenge ingrained beliefs in other communities has not analysed a philosophy that has significantly impacted their own way of life. Is the research-teaching relationship a myth? If it is not a myth, what specific link is there between research and teaching[1]? Further, for which research, and which aspect of teaching (for example content, strategy or method), can linkage statements be made? Indeed, the stereotypical academic is an absent-minded, research-focussed professor to whom no sane, worldly person can relate.

An attempt to more specifically explain an expectation that research activity produces higher teaching quality is faced with many problems. For example, general statements that make claims about the beneficial impact of research on teaching do not normally clarify:

- What aspect of teaching they refer to (for example, what is taught, how it is taught or the tools and materials used in teaching);
- Whether the statement relates to teaching in general or the teaching of that specific researcher;
- Which research can have this beneficial impact on teaching; and
- How research can improve teaching.

This chapter focuses on the use of research in improving academic teaching outcomes. The range of meanings commonly adopted for 'teaching' in this context resembles a formal definition of curriculum. Consequently, to examine the way that research can influence university teaching and learning in their broadest sense, this chapter considers the differing nature of 'curriculum' and the differing nature of 'research' since, in this context, both of these terms can have different meanings to the user. In fact, it appears to the writer that the discussants in many conversations about using research in curriculum development experience a totally different understanding of their discussion.

The objective of this chapter is to clarify which research can inform curricula at different levels. An outcome of this analysis is the ability of academics, both as researchers and as teachers, to identify the use of research in curricula and its development. Conversely, the findings may be used as a guide to select research projects.

The initial analysis in this chapter is of curricula and their development. The analysis is then extended specifically to discuss accounting curricula development. First the chapter identifies different levels of curricula and then highlights key influences on curricula requirements before explaining curriculum development through its four categories of nondiscrete decisions and their evaluation. Next, the chapter specifies four ways in which research can have an impact on curricula development. Finally, the chapter discusses specific research topics that have impacted, or can impact upon curriculum development in accounting courses. These research topics are categorised in the context of the preceding analyses.

Defining terms frequently provides us with a logical process in the derivation of answers. In this case, possible relationships between research and curriculum are being examined. A review of recent articles and books that discuss 'curriculum' show that they typically do not specify the writer's meaning of the term. The implied meaning can include course content, lecturing materials and tutoring method, among others. For example, Arya et al (2003) write specifically of the structure and content of accounting programmes, while Entwhistle (2003), in a chapter about 'The Research Curriculum', focuses on the delivery materials used in an accounting programme.

Marsh and Willis (1999) describe the broadening of the meaning of 'curriculum' through the twentieth century while

Beyer and Apple (1998) describe a shift in the focus of curriculum theory and practice, away from 'what' and 'why' towards 'how'. Some definitions in texts have become esoteric, including 'Curriculum as *Currere*' (*i.e.* in its verb form rather than as a noun), 'Curriculum as Complexity', 'Curriculum as Cosmology', 'Curriculum as Conversation', 'Curriculum as Community' (Doll and Gough, 2002), and 'Curriculum as Social Conflict' (Goodson, 1997). Among other texts that appear to identify curriculum as an activity in itself are Kincheloe (1991) with *Curriculum as Social Psychoanalysis: the significance of place* and van Lier (1996) with *The Curriculum as Interaction*. Notice also other uses of this word, such as 'Television is a curriculum that...' (Postman cited in OECD 1994, p. 43)

Returning to standard definitions that precede moves that broaden the meaning of curriculum (Doll and Gough, 2002 p.43), esotericism and assumptions of shared meanings, useful definitions for the purposes of this chapter include:

> *Planned experiences offered to the learner under the guidance of the school. (Wheeler, 1967) and*
>
> *A plan for achieving intended learning outcomes. (Unruh, 1975).*

However, university students gain much useful knowledge from experiences that are not carefully planned and Unruh's definition is restricted to the plan itself. Marsh and Stafford (1988) provide a table of curriculum definitions and ultimately develop the definition that is adopted both in this chapter and by Marsh and Willis (1999): An interrelated set of plans and experiences which a student completes under the guidance of the school.

Stenhouse (1987) identifies teaching as 'not merely instruction, but the systematic promotion of learning *by whatever means*. And teaching strategy is an important aspect of curriculum...[Teaching strategy] involves developing a policy and putting that policy into practice' (p.24, emphasis added).

Marsh and Stafford (1988, p.3) and Markee (1997, p.21) clarify the place of 'syllabus' as also being subsumed by 'curriculum'.

Marsh and Willis (1999, p.11) also explain that it is both unnecessary and undesirable to separate instruction from curriculum. Instruction, as the means by which defined ends should be achieved, is entirely interwoven with the other aspects of curriculum. With such broad definitions underpinning curriculum studies it is understandable why the word 'curriculum' has been used in a variety of contexts and appears, in fact, to have a plethora of different meanings. The diverse meanings and uses can be better understood by reference to four levels of curricula. This hierarchy of curricula also assists in the identification of *which* research can inform curriculum development, and *how* that research can impact the curriculum.

The terms used by writers differ but a representative curricula hierarchy is: broad, core, subject, and activity levels (for example, Wheeler (1967) writes of broadfield, core, subject and activity levels). This concept of curricula, written about in the context of primary and secondary education, can be adapted to a tertiary education setting. Broad level.

In the first approach, pre-2005 graduates would be better equipped to work as an accountant in a range of countries, or supervise the preparation of financial statements in the national branches of a multi-national company. The latter approach could examine issues such as the design of an effective control system for the operations of international subsidiaries, and performance evaluation measures for national branch managers.

Both of these kinds of course could have been offered by the same university, possibly with the first in the undergraduate programme and the latter in a postgraduate master's programme. This specific focus of a course arises from decisions about its objective. Further decisions are then made about the particular content of the course. As a case in point, for a management accounting course subject level decisions must be made about incorporating topics such as cost-volume-profit analysis, contemporary performance evaluation methods and inventory management methods. Some topics are best suited to cost analysis courses. Yet some cost analysis topics could also appropriately be incorporated in a subsequent Strategic Management Accounting course. Content decisions therefore need to be made in the interests of minimising the overlap of course content.

Activity Level

The teaching content of a course can be called the *activity* curriculum level. At this level, decisions can cover issues such as the use of case studies, the nature of progressive evaluation, the lecturing style, the content of PowerPoint presentations, and so on. At the activity level the decisions relate to '*how* we try to get the message across'. '*What* message we are trying to get across' is the outcome of decisions at the subject level.

Influences on Curriculum Requirements

Four distinct sources of influence on the requirements of the curricula are those of society in general; select groups; the school (*i.e.* the institution and its academic staff); and the scholar. It will be seen that each of these can provide a source of research ideas. However, research itself is not presented as an influence on curricula since research ideally acts as one of the media for communication between the influencers and the change agents (curriculum developers at all four levels), often analysing desires, wants and needs and the likely outcomes of alternative options.

Society

Society's needs are always in a state of flux. The problems confronting society change rapidly and recurring issues change in the level of importance that society places on them. Furthermore, society's members become increasingly knowledgeable about problems. Consequently, the demands they place on academia, and the accounting profession, become more sophisticated.

The most general, overarching level of curriculum can be termed *broad*. In the context of university curricula this can be as wide-ranging as the content of a degree programme, or even the programmes offered by the university and their general structure. In business and accounting degrees there are general decisions to be made about the courses that must be studied by students to qualify for the degree. There are usually some compulsory courses and a structure of major and minor sequences of study. These decisions are influenced, to a large extent, by accounting's professional bodies.

Core Level

The content of a major or minor sequence of study, and the offerings within a discipline, can be regarded as the *core* level of curricula. Decisions include: which courses will be offered for study by the faculty, which of these are essential for the sequence, which courses are electives from which students can select the rest of the major/minor sequence, and which courses provide knowledge essential for the study of subsequent courses (prerequisite courses of study).

Subject Level

At the *subject* level, the content of courses is determined. Given a focus on international accounting, for instance, decisions used to be made about whether the content would examine and compare the different accounting approach adopted in a variety of countries—studying the national accounting standards—or whether students should take a managerial perspective that reflected on the impact of accounting on managing international operations.

Hilda Taba (1902–1967)

Although Ernest Hemingway once stated that in each port of the world you could meet at least one Estonian, it is a rare occurrence when the existence and achievements of great personalities originating from this 1 million strong nation are associated with their native country and nation in the minds of their foreign colleagues. In this sense **Hilda Taba** is not an exception. She is known worldwide as an outstanding American educator and **curriculum** theorist, but very few know that she was born, brought up and educated in Estonia. Probably, even more surprising is the fact that **Taba**, belonging to the list of the most outstanding educators of the twentieth century and whose academic work climaxed with the publication of the monograph ***Curriculum** development: theory and practice* (1962), remained unknown in her native country for decades.

So, in spite of the fact that Taba's approach to **curriculum** design spread throughout the world and her monograph took an honourable position on the bookshelves of European education libraries in the 1960s, her educational ideas reached Estonian educators only at the end of the 1980s.

The above-mentioned circumstance is one of the many controversial aspects in **Hilda** Taba's life that evidently played an important role in her development as a scientist and gave a unique colouration to her educational ideas. Another controversy, undoubtedly playing a major role in the formation of Taba's theoretical ideas and thinking, was the collision between German and American educational traditions that she experienced in her studies of pedagogy. For instance, the undergraduate educational preparation that she received at the University of Tartu had a strong disposition towards German didactics and educational philosophy.

However, her subsequent post-graduate studies in the United States of America were strongly influenced by the ideas of progressive education, which she came to admire and which became a cornerstone of her educational thinking.

It remains unknown whether **Taba** had dreamed of pursuing her academic career in the United States or of returning to Estonia after her post-graduate studies abroad. However, the fact that she competed for the professorship in education at the University of Tartu in 1931 rather points to her intention to bind her working career and life to Estonia. These plans did not comeabout, as she was not selected for this position. But what is even more amazing was that she could not find any other job in Estonia worthy of her qualifications. So, the author of the doctoral dissertation *The dynamics of education: a methodology of progressive educational thought*(1932), which later earned wide recognition among educators, decided to return to North America. This unexpected change in her plans and the subsequent move caused **Taba** to experience serious difficulties and misery at the beginning of her career. **Hilda** Taba's road to excellence was in some parts due to chance, her enormous desire to succeed and the favourable conditions for educational research in the United States, and she became one of the brightest stars in the educational constellation of the 1960s. Nowadays, her work in the field of **curriculum**design, alongside that of Ralph W. Tyler, belongs to the classics of pedagogy. Several contemporary authors still frequently refer to **Hilda** Taba's ideas and base their work in the field of **curriculum** theory and practice on her conceptions developed decades ago (see, for example, articles in the handbooks edited by Shaver, 1991; and Leawy, 1991; and in academic journals by Klarin, 1992; Fraenkel, 1994; Parry et al., 2000). There are over 100 recent articles and monographs referring to the work of **Taba** in the ERIC database. Furthermore, countless references to her name and educational ideas on the Internet are additional proof that her academic contribution to the field of education has lasting value.

Some ideas about **Hilda Taba** as a person can be found in Elizabeth H. Brady's (1992) commemorative article. Brady, one of her closest colleagues during the days of intergroup education projects (1945–51), wrote: 'Taba was very energetic, enthusiastic, active, seemingly tireless; she led life at a tempo which sometimes led to misunderstandings and often wore out friends and staff. She was small in stature, perky in manners and in dress, and always intent on the next thing' (Brady, 1992, p. 9).

Hilda Taba's Childhood and University Studies

The future prominent educator **Hilda Taba** was born in Kooraste, a small village in the present Põlva county, in south-east Estonia, on 7 December 1902. She was the first of nine children of Robert **Taba**, a schoolmaster. **Hilda** was first educated at her father's elementary school, and then at the local parish school.

In 1921, after graduating from Võru High School for Girls, she decided to become an elementary school-teacher. In the autumn of the same year **Hilda** passed the final examination for elementary teacher certification at the Didactic Seminar of Tartu, but she did not begin work at a primary school. Instead, she became a student of economics at the University of Tartu. Economics, however, did not appeal to **Taba** and a year later she applied to be transferred to the Faculty of Philosophy where she majored in history and education. As her father's schoolmaster income was too modest for maintaining a big family and supporting Hilda's studies, the tutoring of young students became her main after-school activity and source of income. A dedication in her dissertation to Maria Raudsepp, a pupil she coached during her university studies in Tartu, commemorates this aspect of Taba's biography.

After graduating from the University of Tartu in 1926, **Taba** had the opportunity to undertake her post-graduate studies in the United States, supported by a grant from the Rockefeller Foundation. Her excellent knowledge of educational subjects acquired at Tartu University made it possible for her to complete a master's degree at Bryn Mawr College in a year. During her studies at Bryn Mawr, she started to visit progressive schools and became interested in the practice of the Dalton Plan (Klarin, 1989). Surveying American educational literature, **Taba** discovered *Fundamentals of education* by Boyd. H. Bode (1921), a then widely known author and educator in the United States.

Taba was very impressed by Bode's (1873–1953) approach and she grew interested in the philosophy of progressive education. In particular, she enjoyed the child-centredness and the novelty and flexibility of this educational approach. In 1927 she applied for doctoral studies in educational philosophy at Columbia University. During the following five years of studies **Taba** met many American scientists of world renown, among them the psychologist E.L. Thorndike (1874–1949), the educator and historian P. Monroe (1869–1947), the sociologist G.C. Gounts, and the founder of the Winnetka Plan, C. Washburne (1889–1968). Nevertheless, the person to affect **Hilda** Taba's educational thinking most was John Dewey (1859–1952)—a philosopher and educator with a global reputation, and one of the initiators of the progressive educational movement whose lectures she attended and whose writings she studied carefully (Isham, 1982; **Taba**, 1932, p. vii). The principal advisor of her doctoral work became William H. Kilpatrick (1871–1965), one of John Dewey's colleagues, known in the history of education as the initiator of the project method. Kilpatrick ended his foreword to Taba's dissertation with prophetic words about its author, stating that 'hard will be that reader to please and far advanced his previous thinking who does not leave this book feeling distinctly indebted to its very capable author' (Kilpatrick, 1932). Kilpatrick was right in assessing the value of this work, and his opinion was proved by the fact that some fifty years later Telegraph Books reprinted the monograph in 1980.

In 1931, having completed her doctoral dissertation, **Hilda Taba** returned to Estonia in order to apply for the professorship left vacant through the untimely death of Peeter Põld, her professor of education when she studied at the University of Tartu. Unfortunately, **Taba** was not elected and evidently was badly disappointed. Although she found employment at a college of household economics in Estonia, she decided shortly thereafter to return to the United States.

Taba's Scientific Career in the United States

Once back in the United States, **Hilda Taba** experienced serious hardships. In the beginning she did not find any employment corresponding to her qualifications, and so she had to undertake some casual jobs. Later, she worked for a wealthy American family coaching their children—an activity she was used to already in Estonia. In addition, her stay in the United States was complicated by the fact that she did not have American citizenship, and because of this she was permanently threatened with deportation by the Department of Immigration. Finally, in 1933

Taba was given a post as a German teacher, and later on she became the director of **curriculum** in the Dalton School, in Ohio.

It is of interest to mention that **Hilda Taba** became involved in educational research by a lucky chance. She was hired just at the start of the Eight-Year Study in which the Dalton School was actively involved. Taba's participation in the study brought her together with Ralph Tyler, who was the head of the field evaluation staff of the study. Tyler was impressed by her devotion to scientific research and by her profound understanding of educational processes, and he hired **Taba** to form part of the evaluation staff (located at the University of Ohio) as the co-ordinator of the social studies **curriculum**. In 1939, when the evaluation staff was transferred to the University of Chicago, **Taba** became the director of the **curriculum** laboratory, which she headed until 1945.

By the mid-1940s **Taba** had become a capable and widely recognized educational researcher. She initiated, designed and directed several research projects centred on two major topics: intergroup education (1945–51); and the reorganization and development of social studies curricula in California (1951–67). **Hilda Taba** also served as a consultant to many local institutions and school districts, and she took part in UNESCO seminars in Paris and Brazil (Harshbarger, 1978).

Studies in The Field of Intergroup Education

Intergroup education became topical in the United States following the Second World War. The reorganization of American industry for the needs of war had caused a significant migration of workers from rural areas to the cities. As a result, major changes in people's way of life and in the composition of their neighbourhoods took place, and these changes contributed to a growing tension. In 1944, quite serious interracial riots took place in Detroit. This was the drop that made the cup run over, and more than 400 public organizations were founded in the United States in response to these events (Klarin, 1989). Taba's research group submitted to the American Council on Education one of many proposals aimed at the investigation of possibilities for increasing the level of tolerance between students from different ethnic and cultural backgrounds. The Intergroup Education Project was accepted and launched in New York City in 1945.

Hilda Taba became its director. The success of the experimental project led to the establishment of the Center of Intergroup Education at the University of Chicago, which was headed by **Taba** (1948–51).

The study began with an extensive investigation of the socio-psychological causes of intergroup tensions, and it ended with the approval of school curricula for intergroup tolerance education between students. These curricula focused on the four main issues related to social life that proved to be essential in the formation of stereotypes and prejudices: (1) differences in the style of family life; (2) differences in the life-styles of the communities; (3) ignorance of American culture; and (4) development of peaceful relations between individuals (**Taba** et al., 1952). In order to foster better knowledge, understanding and attitudes in these life spheres, special education programmes were developed.

For example, the education programme aimed at the development of personal relations taught children how to handle conflicts without resorting to violence. From today's perspective, intergroup education can be considered as a forerunner of intercultural or multicultural education. When taking a closer look at Taba's work on intergroup education, it is difficult to disagree with Elizabeth H. Brady's comment that one of Taba's 'major contributions was to recognize that social science could provide a strong foundation for education, with sociology, social pedagogy and cultural anthropology in particular illuminating issues in human relations education' (Brady, 1992, p. 8).

Development of Social Studies Curricula

The second and final period of **Hilda** Taba's independent scientific career began in 1951, when she accepted a proposal for the reorganization and development of social studies curricula in Contra Costa county, in the San Francisco Bay area. At the same time, she became a full professor of education at San Francisco State University. This was the period when her expertise in the areas of **curriculum** design, intergroup education and development of cognitive processes won her international recognition.

Mary Durkin (1993, p. ix), the former social studies **curriculum** co-ordinator for the county, describes the beginning of Taba's research and its character in Contra Costa as follows: It was a fortunate coincidence that Dr. **Hilda Taba** joined the staff of San Francisco State at the same time as the Director of **Curriculum** of Contra Costa County Department of

Education in California was searching for a consultant whose mode of thinking was compatible with staff's to write a social studies teacher guide.

The Contra Costa County Board of Education provided **Taba** with ample time by not setting a deadline for the guides. Seven years were spent on two studies of children's thinking and the guides. The process included conferences with content specialists, in-service workshops, and the writing, testing and rewriting of the guides.

In her turn, **Taba** (1962, p. 482) saw the problems connected with the social studies **curriculum** and the reasons for selecting a specific strategy for **curriculum** development in this way:

> *The analysis of the problems required change in the* ***curriculum*** *and the approach to making this change was made by the county* ***curriculum*** *staff in co-operation with the school principals. This analysis suggested that the usual efforts—institutes, lectures, required attendance of college classes—had not over a period of years produced much* ***curriculum*** *improvement and did not seem promising for making changes in the structure of* ***curriculum****. Furthermore, since the county staff had been responsible for developing* ***curriculum*** *guides and units, the teachers in various districts tended to regard the county as authoritarian and it was difficult to kindle their initiative for* ***curriculum*** *improvement. For these reasons, the county staff was searching for some kind of grass-roots approach that would promise greater participation and involvement in the whole process of* ***curriculum*** *improvement, and at the same time improve the human relations between the schools and the county office.*

So, the beginning of the study was largely concerned with the identification and analysis of teachers' problems in the field of social studies. The teachers, after they had identified mismatches in the curricula they were using with their expectations for them, were asked to develop their own teaching/learning units. As the teachers' expertise was not sufficient for **curriculum** development, seminars and consultancy sessions were organized. The members of the research team primarily provided this kind of in-service training for co-operating teachers. Later on, this function was gradually taken over by the county staff as their expertise through in-service training that was especially organized for them increased. Teachers who developed the new teaching/learning units first checked them in school practice. Then they underwent a critical revision and were again tried out, but this time by a larger number of teachers. This procedure was applied many times, until results satisfying the needs of teachers at different schools were achieved. Usually, the **curriculum** for an entire grade involved from five to eight units.

The planning of general steps and procedures of **curriculum** development were the responsibility of Taba's research team at the beginning of the study. Then, similarly to the development of teacher guidance abilities, this function was gradually taken over by the county **curriculum** staff as its expertise increased. Consequently, the research programme was aimed at the re-education of the whole staff and at producing pilot models of **curriculum** development and teaching (**Taba**, 1962, p. 482–93).

The main purpose of the study was to provide a flexible model of **curriculum** renewal, based on conjoint efforts of practising teachers and educational administrators responsible for school curricula. It is important to mention that many ideas underlying Taba's **curriculum** model, such as the notion of a 'spiral' **curriculum**, inductive teaching strategies for the development of concepts, generalizations and applications; organization of content on three levels—key ideas, organizational ideas and facts—and her general strategy for developing thinking through the social studies **curriculum** significantly influenced **curriculum** developers during the 1960s and early 1970s. Many general principles and ideas of **curriculum** design developed by **Hilda Taba** belong to the foundations of modern **curriculum** theories, and are frequently referred to by other authors.

Many of Taba's ideas on **curriculum** design can be considered as a further elaboration of Ralph Tyler's rather psychological principles of **curriculum** development: attributing to them a more pedagogical and practical nature. This is well evidenced by reconsidering the meaning and nature of Tyler's (1969) rationale of **curriculum** design: (1) stating educational objectives; (2) selecting and (3) organizing learning experiences; and (4) assessing the achievement of objectives. In her version, **Taba** introduced notions of multiple educational objectives and four distinct categories of objectives (basic knowledge, thinking skills, attitudes and academic skills).

This approach allowed **Hilda Taba** to relate specific teaching/learning strategies to each category of objectives. In this sense, her classification of educational objectives has some similarities with Gagné's (1985) system of learning outcomes and the conditions of learning which explain the ways for reaching desired outcomes.

Also, the sophisticated classification of educational objectives allowed **Taba** to give to Tyler's notion of learning experiences a more specific and practical meaning by considering separately the selection and organization of instructional content and strategies of learning. As stated by **Hilda Taba** in her teacher handbook for elementary social studies: the selection and organization of content implements only one of the four areas of objectives—that of knowledge.

The selection of content does not develop the techniques and skills for thinking, change patterns of attitudes and feelings, or produce academic and social skills. These objectives only can be achieved by the way in which the learning experiences are planned and conducted in the classroom. [...] Achievement of three of the four categories of objectives depends on the nature of learning experiences rather than on the content (**Taba**, 1967, p. 11).

Hilda Taba died unexpectedly on 6 July 1967, at the peak of her academic capabilities and power.

Some of Taba's Philosophical Ideas on Curriculum Development

There are many academic papers in English and in Estonian describing **Hilda** Taba's ideas and research on specific areas of education. But there are fewer writings on Taba's general principles and beliefs regarding research and education that made her work unique, inventive and original. Many of the ideas that made **Taba** world famous kept developing and evolving gradually throughout her career. A preliminary, and therefore incomplete, analysis of her scientific heritage suggests at least four principles that seem to govern her vision of **curriculum** theory and **curriculum** development (Krull & Kurm, 1996, p. 11–12):

1. Social processes, including the socialization of human beings, are not linear, and they cannot be modelled through linear planning. In other words, learning and development of personality cannot be considered as one-way processes of establishing educational aims and deriving specific objectives from an ideal of education proclaimed or imagined by some authority.
2. Social institutions, among them school curricula and programmes, are more likely to be effectively rearranged if, instead of the common way of administrative reorganization— from top to bottom—a well-founded and co-ordinated system of development from bottom to top can be used.
3. The development of new curricula and programmes is more effective if it is based on the principles of democratic guidance and on the well-founded distribution of work. The emphasis is on the partnership based on competence, and not on administration.
4. The renovation of curricula and programmes is not a short-term effort but a long process, lasting for years.

The principle of considering social processes as non-linear is the most important one, and it probably governs all of **Hilda** Taba's educational work. **Taba** pointed out already in her doctoral dissertation that 'ends and aims, as they are in actual life, seldom present themselves as simple and easily comprehensible units' (1932, p. 142) and, therefore, 'a purposive act must be regarded primarily as an outgrowth of previous activity and not as an independent unit starting and activating because of some end or purpose clamoring for actualization'

(1932, p. 143). Applying the principle to **curriculum** design, this means that it is unreal and impossible to set up rigid general goals of education from which more specified objectives would be derived for a concrete plan. The general goals are also subject to modification in order to become adapted to the real circumstances, whereby they are dependent more or less on the content and character of the educational step planned.

The second principle of the efficiency of the bottom-up approach suggests the most convenient way to help individuals and human social organizations to accept and to adapt to new situations and ideas. Taba's view can be well interpreted in the light of Donald Schön's concept of 'dynamic conservatism' (Schön, 1971), which expresses the tendency of individuals and social organizations to oppose energetically changes that derange or offend their convictions and understandings by building up structures and mechanisms that will interfere with these changes.

The expected changes in the individual or social consciousness will take place only if individuals or groups, under pressure to introduce these changes, conserve or acquire the ability to learn. So, the changes and learning underlying it take place more easily, and meet less opposition if they are not imposed by the central institutions but are initiated in the periphery, and gradually spread all over the structure.

The third and fourth principles underline the necessity for the democratic guidance of **curriculum** development and the long-term nature of this process, and are essentially derived from the first two principles. They are explicitly spelled out in the description of the organization for social studies **curriculum** development used in Contra Costa county.

Probably the most characteristic feature of **Hilda** Taba's educational thinking was the ability to see the forest for the trees, pointing to her capability to discriminate between the essential and the non-essential or the important and the unimportant. She was never misled by the outside lustre of an idea even when facing the most advanced educational innovations of the day, and she always scrutinized them for their educational purpose or value. An episode described in the commemorative article by A.L. Costa and R.A. Loveall (2002) is good evidence of this aspect of Taba's thinking.

Taba, when visiting a prestigious American university in the 1960s, was led to a computer centre where a huge mainframe computer was used for developing one of the first teaching machines. Her judgement on the value of this enterprise was fast and rather disappointing: 'Million-dollar machine, ten cent idea' (Costa & Loveall, 2002, p. 61)

UNIT-IV

Curriculum Transaction

Strategies for Curriculum Transaction

The changes reflected in the Conceptual Framework of Population Education will require identification and adoption of suitable strategies of curriculum transaction. The strategy of integration of population education contents into the syllabi and textbooks of selected subjects at the school level has been adopted. The textbooks are considered effective instruments for exposing students to population education ideas and messages that are essential for making their understanding of population phenomena better. In this context the follcwing strategies may be useful:

(i) Attempt has to be made to include only those contents that could receive comprehensive and effective treatment in the syllabi and textbooks of concerned subjects. Those natural entry points be selected that have potentiality of providing comprehensive treatment to relevant population education contents. The most crucial aspect of effective integration would be to integrate maximum contents at minimum points in most comprehensive way. Only those subjects should be given priority that have greater potentiality to incorporate these contents.

(ii) Some contents of population education may not find suitable entry into the existing syllabi and textbooks because of the limitation of the subject areas. For such contents supplementary reading materials and 'audio-visual materials may be developed. Classroom teaching needs to be supplemented by a variety of co-curricular activities such as project assignments, play way activities, demonstration, group discussion, painting, essay writing, debate, elocution, question box, quiz competition, etc.

(iii) Any curriculum remains a futile exercise unless it is put into practice. Teacher occupies an important place in the implementation of this area. It is the teacher who has to use the material, create learning situations in the classroom for their students and help them to learn. Their orientation to the new curriculum is, therefore, absolutely essential. Both in-service and pre-service orientation should be organized. The teacher should be fed with suitable instructional materials like teacher's guide, handbooks with update information and audio-visual materials.

Population education taught by an imaginative teacher could enable students to creative thinking and action in relation to a number of problems and issues that surround them. Problem solving/discovery approach and value clarification approaches are regarded to be more functional.

(iv) The population education contents integrated in different subject areas, other materials developed for promoting effective integration, teacher training organized and activities conducted in schools should be evaluated to find out whether the desired outcomes in terms of awareness and attitude have been achieved. Being value-laden, continuous and comprehensive evaluation should be followed so that necessary improvements are made in the curriculum and materials and its transaction.

Implementing Strategies for Learners with Special Needs

Segregation or isolation is good neither for learners with impairments nor for general learners without impairment. Societal requirement is that learners with special needs should be educated along with other learners in 'inclusive schools'; which are cost effective and have sound pedagogical practices.

The process of bringing learners with special needs into the mainstream in an inclusive school starts with the assessment of their educational needs and preparation of an Individual Education Plan for each one of them in consultation with their parents. Teaching then becomes learner centred. Besides, group learning or cooperative learning and peer tutoring would also be encouraged in an inclusive school. This would bring the learners with special needs into the mainstream, create positive attitude among learners without impairment and foster the attitude and skill of learning together without complexes.

Definite action at the level of **curriculum** makers, teachers, writers of teaching-learning materials and evaluation experts is required for the success of this strategy. This has to include:

developing appropriate supplementary instructional material for learners with special needs;

making appropriate modifications in the content, its presentation and ***transaction strategies*** *to facilitate conceptual clarity among learners with different special needs; developing and working out appropriate learner friendly evaluation procedures for learners with different special needs;*

preparing teachers with initial induction and sensitising them through in-service education programmes to help them attend to the special needs of the learners with various challenges and equipping these teachers with skills, competencies and ***strategies*** *required to cater to the diversity in an inclusive setting;*

developing comprehensive guidelines for teachers to define educational goals for all learners in the inclusive setting; and mobilising community resources for support to learners with special needs. These could be in the form of resource centres.

Vocational guidance and counselling would assume an extremely significant role to play. The entire process would produce appropriately equipped functionaries to make their contribution in all the departments of the stream effectively.

Implementing Evaluation Strategies

Successful implementation of any reform requires a combination of strong will and commitment of all the people involved in the process. Reform in the implementation of evaluation **strategies** requires the following measures:

Climate building

Material development

Capacity building

Resource mobilisation

Climate Building

Proper and adequate awareness among the masses is the first pre-requisite for the success of any effort at bringing in reform in the area of school education. Conscious efforts, therefore, need to be made through media blitz to educate the community regarding the merits of the proposed reforms and bring about change in people's mind set.

Material Development

Materials have to be developed in keeping with the local specificities and requirements. These will have to be:

conceptual materials on various reforms like continuous and comprehensive evaluation, grading, semesterisation, question banking etc.;

tools of evaluation like diagnostic tests, criterion-referenced tests, achievement tests, rating scales, observation schedules, checklists, inventories etc.;

question banks in various curricular areas;

detailed schemes of continuous and comprehensive evaluation for every stage of school education;

detailed schemes of semesterisation at secondary and higher secondary stages of school education;

modularisation of courses of secondary and higher secondary stages for the purpose of semesterisation;

teacher education materials on evaluation both for pre-service and in-service programmes; and guidelines for schools and boards for implementing various reforms.

Capacity Building

All the functionaries involved in the implementation of the proposed reforms, right from the managers to teachers, will need capacity building interventions. These programmes will have to be tailor made in view of the specific requirements of different target groups.

Resource Mobilisation

All out efforts shall have to be made to mobilise all the possible and probable resources available at any level — national, state, district, institutional or even individual — for the implementation of the proposed reforms.

The Role of Different Agencies

The various agencies responsible for qualitative improvement in school education, both at the national and the state levels, have to work hand-in-hand to bring about reforms in the evaluation system.

School

In any venture of educational reform schools play the most crucial role because they are the agencies that transact **curriculum** and deal with the growth of the learners directly. Therefore, each school will have to develop its own scheme and strategy of evaluation for Classes I to XII which will include the frequency of assignments, tests and examinations, the specific cognitive and non-cognitive areas to be covered, the types of tests to be employed for assessing both the kinds of learning outcomes, maintenance of records and reporting of results. The schools will also develop remediation materials in order to upgrade teaching and learning in the classrooms and encourage teachers to take up action research with a view to improving upon the evaluation procedures. These activities will have to be taken up either individually or collectively by forming school clusters in order to sustain the best of their human and physical resources.

Boards of School Education

The objective of state boards of education in promoting reforms in evaluation will be to improve not only the reliability, validity and management of their own examinations but also the quality of school evaluation in general. Besides, the boards would also have to accept the responsibility of validating educational objectives and identifying hard spots of learning by undertaking performance analysis of the examination results.

Since the boards have the expertise which may not be available with the individual schools for preparing quality test material, they may develop prototypes and make them available to schools. They will have to organise teachers' orientation programmes in educational evaluation with a view to building capabilities at the school level. The boards must also conduct research in the area of educational evaluation, carry out achievement surveys to obtain census-like data and make their results available to individual schools so as to make them realise their strengths and weaknesses.

State Level Agencies

State agencies like Directorates of Education, State Councils of Educational Research and Training, DIETs and voluntary agencies will have to shoulder the responsibility of assisting and guiding schools in developing and selecting appropriate instructional materials and selecting suitable transactional **strategies** with a view to realising the educational objectives. Besides, they must also help schools develop tests which can be used for assessing cognitive and non-cognitive learning outcomes and organise regular in-service training programmes for their teachers. They also have to provide to schools the logistics for maintaining students' records, conducting achievement surveys, undertaking innovations, conducting research besides monitoring the progress of individual schools and providing them necessary feedback and guidelines.

Teacher Education Institutions

The institutions responsible for imparting pre-service teacher education in the country can play a vital role in bringing about reform in evaluation practices. For this, they will have to make evaluation a core component in their curricula and review the existing ones thoroughly. Apart from undertaking research they will also have to conduct in-service teacher orientation programmes in evaluation for the teachers belonging to the schools in their vicinity.

National Agencies

National agencies like the National Council of Educational Research and Training, the proposed National Evaluation Organisation and the Council of Boards of School Education need to undertake the task of:

laying down the expected levels of attainment in each curricular area of all the stages of school education;
developing conceptual materials and prototypes on child-centred, activity oriented and competency based teaching-learning materials;
generating various kinds of tests, which could be meaningfully employed for assessing cognitive and non-cognitive learning outcomes, and making them available to the state agencies;
conducting orientation programmes for key resource persons;
organising training programmes for paper setters of different boards;
inventing and suggesting logistics of maintaining records and reporting of results;
conducting research for finding out better ways and means for evaluating learning outcomes;
conducting achievement surveys for obtaining census-like data; and dissemination of information

Organisation of Instruction

Curriculum and instruction is the method in which to design a set of instructions on how to provide instruction within a formal classroom.

This also includes how to prepare and administer exams to students. These exams must meet a set of criteria in order to provide a fair and accurate measurement of a student's comprehension of the class materials presented.

Curriculum Theory and Practice

The organization of schooling and further education has long been associated with the idea of a curriculum. But what actually is curriculum, and how might it be conceptualized? We explore curriculum theory and practice and its relation to informal education.

The idea of curriculum is hardly new-but the way we understand and theorize it has altered over the years-and there remains considerable dispute as to meaning. It has its origins in the running/chariot tracks of Greece. It was, literally, a course. In Latin curriculum was a racing chariot; currere was to run.

A useful starting point for us here might be the definition offered by John Kerr and taken up by Vic Kelly in his standard work on the subject. Kerr defines curriculum as, 'All the learning which is planned and guided by the school, whether it is carried on in groups or individually, inside or outside the school. (quoted in Kelly 1983: 10; see also, Kelly 1999). This gives us some basis to move on-and for the moment all we need to do is highlight two of the key features:

Learning is planned and guided. We have to specify in advance what we are seeking to achieve and how we are to go about it. The definition refers to schooling. We should recognize that our current appreciation of curriculum theory and practice emerged in the school and in relation to other schooling ideas such as subject and lesson. In what follows we are going to look at four ways of approaching curriculum theory and practice:

1. *Curriculum as a body of knowledge to be transmitted.*
2. *Curriculum as an attempt to achieve certain ends in students-product.*
3. *Curriculum as process.*
4. *Curriculum as praxis.*

It is helpful to consider these ways of approaching curriculum theory and practice in the light of Aristotle's influential categorization of knowledge into three disciplines: the theoretical, the productive and the practical.

Here we can see some clear links-the body of knowledge to be transmitted in the first is that classically valued as 'the canon'; the process and praxis models come close to practical deliberation; and the technical concerns of the outcome or product model mirror elements of Aristotle's characterization of the productive. More this will be revealed as we examine the theory underpinning individual models.

Curriculum as a syllabus to be transmitted Many people still equate a curriculum with a syllabus. Syllabus, naturally, originates from the Greek (although there was some confusion in its usage due to early misprints). Basically it means a concise statement or table of the heads of a discourse, the contents of a treatise, the subjects of a series of lectures. In the form that many of us will have been familiar with it is connected with courses leading to examinations-teachers talk of the syllabus associated with, say, the Cambridge Board French GCSE exam. What we can see in such documents is a series of headings with some additional notes which set out the areas that may be examined. A syllabus will not generally indicate the relative importance of its topics or the order in which they are to be studied.

In some cases as Curzon (1985) points out, those who compile a syllabus tend to follow the traditional textbook approach of an 'order of contents', or a pattern prescribed by a 'logical' approach to the subject, or—consciously or unconsciously-a the shape of a university course in which they may have participated. Thus, an approach to curriculum theory and practice which focuses on syllabus is only really concerned with content. Curriculum is a body of knowledge-content and/ or subjects. Education in this sense, is the process by which these are transmitted or 'delivered' to students by the most effective methods that can be devised (Blenkin et al 1992: 23). Where people still equate curriculum with a syllabus they are likely to limit their planning to a consideration of the content or the body of knowledge that they wish to transmit.

'It is also because this view of curriculum has been adopted that many teachers in primary schools', Kelly (1985: 7) claims, 'have regarded issues of curriculum as of no concern to them, since they have not regarded their task as being to transmit bodies of knowledge in this manner'.

Curriculum as product The dominant modes of describing and managing education are today couched in the productive form. Education is most often seen as a technical exercise. Objectives are set, a plan drawn up, then applied, and the outcomes (products) measured. It is a way of thinking about education that has grown in influence in the United Kingdom since the late 1970s with the rise of vocationalism and the concern with competencies.

Thus, in the late 1980s and the 1990s many of the debates about the National Curriculum for schools did not so much concern how the curriculum was thought about as to what its objectives and content might be. It is the work of two American writers Franklin Bobbitt (1918; 1928) and Ralph W. Tyler (1949) that dominate theory and practice within this tradition. In The Curriculum Bobbitt writes as follows: The central theory [of curriculum] is simple. Human life, however varied, consists in the performance of specific activities. Education that prepares for life is one that prepares definitely and adequately for these specific activities.

However numerous and diverse they may be for any social class they can be discovered. This requires only that one go out into the world of affairs and discover the particulars of which their affairs consist. These will show the abilities, attitudes, habits, appreciations and forms of knowledge that men need. These will be the objectives of the curriculum. They will be numerous, definite and particularized. The curriculum will then be that series of experiences which children and youth must have by way of obtaining those objectives. (1918: 42) This way of thinking about curriculum theory and practice was heavily influenced by the development of management thinking and practice.

The rise of 'scientific management' is often associated with the name of its main advocate F. W. Taylor. Basically what he proposed was greater division of labour with jobs being simplified; an extension of managerial control over all elements of the workplace; and cost accounting based on systematic time-and-motion study. All three elements were involved in this conception of curriculum theory and practice. For example, one of the attractions of this approach to curriculum theory was that it involved detailed attention to what people needed to know in order to work, live their lives and so on.

A familiar, and more restricted, example of this approach can be found in many training programmes, where particular tasks or jobs have been analyzed-broken down into their component elements-and lists of competencies drawn up. In other words, the curriculum was not to be the result of'armchair speculation' but the product of systematic study. Bobbitt's work and theory met with mixed responses. One telling criticism that was made, and can continue to be made, of such approaches is that there is no social vision or programmed to guide the process of curriculum construction.

As it stands it is a technical exercise. However, it wasn't criticisms such as this which initially limited the impact of such curriculum theory in the late 1920s and 1930s. Rather, the growing influence of'progressive', child-centred approaches shifted the ground to more romantic notions of education. Bobbitt's long lists of objectives and his emphasis on order and structure hardly sat comfortably with such forms. The Progressive movement lost much of its momentum in the late 1940s in the United States and from that period the work of Ralph W. Tyler, in particular, has made a lasting impression on curriculum theory and practice.

He shared Bobbitt's emphasis on rationality and relative simplicity. His theory was based on four fundamental questions: 1. What educational purposes should the school seek to attain? 2. What educational experiences can be provided that are likely to attain these purposes? 3. How can these educational experiences be effectively organized? 4. How can we determine whether these purposes are being attained? (Tyler 1949: 1) Like Bobbitt he also placed an emphasis on the formulation of behavioral objectives. Since the real purpose of education is not to have the instructor perform certain activities but to bring about significant changes in the students' pattern of behavior, it becomes important to recognize that any statements of objectives of the school should be a statement of changes to take place in the students. (Tyler 1949: 44)

Models of Teaching

Behavioral Systems

The focus of the methods associated with this category is on observable skills and behaviors. These methods have generally proved more likely to positively impact scores on standardized tests of basic skills than models in other categories.

- Direct Instruction—highly structured, teacher-directed; maximization of student learning time
- Mastery Learning—given enough time and quality instruction, nearly all students can master any set of objectives

Information-Processing Approaches

The focus of the methods associated with information processing approaches are more linked to concepts and principles developed in cognitive psychology. Many of the tests used to measure school learning are being modified so that they consider important mental processing skills that these models are designed to address.

- Inquiry Training/Inductive Thinking—focus on concept formation, interpretation of data, and formation of principles and theories
- Concept Attainment—focus on categorizing, concept formation, and concept attainment
- Intellectual Development—based on the cognitive developmental theory of Jean Piaget

Personal Development

The focus of these models is on those outcomes held in high regard by humanistic educators: high self-concept and self-esteem; positive self-direction and independence; creativity and curiosity; and the development of affect and emotions. Most of the methods used are associated with open education. While these models have not demonstrated an ability to impact outcomes associated with traditional education, they do show promise in impacting other outcomes important for the information age.

- Facilitative teaching—student-centered; based on the methods of Carl Rogers
- Increasing Personal Awareness—focus is on developing an awareness and fullfillment of individual potential
- Synectics—focus on the development and application of creativity

Social Interaction

The models associated with the social interaction family are focused on developing the concepts and skills needed to work in groups. Cooperative learning has demonstrated an ability to impact standard achievement measures as well as group interaction.

- Cooperative Learning—focus is on working in groups; based on the methods of Slavin and Johnson and Johnson
- Role playing—focus is on the study and development of social behavior and values

Summary

In my review of the research literature on effective instruction, it is my opinion that most teachers will work with most students more effectively using the direct or explicit instruction model when the desired outcome is a score on a standardized test of basic skills. When this basic method is used as the foundation for instruction and supplemented with techniques used in the others (*e.g.*, asking higher-level questions, using facilitiative teaching techniques, and using cooperative learning activities for guided and independent practice), I believe classroom teachers will use the best educational practices as we now understand them.

Team Teaching

In many higher education institutions, including CityU, the usual pattern of teaching is still largely based on an individual lecturer bearing responsibility for students in a course module or unit, possibly supported by part-time staff tutors. At some levels of learning though, for example in postgraduate seminars, this model is replaced by a team teaching approach which involves a number of lecturers (usually between two and five) and possibly non-teaching professional support staff as well. To carry out effective team teaching requires a re-orientation on the part of individual staff members and departmental administrators.

What is Team Teaching?: In team teaching a group of teachers, working together, plan, conduct, and evaluate the learning activities for the same group of students. In practice, team teaching has many different formats but in general it is a means of organising staff into groups to enhance teaching. Teams generally comprise staff members who may represent different areas of subject expertise but who share the same group of students and a common planning period to prepare for the teaching. To facilitate this process a common teaching space is desirable. However, to be effective team teaching requires much more than just a common meeting time and space.

Why Should I Use Team Teaching?: In view of the additional complexity which team teaching initiatives introduce into departmental organisation and in view of the time needed for staff to adapt to the new structures, it is relevant to ask what benefits accrue from team teaching. How, for instance, does team teaching benefit lecturers, part-time tutors, students, and departments as a whole?

- For Lecturers, who so often work alone, team teaching provides a supportive environment that overcomes the isolation of working in self-contained or departmentalized class-rooms. Being exposed to the subject expertise of colleagues, to open critique, to different styles of planning and organisation, as well as methods of class presentation, teachers can develop their approaches to teaching and acquire a greater depth of understanding of the subject matter of the unit or module.

- Part-time staff can be drawn more closely into the department as members of teams than is usually the case, with a resulting increase in integration of course objectives and approaches to teaching.
- Team teaching can lead to better student performance in terms of greater independence and assuming responsibility for learning. Exposure to views and skills of more than one teacher can develop a more mature understanding of knowledge often being problematic rather than right or wrong. Learning can become more active and involved. Students could eventually make an input into team planning.
- Team teaching aids the professional and interpersonal dynamics of departments leading to closer integration of staff.

In the following extract, the authors describe the instructional advantages of working in teams.

Team Teaching: An Alternative to Lecture Fatigue.

Team teaching is an approach which involves true team work between two qualified instructors who, together, make presentations to an audience. The instructional advantages of team teaching include:

(1) Lecture-style instruction is eliminated in favour of a dynamic interplay of two minds and personalities.

Lectures require students to act as passive receptors of communicated information, but team teaching involves the student in the physical and mental stimulation created by viewing two individuals at work. . . .

(2) Teaching staff act as a role models for discussion and disagreement.

Teaching staff members demonstrate modes of behaving in a disagreement as well as exposing students to the course content.

(3) Team teaching makes effective use of existing human resources.

Acquisition of additional expensive resources or equipment is not required to implement this method: only reorganisation is required to put the team into operation.

(4) Team teaching has the potential for revitalizing instructional capabilities through a process of dialogue.

Team teaching begins with the recognition that the instructor/student link is critical and offers an approach that has been shown to stimulate and provoke, while expanding and enriching student understanding.

(5) Interest in traditional courses can be stimulated as students share the enthusiasm and intellectual discourse that the lecturers communicate.

Team teaching is not boring. Students are drawn into the situation from the first moment.

(6) The effective use of facilities is possible.

The impersonal nature of large lecture halls can be brought to life by an interactive and dynamic situation.

(7) Team teaching provides opportunities for interaction with the audience.

Implementation

Implementing a team teaching approach requires administrative encouragement, acceptance of an initial experimental quality, and willingness to take risks. Proof that team teaching works comes not only from the instructors' self-judgment, but from students' evaluations. Above all, team teaching cannot be accomplished by administrative fiat — but administrators need to encourage it.

Adapted From: Quinn, S. and Kanter, S. (1984) "Team Teaching: An Alternative to Lecture Fatigue", Innovation Abstracts, Volume 6, No. 34, Eric Document: ED 251 159.

Is there Only One way to Team Teach?: In its fullest sense, team teaching is where a group of lecturers works together to plan, conduct, and evaluate the learning activities of the same group of students. However, it would be a mistake to think that team teaching is always practised in the same way. Its format needs to be adapted to the requirements of the teaching situation. Some possible options are where:

- two or more teachers teach the same group at the same time;
- team members meet to share ideas and resources but generally function independently;
- teams of teachers share a common resource centre;
- a team shares a common group of students, shares planning for instruction but team members teach different sub-groups within the whole group;
- certain instructional activities may be planned for the whole team by one individual, for example planning and developing research seminars;
- planning is shared, but teachers each teach their own specialism or their own skills area to the whole group;
- teams plan and develop teaching resource materials for a large group of students but may or may not teach them in a classroom situation.

Planning to Implement Team Teaching

Planning, conducting and evaluating team teaching are all important activities. Some of the most important aspects of planning which need to consider in advance of implementing teams are the concerns of staff; the selection of team members; and setting realistic goals for any teaching team in the first instance.

Understanding Staff Concerns

Like any other change or innovation in a department, team teaching will raise concerns among staff members. The full range of concerns will only become clear over time after initial worries are dealt with and team members become comfortable with the innovation. A basic premise of team teaching is that its adoption is not something that happens at one point in time—it extends over time. As users go through the adoption process there will be changes in their concerns.

From a team perspective, the ultimate aim will be to have individual team members reach a stage where they accept joint responsibility for the basic instruction of a group of students. There will be concerns, however, the relevant literature suggests that one way of dealing with these concerns is to recognise that they seem to follow a time cycle. Early concerns usually appear to be procedural *e.g.*, determining roles, setting agendas, keeping records, setting procedures for communicating with outside people, and scheduling teamwork, etc.

Next to appear are student-related concerns such as meeting students' needs, planning to deal with individual students, etc. These are followed by concern among team members for their own professional growth and finally there is concern for the collective well being of the team. This last level is reached when teams are seen as (i) a means of professional self development, (ii) a forum at which ideas about instruction and coordinating curriculum can be shared, and (iii) when students are involved in decision making.

Here are some common concerns about team teaching along with suggestions of what to do to improve the likelihood of overcoming them. The first three of these concerns are usually expressed before the team actually begins functioning while the last is usually expressed after it has functioned for a time.

I do not know enough about team teaching.

Explain the concept of team organisation and the rationale for implementing it. This should include an explanation of how it is envisaged that team teaching will fit with the rest of the departmental programme. Staff need to have a clear idea of the kinds of teaching teams envisaged, what their responsibilities will be and how much of their time will be occupied in teaching in this way.

How Will I Manage My Teaching in the Light of the Proposed Change?

Supplying information usually leads teachers to express personal concerns. Take these concerns seriously. If you do not they become potential barriers to effective implementation. Personal concerns usually expressed about team teaching include:

- not all team members will contribute equally;
- teachers do not understand how to make the team work;
- there will be personality conflicts to deal with in addition to the teaching itself;
- a preference for working alone;
- all the work will fall on the team leader/senior subject expert;
- it will be too difficult to cover all the course content;
- team meetings will be a waste of time.

All in all, concerns usually revolve about inter-personal problems — issues of self doubt, team management and group processes in addition to whether the teaching carried out by this method will be worthwhile.

How is the Team Going to be Managed?

Management questions are concerned with who will be on the team, who will lead it, what will be expected and in what timeframe, how meetings will be conducted, how teaching activities and events will actually be planned, and so on. These should be dealt with as early as possible and not in a casual manner, so that everyone is clear about what their roles and responsibilities will be. As well, once the team begins to function, more routine issues will surface: staff may be bothered by the amount of time involved, the difficulty of keeping track of students, coordinating materials and the work of other team members.

Concern may arise and have to be dealt with while the team is actually functioning or at the time of periodic course reviews. Rather than a single concern, it may be more useful to see it as a category of concerns that focus on **the consequences of team actions.**

It would be most unusual for the team to find that everything has proceeded as they planned. More usually, they find that there are outcomes as a result of team teaching which they had not anticipated. These outcomes may be to do with student learning or with how the team is functioning. If there are differences between what was planned and what the students are achieving then the team will need to **refocus on what is important.** To do this the team will have to monitor continually how students are reacting to the team teaching experience. Conscious decisions will have to be taken to emphasise points that may have been missed or correct mistaken impressions. However, concerns may arise apart from those related to student learning.

There may be a need for the team to **deal with issues of collaboration** among its own members. In the same way that the goals associated with student learning need to be monitored and reviewed where necessary, so too do aspects of team behaviour. In both these examples it is apparent that regular meetings of the team need to take place where constructive, professional reflection is encouraged which is itself a team teaching strength.

Selecting Team Members: The composition of any teaching team is a matter which must be considered carefully if that particular team is going to function effectively. While it is possible that teams can be arbitrarily formed it is far more fruitful if they come together in response to needs and interests. Thought needs to be given to selecting team members and defining team roles and these decisions need to be evaluated periodically. The following questions are indicative of the sorts of issues which should be considered:

- on what basis should team members be selected?

  Team members should not be clones of each other. Why? Because differences in subject expertise, interests, perspectives, back-grounds, and qualification levels, can contribute to the collective strength of a team and the growth of individual team members. Furthermore, the 'mix' of personalities and characteristics add to the experience the students get from interacting with the team.

- What is the role of the team leader?

  Basically the team leader will be concerned with (i) internal functioning — setting agendas, keeping records, coordinating schedules ensuring the team 'stays on task' *i.e.* that it achieves what it sets out to achieve; and (ii) external functioning — communicating with department heads to ensure that the team is resourced, supported, and meeting departmental goals/ expectations, etc.

- What is the role of team members?

  Team members need to contribute to the team in ways other than simply turning up for classes and meetings. It is essential that all team members contribute to formulating and achieving team goals. To do this, each member must take responsibility for participating in team discussions and planning session and following through on decisions made by the team within the timeframes decided by the team. It is only in this way that a spirit of co-operation and collaboration can be maintained.

Setting Realistic Team Goals: Teams need to have a sense of direction. One finding from the relevant literature of particular interest relates to the time required to develop an effective level of team teaching. When teams are formed from teachers with no previous team experience, it seems to take about three years for them to develop the team teaching process to an efficient and effective level. Hence in setting a time line for teams to achieve realistic goals it is important to ask what will be the aims of team teaching during the first year or semester and what are the longer term goals? The answers to such questions are important in determining priorities for the development of teams. It is unrealistic to expect that all goals and expectations will be met immediately. Rather it is better to consider what it is reasonable to undertake as teachers and to expect from students and at what stage?

The Team in Action

Planning for Teaching: Assume that it has been decided that team teaching will go ahead in your department and that you have agreed and been selected to be a member of a team. Assume also that the issues surrounding teams discussed earlier have been attended to and the team is now ready to begin work. Decisions facing yourself and your teaching partners now will focus undoubtedly on planning teaching/learning activities.

You may ask, for instance, in what way will the team use small and large group contexts or independent study? Will it use a large group in an auditorium setting to introduce a topic or convey basic information and background material which all the students need to know? Will the team decide to use a single teacher to make the presentation or will several teachers be used? Will small group discussions relate to large group presentations, or demonstrate skills, or develop a seminar discussion group etc? What of independent study? It is not always taken into consideration but it provides a student or group of students with the opportunity to research or explore a topic of special interest in greater depth outside the formal teaching situation. How will the team use independent study?

This short list of questions underlines the decisions to be made in this area.

- What are the programme, unit, and lesson objectives?
- What lesson content is to be presented and in what order?
- Which content is to be presented by large group presentation?
- Which methods and resources are to be used to present the content?
- Who will make large group presentations?
- What will be discussed during small group meetings?
- How will small groups be organized?
- Who will be assigned to each small group?
- What types of independent study will be appropriate?
- What blocks of time will be assigned to large-group, small group and independent study activities?
- How will students be assessed?

All of these questions are to do with ongoing interaction with students. A little later the team will have to consider questions such as:

- How can the activities be improved?
- What specific problems have arisen with particular groups of students and how can they be solved?

Irrespective of who asks these questions, they are very realistic and they need to be answered, but the critical issue is who by and how.

Assigning Roles and Responsibilities: Effective teams are systematic in their division of labour, not forgetting that roles may be rotated on a regular basis. In allocating roles, strengths and weaknesses of individual team members need to be taken into account. A brief questionnaire gathering an idea of these strengths and weaknesses might be a good idea before a draft list of responsibilities for the team is discussed.

Catering for Students: While team teachers and their students are usually happy with the community spirit that teams can provide, teamwork also has a considerable effect on classroom management. For example, by planning together, team teachers can clarify teaching policies and behavioural expectations that are applied to students. Difficult management situations can be analyzed and resolved together resulting in richer discussions and sounder solutions. Teams of teachers can think of ways of improving student motivation, a sense of responsibility, and overall student performance.

Conducting Meetings: Team teaching is group work and as such teams need to develop as functioning groups. In dealing with other team members teamwork is seldom without conflict — professional or personal points of view may clash. Blending differences constructively is a challenge to all team members. To do this it is important to acknowledge team members' strengths, interests, personal and professional goals both in assigning responsibilities and in the conduct of meetings.

Running Meetings

For a team to function effectively the team meetings need to run well. They need to clarify expectations for how the team will operate, *i.e.* clarify management issues and set ground rules for meetings such as:

- how will items get on the agenda?
- what should be recorded in the minutes?
- who will do the recording?
- how will decisions be reached?
- how should communication with other teams and members of the department be managed?
- how will a team calendar/schedule be compiled?

Making Decisions

The main problem encountered in meetings which prevents decisions from being made effectively and efficiently is the difficulty of keeping all team members on task. The team leader needs to ensure that:

- problems are defined clearly;
- there is time for brainstorming alternatives for action;
- each alternative is subject to critique
- a plan of action is selected, implemented and subsequently evaluated

Evaluating Progress

In a small team, a formal evaluation of progress often seems inappropriate. However, all teams need to set aside some time to evaluate their progress in terms of both teaching the module and with their own development as an effective team. An outside facilitator could be called in to manage this where appropriate. Some questions which might be asked in the context of such an evaluation are:

- are the goals set for the team's work realistic?
- have the goals been achieved? to what extent?
- do all team members participate equally in team decisions?
- have decisions been carried out?
- are responsibilities shared among team members?
- do students benefit from the team's work?
- what areas need more attention?

Maintaining Continuity From Year to Year

In order to ensure the continuity of the module/course when it is presented a second and subsequent times the team needs to maintain clear documentation of the course including:

- the course outline or syllabus;
- weekly timetables;
- teachers' notes for each unit;
- students' notes;
- teaching materials/written bulletins;
- copies of tests and examinations;
- final course evaluations;
- student evaluations.

Carefully maintaining these course documents will ease the task of the course leaders, facilitate the induction of new teachers into the team, and simplify the task of revising the course/module in a rational manner.

Conclusion

Teams take a variety of forms in different contexts, however, successful team teaching must go beyond sharing a group of students and scheduling a common meeting time if it is to make positive contributions to the quality of learning and staff development.

Effective team teaching takes time to develop to its fullest potential. Staff who are unfamiliar with it need time to work through the basic issues and routine matters before they can turn their attention fully to issues which affect students and to the impact which their teaching has on the department as a whole. This is time well spent because team teaching can be a valuable source of personal and professional development for those who engage in it. It can also be a source of considerable frustration if its goals are unrealistic, meetings are not productive and decision making is not well handled by team leaders.

These pitfalls and others can be avoided or at least not encountered more than once if adequate staff development support is available and the relative complexity of demands which team teaching places on people is recognized both by the individuals themselves and their departmental leaders.

Individualizing the Curriculum

Goals for students who are gifted or may be gifted should provide opportunities to master the knowledge and skills of the general curriculum. In addition, areas of giftedness should be developed and extended in a conducive learning environment. This includes having differentiated learning alternatives that emphasize and expand thinking abilities, expand independent learning skills, expand understanding and acceptance of others, and assists students in solving real-life problems, developing products, and sharing information with others.

The student outcomes that will result from working toward these goals include:

- increased academic learning.
- increased self-directed learning behaviors.
- enhanced talent development
- increased intrinsic motivation for learning.

The strategies that assist students in attaining the goals listed above include:

- Strength and Preference Assessment-observe and survey students to identify their interests, learning styles, strength areas, past accomplishments, goals to the future, and product preferences.
- Curriculum Modification-Analyze and modify existing curriculum units.
- Differentiation-Anticipate differences among students by planning instruction that accommodates a variety of levels and styles.
- Enrichment-Plan options that stretch the curriculum and challenge students to explore related areas and interests.

Individualizing The General Curriculum

When individualizing the general curriculum for students who are gifted a focus must be made on curriculum design; *i.e.*, a focus on the content, instruction, and assessment. In addition it must be determined if the curriculum is being modified or differentiated. Curriculum modification involves the analysis, evaluation, and improvement of existing curriculum units and lesson plans. Modified units increase challenge, authenticity, and active learning to improve learning and achievement.

Curriculum differentiation is a process teachers use to enhance learning to improve the match between the learner's unique characteristics and various curriculum components. Differentiation involves making changes to the depth or breadth of student learning. Differentiation is enhanced with the use of appropriate classroom management, varied pedagogy, pre-testing, flexible small groups, access to support personnel, and the availability of appropriate resources.

The plan to be used to assist students in achieving the goals and outcomes in the general curriculum must include a focus on three areas: content, process, and product. The learning environment is also a factor in developing an effective programme plan.

Distance Learning Models

A growing number of Masters programmes can be studied by distance learning, where instructors and students communicate online rather than face to face. A wide variety of educational media and modes of communication and teaching are used. One of the hallmarks of many distance-learning programmes is that, via flexible, modular class offerings, students can progress through them at their own pace. Distance-learning programmes have a longer duration than their full-time equivalents. For postgraduate programmes, these typically usually last two to five years instead of one year full time. Some distance-learning courses require a combination of online and physical communication, where students attend residential sessions.

The Distance-learning Experience

To be a distance-learning success, you must have what it takes. This type of studying does have different requirements and pressures from full-time study, which you should be aware of if you want to go down this route. The institution will agree with you a timetable of study and deadlines for supplying essays and assignments, with videos, audio tapes and written materials sent regularly by post or available online to give you the raw materials for your studies. You can keep in regular contact with your tutor via e-mail or telephone and it is usual to e-mail your essays to them. However, much will be up to you:

- First, you will need to be self-motivated or a self-starter. Even though you are not on a campus, you will still have to undertake study and provide essays to an agreed timetable. Without the structure of full-time study, it will be up to you to ensure that you keep the ball rolling. Your institution and tutor can give you advice and support, but ultimately it is your game.
- You will also need dedication and discipline as a distance-learning programme can be a long haul (usually twice as long as the full-time equivalent). It might be daunting, after a long day at work, to then have to undertake several hours of study, but persevere – this is the only way you will attain your goal of gaining a qualification.
- You must also be organised and be able to multi-task in order to ensure that your other commitments (often the reason for distance learning in the first place) do not impinge on the time you need for study. Some students spend up to 15 hours a week studying and preparing assignments, so you will have to find a way of fitting this in. If you are able to establish a routine and settle into a rhythm, then this will become easier.

Although this may sound daunting, many distance-learning students go on to successfully complete their courses. Once you get the knack, there will be no stopping you.

Resources for Curriculum Transaction—Computer and the Internet

Although mechanical examples of computers have existed throughout history, the first resembling a modern computer were developed in the mid-20th century (1940–1945). The first electronic computers were the size of a large room, consuming as much power as several hundred modern personal computers (PC). Modern computers based on tiny integrated circuits are millions to billions of times more capable than the early machines, and occupy a fraction of the space. Simple computers are small enough to fit into a wristwatch, and can be powered by a watch battery. Personal computers in their various forms are icons of the Information Age, what most people think of as a "computer", but the embedded computers found in devices ranging from fighter aircraft to industrial robots, digital cameras, and toys are the most numerous.

The ability to store and execute lists of instructions called programmes makes computers extremely versatile, distinguishing them from calculators. The Church–Turing thesis is a mathematical statement of this versatility: any computer with a certain minimum capability is, in principle, capable of performing the same tasks that any other computer can perform. Therefore computers ranging from a personal digital assistant to a supercomputer are all able to perform the same computational tasks, given enough time and storage capacity.

History of Computing

The first use of the word "computer" was recorded in 1613, referring to a person who carried out calculations, or computations, and the word continued to be used in that sense until the middle of the 20th century. From the end of the 19th century onwards though, the word began to take on its more familiar meaning, describing a machine that carries out computations.

The history of the modern computer begins with two separate technologies—automated calculation and programmability—but no single device can be identified as the earliest computer, partly because of the inconsistent application of that term. Examples of early mechanical calculating devices include the abacus, the slide rule and arguably the astrolabe and the Antikythera mechanism (which dates from about 150–100 BC). Hero of Alexandria (c. 10–70 AD) built a mechanical theater which performed a play lasting 10 minutes and was operated by a complex system of ropes and drums that might be considered to be a means of deciding which parts of the mechanism performed which actions and when. This is the essence of programmability.

The "castle clock", an astronomical clock invented by Al-Jazari in 1206, is considered to be the earliest programmable analog computer. It displayed the zodiac, the solar and lunar orbits, a crescent moon-shaped pointer travelling across a gateway causing automatic doors to open every hour, and five robotic musicians who played music when struck by levers operated by a camshaft attached to a water wheel. The length of day and night could be re-programmed to compensate for the changing lengths of day and night throughout the year.

The end of the Middle Ages saw a re-invigoration of European mathematics and engineering. Wilhelm Schickard's 1623 device was the first of a number of mechanical calculators constructed by European engineers, but none fit the modern definition of a computer, because they could not be programmed.

In 1801, Joseph Marie Jacquard made an improvement to the textile loom by introducing a series of punched paper cards as a template which allowed his loom to weave intricate patterns automatically. The resulting Jacquard loom was an important step in the development of computers because the use of punched cards to define woven patterns can be viewed as an early, albeit limited, form of programmability.

It was the fusion of automatic calculation with programmability that produced the first recognizable computers. In 1837, Charles Babbage was the first to conceptualize and design a fully programmable mechanical computer, his analytical engine. Limited finances and Babbage's inability to resist tinkering with the design meant that the device was never completed.

In the late 1880s Herman Hollerith invented the recording of data on a machine readable medium. Prior uses of machine readable media, above, had been for control, not data. "After some initial trials with paper tape, he settled on punched cards ...” To process these punched cards he invented the tabulator, and the key punch machines. These three inventions were the foundation of the modern information processing industry. Large-scale automated data processing of punched cards was performed for the 1890 United States Census by Hollerith’s company, which later became the core of IBM. By the end of the 19th century a number of technologies that would later prove useful in the realization of practical computers had begun to appear: the punched card, Boolean algebra, the vacuum tube (thermionic valve) and the teleprinter.

During the first half of the 20th century, many scientific computing needs were met by increasingly sophisticated analog computers, which used a direct mechanical or electrical model of the problem as a basis for computation. However, these were not programmable and generally lacked the versatility and accuracy of modern digital computers.

George Stibitz is internationally recognized as a father of the modern digital computer. While working at Bell Labs in November of 1937, Stibitz invented and built a relay-based calculator he dubbed the “Model K” (for “kitchen table”, on which he had assembled it), which was the first to use binary circuits to perform an arithmetic operation. Later models added greater sophistication including complex arithmetic and programmability.

A succession of steadily more powerful and flexible computing devices were constructed in the 1930s and 1940s, gradually adding the key features that are seen in modern computers. The use of digital electronics (largely invented by Claude Shannon in 1937) and more flexible programmability were vitally important steps, but defining one point along this road as “the first digital electronic computer” is difficult (Shannon 1940). Notable achievements include:

- Konrad Zuse’s electromechanical “Z machines”. The Z3 (1941) was the first working machine featuring binary arithmetic, including floating point arithmetic and a measure of programmability. In 1998 the Z3 was proved to be Turing complete, therefore being the world’s first operational computer.

- The non-programmable Atanasoff–Berry Computer (1941) which used vacuum tube based computation, binary numbers, and regenerative capacitor memory. The use of regenerative memory allowed it to be much more compact then its peers (being approximately the size of a large desk or workbench), since intermediate results could be stored and then fed back into the same set of computation elements.
- The secret British Colossus computers (1943), which had limited programmability but demonstrated that a device using thousands of tubes could be reasonably reliable and electronically reprogrammable. It was used for breaking German wartime codes.
- The Harvard Mark I (1944), a large-scale electromechanical computer with limited programmability.
- The U.S. Army's Ballistics Research Laboratory ENIAC (1946), which used decimal arithmetic and is sometimes called the first general purpose electronic computer (since Konrad Zuse's Z3 of 1941 used electromagnets instead of electronics). Initially, however, ENIAC had an inflexible architecture which essentially required rewiring to change its programming.

Several developers of ENIAC, recognizing its flaws, came up with a far more flexible and elegant design, which came to be known as the "stored programme architecture" or von Neumann architecture. This design was first formally described by John von Neumann in the paper *First Draft of a Report on the EDVAC*, distributed in 1945.

A number of projects to develop computers based on the stored-programme architecture commenced around this time, the first of these being completed in Great Britain. The first to be demonstrated working was the Manchester Small-Scale Experimental Machine (SSEM or "Baby"), while the EDSAC, completed a year after SSEM, was the first practical implementation of the stored programme design. Shortly thereafter, the machine originally described by von Neumann's paper—EDVAC—was completed but did not see full-time use for an additional two years.

Nearly all modern computers implement some form of the stored-programme architecture, making it the single trait by which the word "computer" is now defined. While the technologies used in computers have changed dramatically since the first electronic, general-purpose computers of the 1940s, most still use the von Neumann architecture.

Computers using vacuum tubes as their electronic elements were in use throughout the 1950s, but by the 1960s had been largely replaced by transistor-based machines, which were smaller, faster, cheaper to produce, required less power, and were more reliable. The first transistorised computer was demonstrated at the University of Manchester in 1953. In the 1970s, integrated circuit technology and the subsequent creation of microprocessors, such as the Intel 4004, further decreased size and cost and further increased speed and reliability of computers. By the 1980s, computers became sufficiently small and cheap to replace simple mechanical controls in domestic appliances such as washing machines. The 1980s also witnessed home computers and the now ubiquitous personal computer. With the evolution of the Internet, personal computers are becoming as common as the television and the telephone in the household.

Modern smartphones are fully-programmable computers in their own right, and as of 2009 may well be the most common form of such computers in existence.

Internet

The **Internet** is a global network of interconnected computers, enabling users to share information along multiple channels. Typically, a computer that connects to the Internet can access information from a vast array of available servers and other computers by moving information from them to the computer's local memory. The same connection allows that computer to send information to servers on the network; that information is in turn accessed and potentially modified by a variety of other interconnected computers. A majority of widely accessible information on the Internet consists of inter-linked hypertext documents and other resources of the World Wide

Web (WWW). Computer users typically manage sent and received information with web browsers; other software for users' interface with computer networks includes specialized programmes for electronic mail, online chat, file transfer and file sharing.

The movement of information in the Internet is achieved via a system of interconnected computer networks that share data by packet switching using the standardized Internet Protocol Suite (TCP/IP). It is a "network of networks" that consists of millions of private and public, academic, business, and government networks of local to global scope that are linked by copper wires, fiber-optic cables, wireless connections, and other technologies.

Terminology

The terms Internet and World Wide Web are often used in every-day speech without much distinction. However, the Internet and the World Wide Web are not one and the same. The Internet is a global data communications system. It is a hardware and software infrastructure that provides connectivity between computers. In contrast, the Web is one of the services communicated via the Internet. It is a collection of interconnected documents and other resources, linked by hyperlinks and URLs.

The term the Internet, when referring to the Internet, has traditionally been treated as a proper noun and written with an initial capital letter. There is a trend to regard it as a generic term or common noun and thus write it as "the internet", without the capital.

History

Creation: The USSR's launch of Sputnik spurred the United States to create the Advanced Research Projects Agency, known as ARPA, in February 1958 to regain a technological lead. ARPA created the Information Processing Technology Office (IPTO) to further the research of the Semi Automatic Ground Environment (SAGE) programme, which had networked country-wide radar systems together for the first time.

J.C.R. Licklider was selected to head the IPTO, and networking as a potential unifying human revolution.

Licklider moved from the Psycho-Acoustic Laboratory at Harvard University to MIT in 1950, after becoming interested in information technology. At MIT, he served on a committee that established Lincoln Laboratory and worked on the SAGE project. In 1957 he became a Vice President at BBN, where he bought the first production PDP-1 computer and conducted the first public demonstration of time-sharing.

At the IPTO, Licklider got Lawrence Roberts to start a project to make a network, and Roberts based the technology on the work of Paul Baran, who had written an exhaustive study for the U.S. Air Force that recommended packet switching (as opposed to circuit switching) to make a network highly robust and survivable. After much work, the first two nodes of what would become the ARPANET were interconnected between UCLA and SRI (later SRI International) in Menlo Park, California, on October 29, 1969. The ARPANET was one of the "eve" networks of today's Internet.

Following on from the demonstration that packet switching worked on the ARPANET, the British Post Office, Telenet, DATAPAC and TRANSPAC collaborated to create the first international packet-switched network service. In the UK, this was referred to as the International Packet Switched Service (IPSS), in 1978. The collection of X.25-based networks grew from Europe and the US to cover Canada, Hong Kong and Australia by 1981. The X.25 packet switching standard was developed in the CCITT (now called ITU-T) around 1976.

X.25 was independent of the TCP/IP protocols that arose from the experimental work of DARPA on the ARPANET, Packet Radio Net and Packet Satellite Net during the same time period. Vinton Cerf and Robert Kahn developed the first description of the TCP protocols during 1973 and published a paper on the subject in May 1974. Use of the term "Internet" to describe a single global TCP/IP network originated in December 1974 with the publication of RFC 675, the first full specification of TCP that was written by Vinton Cerf, Yogen

Dalal and Carl Sunshine, then at Stanford University. During the next nine years, work proceeded to refine the protocols and to implement them on a wide range of operating systems.

The first TCP/IP-based wide-area network was operational by January 1, 1983 when all hosts on the ARPANET were switched over from the older NCP protocols. In 1985, the United States' National Science Foundation (NSF) commissioned the construction of the NSFNET, a university 56 kilobit/second network backbone using computers called "fuzzballs" by their inventor, David L. Mills. The following year, NSF sponsored the conversion to a higher-speed 1.5 megabit/second network. A key decision to use the DARPA TCP/IP protocols was made by Dennis Jennings, then in charge of the Supercomputer programme at NSF.

The opening of the network to commercial interests began in 1988. The US Federal Networking Council approved the interconnection of the NSFNET to the commercial MCI Mail system in that year and the link was made in the summer of 1989. Other commercial electronic e-mail services were soon connected, including OnTyme, Telemail and Compuserve. In that same year, three commercial Internet service providers (ISP) were created: UUNET, PSINet and CERFNET. Important, separate networks that offered gateways into, then later merged with, the Internet include Usenet and BITNET. Various other commercial and educational networks, such as Telenet, Tymnet, Compuserve and JANET were interconnected with the growing Internet.

Telenet (later called Sprintnet) was a large privately funded national computer network with free dial-up access in cities throughout the U.S. that had been in operation since the 1970s. This network was eventually interconnected with the others in the 1980s as the TCP/IP protocol became increasingly popular. The ability of TCP/IP to work over virtually any pre-existing communication networks allowed for a great ease of growth, although the rapid growth of the Internet was due primarily to the availability of commercial routers from companies such as Cisco Systems, Proteon and Juniper, the availability of commercial Ethernet equipment for local-area networking, and the widespread implementation of TCP/IP on the UNIX operating system.

Growth

Although the basic applications and guidelines that make the Internet possible had existed for almost two decades, the network did not gain a public face until the 1990s. On 6 August 1991, CERN, a pan European organisation for particle research, publicized the new World Wide Web project. The Web was invented by English scientist Tim Berners-Lee in 1989.

An early popular web browser was ViolaWWW, patterned after HyperCard and built using the X Window System. It was eventually replaced in popularity by the Mosaic web browser. In 1993, the National Center for Supercomputing Applications at the University of Illinois released version 1.0 of Mosaic, and by late 1994 there was growing public interest in the previously academic, technical Internet. By 1996 usage of the word Internet had become commonplace, and consequently, so had its use as a synecdoche in reference to the World Wide Web.

Meanwhile, over the course of the decade, the Internet successfully accommodated the majority of previously existing public computer networks (although some networks, such as FidoNet, have remained separate). During the 1990s, it was estimated that the Internet grew by 100% per year, with a brief period of explosive growth in 1996 and 1997. This growth is often attributed to the lack of central administration, which allows organic growth of the network, as well as the non-proprietary open nature of the Internet protocols, which encourages vendor interoperability and prevents any one company from exerting too much control over the network.

Using various statistics, AMD estimated the population of internet users to be 1.5 billion as of January 2009.

University Students' Appreciation and Contributions

New findings in the field of communications during the 1960s, 1970s and 1980s were quickly adopted by universities across North America. Examples of early university Internet communities are Cleveland FreeNet, Blacksburg Electronic

Village and NSTN in Nova Scotia. Students took up the opportunity of free communications and saw this new phenomenon as a tool of liberation. Personal computers and the Internet would free them from corporations and governments (Nelson, Jennings, Stallman).

Graduate students played a huge part in the creation of ARPANET. In the 1960s, the network working group, which did most of the design for ARPANET's protocols, was composed mainly of graduate students.

Today's Internet

The My Opera Community server rack. From the top, user file storage (content of files.myopera.com), "bigma" (the master MySQL database server), and two IBM blade centers containing multi-purpose machines (Apache front ends, Apache back ends, slave MySQL database servers, load balancers, file servers, cache servers and sync masters)

Aside from the complex physical connections that make up its infrastructure, the Internet is facilitated by bi-or multi-lateral commercial contracts (*e.g.*, peering agreements), and by technical specifications or protocols that describe how to exchange data over the network. Indeed, the Internet is defined by its interconnections and routing policies.

By December 31, 2008, 1.574 billion people were using the Internet according to Internet World Statistics.

Internet Protocols

The complex communications infrastructure of the Internet consists of its hardware components and a system of software layers that control various aspects of the architecture. While the hardware can often be used to support other software systems, it is the design and the rigorous standardization process of the software architecture that characterizes the Internet.

The responsibility for the architectural design of the Internet software systems has been delegated to the Internet Engineering Task Force (IETF). The IETF conducts standard-setting work groups, open to any individual, about the various aspects of

Internet architecture. Resulting discussions and final standards are published in Requests for Comments (RFCs), freely available on the IETF web site.

The principal methods of networking that enable the Internet are contained in a series of RFCs that constitute the Internet Standards. These standards describe a system known as the Internet Protocol Suite. This is a model architecture that divides methods into a layered system of protocols (RFC 1122, RFC 1123). The layers correspond to the environment or scope in which their services operate. At the top is the space (Application Layer) of the software application, *e.g.*, a web browser application, and just below it is the Transport Layer which connects applications on different hosts via the network (*e.g.*, client-server model). The underlying network consists of two layers: the Internet Layer which enables computers to connect to one-another via intermediate (transit) networks and thus is the layer that establishes internetworking and the Internet, and lastly, at the bottom, is a software layer that provides connectivity between hosts on the same local link (therefor called Link Layer), *e.g.*, a local area network (LAN) or a dial-up connection. This model is also known as the TCP/IP model of networking. While other models have been developed, such as the Open Systems Interconnection (OSI) model, they are not compatible in the details of description, nor implementation.

The most prominent component of the Internet model is the Internet Protocol (IP) which provides addressing systems for computers on the Internet and facilitates the internetworking of networks. IP Version 4 (IPv4) is the initial version used on the first generation of the today's Internet and is still in dominant use. It was designed to address up to ~4.3 billion (10) Internet hosts. However, the explosive growth of the Internet has led to IPv4 address exhaustion. A new protocol version, IPv6, was developed which provides vastly larger addressing capabilities and more efficient routing of data traffic. IPv6 is currently in commercial deployment phase around the world.

IPv6 is not interoperable with IPv4. It essentially establishes a "parallel" version of the Internet not accessible with IPv4 software. This means software upgrades are necessary for every networking device that needs to communicate on the IPv6 Internet. Most modern computer operating systems are already converted to operate with both versions of the Internet Protocol. Network infrastructures, however, are still lagging in this development.

Internet Structure

There have been many analyses of the Internet and its structure. For example, it has been determined that both the Internet IP routing structure and hypertext links of the World Wide Web are examples of scale-free networks.

Similar to the way the commercial Internet providers connect via Internet exchange points, research networks tend to interconnect into large subnetworks such as the following:

- GEANT
- GLORIAD
- The Internet2 Network (formally known as the Abilene Network)
- JANET (the UK's national research and education network)

These in turn are built around relatively smaller networks. See also the list of academic computer network organizations.

Computer network diagrams often represent the Internet using a cloud symbol from which network communications pass in and out.

ICANN

The Internet Corporation for Assigned Names and Numbers (ICANN) is the authority that coordinates the assignment of unique identifiers on the Internet, including domain names, Internet Protocol (IP) addresses, and protocol port and parameter numbers. A globally unified namespace (*i.e.*, a system of names in which there is at most one holder for each possible name) is essential for the Internet to function. ICANN is headquartered in Marina del Rey, California, but is overseen by an international board of directors drawn from across the

Internet technical, business, academic, and non-commercial communities. The US government continues to have the primary role in approving changes to the root zone file that lies at the heart of the domain name system.

Because the Internet is a distributed network comprising many voluntarily interconnected networks, the Internet has no governing body. ICANN's role in coordinating the assignment of unique identifiers distinguishes it as perhaps the only central coordinating body on the global Internet, but the scope of its authority extends only to the Internet's systems of domain names, IP addresses, protocol ports and parameter numbers.

On November 16, 2005, the World Summit on the Information Society, held in Tunis, established the Internet Governance Forum (IGF) to discuss Internet-related issues.

Language

The prevalent language for communication on the Internet is English. This may be a result of the Internet's origins, as well as English's role as a lingua franca. It may also be related to the poor capability of early computers, largely originating in the United States, to handle characters other than those in the English variant of the Latin alphabet.

After English (28.6% of Web visitors) the most requested languages on the World Wide Web are Chinese (20.3%), Spanish (8.2%), Japanese (5.9%), French and Portuguese (4.6%), German (4.1%), Arabic (2.6%), Russian (2.4%), and Korean (2.3%).

By region, 41% of the world's Internet users are based in Asia, 25% in Europe, 16% in North America, 11% in Latin America and the Caribbean, 3% in Africa, 3% in the Middle East and 1% in Australia.

The Internet's technologies have developed enough in recent years, especially in the use of Unicode, that good facilities are available for development and communication in most widely used languages. However, some glitches such as mojibake (incorrect display of foreign language characters, also known as kryakozyabry) still remain.

Internet and the Workplace

The Internet is allowing greater flexibility in working hours and location, especially with the spread of unmetered high-speed connections and Web applications.

The Internet Viewed on Mobile Devices

The Internet can now be accessed virtually anywhere by numerous means. Mobile phones, datacards, handheld game consoles and cellular routers allow users to connect to the Internet from anywhere there is a cellular network supporting that device's technology.

Within the limitations imposed by the small screen and other limited facilities of such a pocket-sized device, all the services of the Internet, including email and web browsing, may be available in this way. Service providers may restrict the range of these services and charges for data access may be significant, compared to home usage.

Common Uses

E-mail

The concept of sending electronic text messages between parties in a way analogous to mailing letters or memos predates the creation of the Internet. Even today it can be important to distinguish between Internet and internal e-mail systems. Internet e-mail may travel and be stored unencrypted on many other networks and machines out of both the sender's and the recipient's control.

During this time it is quite possible for the content to be read and even tampered with by third parties, if anyone considers it important enough. Purely internal or intranet mail systems, where the information never leaves the corporate or organization's network, are much more secure, although in any organization there will be IT and other personnel whose job may involve monitoring, and occasionally accessing, the e-mail of other employees not addressed to them. Today you can send pictures and attach files on e-mail. Most e-mail servers today also feature the ability to send e-mail to multiple e-mail addresses.

The World Wide Web

Many people use the terms Internet and World Wide Web (or just the Web) interchangeably, but, as discussed above, the two terms are not synonymous.

The World Wide Web is a huge set of interlinked documents, images and other resources, linked by hyperlinks and URLs. These hyperlinks and URLs allow the web servers and other machines that store originals, and cached copies of, these resources to deliver them as required using HTTP (Hypertext Transfer Protocol). HTTP is only one of the communication protocols used on the Internet.

Web services also use HTTP to allow software systems to communicate in order to share and exchange business logic and data.

Software products that can access the resources of the Web are correctly termed user agents. *In normal use, web browsers, such as Internet Explorer, Firefox and Apple Safari, access web pages and allow users to navigate from one to another via hyperlinks. Web documents may contain almost any combination of computer data including graphics, sounds, text, video, multimedia and interactive content including games, office applications and scientific demonstrations.*

Through keyword-driven Internet research using search engines like Yahoo! and Google, millions of people worldwide have easy, instant access to a vast and diverse amount of online information. Compared to encyclopedias and traditional libraries, the World Wide Web has enabled a sudden and extreme decentralization of information and data.

Using the Web, it is also easier than ever before for individuals and organisations to publish ideas and information to an extremely large audience. Anyone can find ways to publish a web page, a blog or build a website for very little initial cost. Publishing and maintaining large, professional websites full of attractive, diverse and up-to-date information is still a difficult and expensive proposition, however.

Many individuals and some companies and groups use "web logs" or blogs, which are largely used as easily updatable online diaries. Some commercial organisations encourage staff to fill them with advice on their areas of specialization in the hope that visitors will be impressed by the expert knowledge and free information, and be attracted to the corporation as a result.

One example of this practice is Microsoft, whose product developers publish their personal blogs in order to pique the public's interest in their work.

Collections of personal web pages published by large service providers remain popular, and have become increasingly sophisticated. Whereas operations such as Angelfire and GeoCities have existed since the early days of the Web, newer offerings from, for example, Facebook and MySpace currently have large followings. These operations often brand themselves as social network services rather than simply as web page hosts.

Advertising on popular web pages can be lucrative, and e-commerce or the sale of products and services directly via the Web continues to grow.

In the early days, web pages were usually created as sets of complete and isolated HTML text files stored on a web server. More recently, websites are more often created using content management or wiki software with, initially, very little content. Contributors to these systems, who may be paid staff, members of a club or other organisation or members of the public, fill underlying databases with content using editing pages designed for that purpose, while casual visitors view and read this content in its final HTML form. There may or may not be editorial, approval and security systems built into the process of taking newly entered content and making it available to the target visitors.

Remote Access

The Internet allows computer users to connect to other computers and information stores easily, wherever they may be across the world. They may do this with or without the use of security, authentication and encryption technologies, depending on the requirements.

This is encouraging new ways of working from home, collaboration and information sharing in many industries. An accountant sitting at home can audit the books of a company based in another country, on a server situated in a third country that is remotely maintained by IT specialists in a fourth. These accounts could have been created by home-working bookkeepers, in other remote locations, based on information e-mailed to them from offices all over the world. Some of these things were possible before the widespread use of the Internet, but the cost of private leased lines would have made many of them infeasible in practice.

An office worker away from his desk, perhaps on the other side of the world on a business trip or a holiday, can open a remote desktop session into his normal office PC using a secure Virtual Private Network (VPN) connection via the Internet. This gives the worker complete access to all of his or her normal files and data, including e-mail and other applications, while away from the office. This concept is also referred to by some network security people as the Virtual Private Nightmare, because it extends the secure perimeter of a corporate network into its employees' homes.

Collaboration

The low cost and nearly instantaneous sharing of ideas, knowledge, and skills has made collaborative work dramatically easier. Not only can a group cheaply communicate and share ideas, but the wide reach of the Internet allows such groups to easily form in the first place. An example of this is the free software movement, which has produced Linux, Mozilla Firefox, OpenOffice.org etc.

Internet "chat", whether in the form of IRC chat rooms or channels, or via instant messaging systems, allow colleagues to stay in touch in a very convenient way when working at their computers during the day. Messages can be exchanged even more quickly and conveniently than via e-mail. Extensions to these systems may allow files to be exchanged, "whiteboard" drawings to be shared or voice and video contact between team members.

Version control systems allow collaborating teams to work on shared sets of documents without either accidentally overwriting each other's work or having members wait until they get "sent" documents to be able to make their contributions.

Business and project teams can share calendars as well as documents and other information. Such collaboration occurs in a wide variety of areas including scientific research, software development, conference planning, political activism and creative writing.

File Sharing

A computer file can be e-mailed to customers, colleagues and friends as an attachment. It can be uploaded to a website or FTP server for easy download by others. It can be put into a "shared location" or onto a file server for instant use by colleagues. The load of bulk downloads to many users can be eased by the use of "mirror" servers or peer-to-peer networks.

In any of these cases, access to the file may be controlled by user authentication, the transit of the file over the Internet may be obscured by encryption, and money may change hands for access to the file. The price can be paid by the remote charging of funds from, for example, a credit card whose details are also passed—hopefully fully encrypted—across the Internet. The origin and authenticity of the file received may be checked by digital signatures or by MD5 or other message digests.

These simple features of the Internet, over a worldwide basis, are changing the production, sale, and distribution of anything that can be reduced to a computer file for transmission. This includes all manner of print publications, software products, news, music, film, video, photography, graphics and the other arts. This in turn has caused seismic shifts in each of the existing industries that previously controlled the production and distribution of these products.

Streaming Media

Many existing radio and television broadcasters provide Internet "feeds" of their live audio and video streams (for example, the BBC). They may also allow time-shift viewing or listening such as Preview, Classic Clips and Listen Again features. These providers have been joined by a range of pure Internet "broadcasters" who never had on-air licenses. This means that an Internet-connected device, such as a computer or something more specific, can be used to access on-line media in much the same way as was previously possible only with a television or radio receiver. The range of material is much wider, from pornography to highly specialized, technical webcasts. Podcasting is a variation on this theme, where—usually audio—material is downloaded and played back on a computer or shifted to a portable media player to be listened to on the move. These techniques using simple equipment allow anybody, with little censorship or licensing control, to broadcast audio-visual material on a worldwide basis.

Webcams can be seen as an even lower-budget extension of this phenomenon. While some webcams can give full-frame-rate video, the picture is usually either small or updates slowly. Internet users can watch animals around an African waterhole, ships in the Panama Canal, traffic at a local roundabout or monitor their own premises, live and in real time. Video chat rooms and video conferencing are also popular with many uses being found for personal webcams, with and without two-way sound.

YouTube was founded on 15 February 2005 and is now the leading website for free streaming video with a vast number of users. It uses a flash-based web player to stream and show video files. Registered users may upload an unlimited amount of video and build their own personal profile. YouTube claims that its users watch hundreds of millions, and upload hundreds of thousands, of videos daily.

Internet Telephony (VoIP)

VoIP stands for Voice-over-Internet Protocol, referring to the protocol that underlies all Internet communication. The idea began in the early 1990s with walkie-talkie-like voice applications for personal computers. In recent years many VoIP systems have become as easy to use and as convenient as a normal telephone. The benefit is that, as the Internet carries the voice traffic, VoIP can be free or cost much less than a traditional telephone call, especially over long distances and especially for those with always-on Internet connections such as cable or ADSL.

VoIP is maturing into a competitive alternative to traditional telephone service. Interoperability between different providers has improved and the ability to call or receive a call from a traditional telephone is available. Simple, inexpensive VoIP network adapters are available that eliminate the need for a personal computer.

Voice quality can still vary from call to call but is often equal to and can even exceed that of traditional calls.

Remaining problems for VoIP include emergency telephone number dialling and reliability. Currently, a few VoIP providers provide an emergency service, but it is not universally available. Traditional phones are line-powered and operate during a power failure; VoIP does not do so without a backup power source for the phone equipment and the Internet access devices.

VoIP has also become increasingly popular for gaming applications, as a form of communication between players. Popular VoIP clients for gaming include Ventrilo and Teamspeak, and others. Play Station 3 and Xbox 360 also offer VoIP chat features.

UNIT-V

Evaluation of Curriculum

The Curriculum Cycle—Evaluation as Comparing Objectives and Outcomes

In Exploring How Texts Work, Derewianka describes the **curriculum cycle**, which includes four stages:

1. Building the Field
2. Modeling the Text Type
3. Joint Construction
4. Independent Writing

Stage 1: Building the Field: This gives the children time to gather information about what they will be writing. Activities are listening, speaking, reading, information gathering, note taking, field trips. This stage ties in perfectly with Units of Inquiry. The students are already familiar with the Unit, the concepts, and the vocabulary.

Stage 2: Modeling the Text Type: This gives the students the chance to become familiar with the purpose, overall structure, and linguistic features of the text type they are going to write.

Stage 3: Joint Construction: The teacher and students write a text together, considering both the content and the language

Stage 4: Independent Writing: Students write on their own.

Stage 1: Building the Field

1. Introduce the persuasive text type to the students. Class discussion.
   - Discuss the words persuasive, persuade, convince, argument.
   - What do they know?
   - Have they ever written a persuasive piece before? When? Why?
   - Why would someone want or need to write a persuasive piece?
   - If they had to write a persuasive piece, what would they write about? Why?
2. Give students examples of the same persuasive piece and ask them to rank them from best to worst. They can work in pairs and must justify their reasons. Class discussion.
3. Give students another example of a persuasive piece (for example: a letter to a magazine editor, trying to convince the editor to change the content of the magazine). Read and discuss the reasons. Class discussion.

Stage 2: Modeling the Text Type

1. Explicitly teach the features of the persuasive text type. Create a display in the classroom which contains the following information:

   Purpose: To present a logical argument from a particular point of view

   Structure: Thesis: A statement on the general position (what you are concerned about)

   Arguments: At least two major arguments with supporting evidence for each argument

   Conclusion: Restate your position or point of view

   Language Features: Present tense (unless past or future are necessary)

General Nouns ("the people", "human beings")

Emotive Words

2. Use an example from Stage 1 (for example: the magazine letter) and have students identify the features of the persuasive text. Students can highlight in different colors and debrief as a class.
3. In pairs students do a **text reconstruction** of another persuasive piece. The students receive the text in paragraphs, and they must put it back together.
4. Use a **dictogloss** to give another example of a persuasive piece.

Stage 3: Joint Construction

1. As a class re-read an example of a persuasive piece (for example: the magazine letter).
2. Have students stand up and go to two different sides of the room based on if they are persuaded or not persuaded.
3. Split the class into these two groups. This is a perfect time to collaborate with your ESL specialist, Learning Support specialist, or Classroom Assistant because each teacher can take a group of children and work with them.
4. In pairs, ask students to list reasons why they feel the way they do. Debrief as a whole group-list all the reasons they feel the way they do on a graphic organizer.
5. Together, construct the text. The teacher can prompt with questions such as:
   - What do we need to start with?
   - Is that the best way to say it?
   - Can anyone think of a better word than that?
   - Can you remember what the other persuasive pieces looked like?
   - It's important to note that the teacher must act as a guide at this stage. The ideas must come from the children, but the teacher has a responsibility to point out grammatical or linguistic errors, and

explicitly teach. The point is that the language is in context and not isolated.

6. Come back together as a large group and share writing. This is a great chance for the children to compare what the others wrote.

Stage 4: Independent Writing

1. Divide students into small groups. Have a selection of graphic organizers. Allow each group to chose a statement (for example: We want longer recess. We want less homework. We want to sit where we want in class. We want to argue for no school uniform.)
2. In groups, children complete the graphic organizer of their choice for their statement.
3. The teacher(s) need to provide assistance to the students as they complete the graphic organizers. This is a good time to conference with different groups of students.
4. Share the graphic organizers in the class.
5. Students chose the statement that they feel most strongly about and write a persuasive piece, using a scaffold. (This can be done in pairs or individually).
6. The teacher(s) conference with individual students or pairs.

If the piece is to be published, the teacher must remind the students to follow the steps in the writing process.

Outcome Evaluation

This is the step that is commonly associated with evaluation: determining whether an intervention was successful. It is also the most desirable part of an intervention, although the most difficult to carry out. However, a quick look through the examples will show that it is possible for anyone to carry out outcome evaluation, even with limited means.

First of all, avoid the common mistake made by many project leaders: thinking about defining objectives and outcome indicators too late, when the project has already started or even when it is about to end. The term 'outcome evaluation' indicates the type of data that needs to be collected – information on changes in the target group (intermediate or final); in contrast, the term 'summative evaluation' is derived from *when* (at which stage of the intervention) the data are processed (typically after the project has ended). Thus, outcome evaluation is ideally prepared for at the planning stage of an intervention. If a pre–post evaluation design is required, it is often necessary to obtain data on several indicators (at baseline) *before* the intervention starts.

A more in-depth discussion of evaluation is to be found in the COST-A 6 publication on evaluation.

During the outcome evaluation, you will analyse indicators on specific variables. Some of them–those that describe the target group's behavioural characteristics–will already have been defined in previous steps (defining objectives and contents). Now is the time to define additional variables/indicators, possibly more closely related to drug use and its intensity. Also take into account the inclusion of additional qualitative data. Be sure that the chosen indicators closely mirror your chosen *specific* objectives (not the operational objectives, which belong to process evaluation.

If intensive drug use or any drug use is not very predominant or is difficult to assess in your target group, it is even more important to define mediating variables in addition to those related to drug use. It is more realistic to formulate objectives not exclusively in terms of drug consumption. Most theories propose large sets of intermediate (or mediating) variables that predict or explain drug use. That is why a good theory base is so important. This will also contribute to a theory-based explanation of how you arrived at your results and help to avoid black box phenomena (outcomes for which you have no explanation). Theory-based evaluation (Italian).

Design

Different evaluation designs have different evidence power and different costs (resources, time, preparation, logistics, experts). By now you should have a clear idea (after Step 4) of the scope, setting and content of your intervention and base your decision regarding evaluation design on this.

It is obvious that large and sophisticated evaluation designs are far more difficult to apply for selective prevention than in the well-controlled conditions of classroom-based prevention. In addition, it is not always easy to find, to match and follow a suitable control group if the study setting is outside a school environment.

On the other hand, the effects of interventions are more likely to be significant when the target phenomenon (drug use, social exclusion, problem behaviour) is more frequent or of greater magnitude.

For similar reasons (to increase effect sizes), consider incorporating sensible stratifications (gender, risk groups) within your target group for the evaluation. It is possible that some subgroups will respond much better or worse to certain types of content than others. Leaving these subeffects unrecorded would lead to interesting effects being diluted or lost altogether.

Use of the Evaluation

Be sure that the presentation of the evaluation satisfies the interest and takes into account the understanding of the addressees of this evaluation. Not all stakeholders are interested in the same aspects or indicators or have the same level of understanding of scientific language.

Be aware that an outcome evaluation is also very important for the internal dynamics (staff, stakeholders) of your intervention; it may be seen as a threat to the established modus operandi or as a means to improve performance, to question and remodel the usual approaches.

Again, pull together all relevant information that explains your outcomes in theoretical and factual contexts and shows that they are result of inputs, target group situation, social and other conditions and the evaluation design.

Notes (on Terminology)

Outcome evaluation assesses the result in terms of achievement of objectives set (were the objectives attained?).

Impact evaluation assesses the results beyond the achievement of objectives set (greater range of results which were not explicitly and previously planned).

At the end of this step, you will ideally have achieved the following:

- You will have a data gathering and analysis plan as well an idea of which most evaluation design is most feasible. This is realistic and within the scope of your intervention's resources.
- You will have made a pragmatic decision on the most realistic evaluation to be used (not all interventions have the resources and real-world conditions needed to conduct a randomised controlled trial).
- You will know what 'outcome' means in your intervention, *i.e.* what works best for whom (of the target) under which conditions.
- You will know from whom the outcome information was gathered, whether the intervention had any effect on target group behaviour and in which target (sub)groups, and whether the intervention actually achieved its purpose.

Logic model key questions: Are all indicators now plausibly and logically connected to the objectives set? Is the whole evaluation design and framework linked to and mirroring the theory base and the concrete components of this intervention?

Problems you will face if this phase is not carried out correctly:

- Without an outcome evaluation, your intervention can still be interesting, but it will attract much less attention than a well-thought-out, even simple, outcome evaluation design.
- You will have spent (mostly public) money without showing that you have used it sensibly.
- The staff involved in your project will not know if their efforts have made any real difference and will be less likely to have grown professionally.

- All you can provide are some positive statements about non-quantified and non-attributable improvements after the intervention, which can easily be contested. A pre–post design is much more convincing.
- You continue to act as you always did in the past. You fail to take a critical view that enables you to revamp your evaluation or dynamise your approach. In other words, you lose the opportunity to improve your intervention.
- Your evaluation does not achieve its full potential (*e.g.* the indicators of a life skills programme should be related to life skills components and not just the information level of the target population).
- You have told the stakeholders (and the EMCDDA EDDRA manager) that your intervention has an outcome evaluation, but this is not the case because none of the indicators refers to any variable related to the target group.

What's the Difference Between Learning Outcomes and Learning Objectives?

Learning Objectives:

- tend to describe specific, discrete units of knowledge and skill
- were useful during the 1970's and 1980's when attempts were made to describe workplace activities as specific tasks to be completed
- can be accomplished within a short time frame-still may be relevant for a class period
- tend to be statements of intent; do not necessarily suggest that the behaviour has been demonstrated

Learning Outcomes:

- describe broad aspects of behaviour which incorporate a wide range of knowledge and skill
- increased use in the 1990's when workplace requirements involve broader skillsets which are transferable to a wide range of work settings

- accomplished over time in several learning experiences
- refer to demonstrations of performance

More about the difference between Learning Outcomes and Course Objectives:

Learning outcomes tend to represent the "big picture" as opposed to the specific details and discrete aspects or chunks of performance.

In the 1950's and 60's, the emphasis was on a person doing specific job tasks which required specific knowledge for an extended period of time. In contrast, rapid technological changes of the 1990's require that the worker readily and repeatedly adapt to new job skill requirements which emphasize an ability to focus on broader concepts. As part of this new workplace structure, the ability to work in teams has been increasingly emphasized.

Curriculum design trends have undergone similar transformations. Behavioural objectives of the 60's and 70's which described very specific and detailed aspects of behaviour, have now been replaced with the broader learning outcomes statements that incorporate broader aspects of performances. These performances have a variety of knowledge, skills and attitudes embedded within them.

Contrast the following behavioural objective statement:

- *Given a paragraph of ten sentences, the student will be able to identify ten rules of grammar which are used in its construction* with the Learning Outcomes statement:
- *The student will have reliably demonstrated the ability to use the conventions of grammar when creating paragraphs.*

How might the learning activities and methods of assessment differ in view of the two statements?

As another example, consider the following statements:

Learning Objective:

At the end of this class, the learner will be able to:

- Define affirmative action;

- Describe three factors which promote affirmative action in the workplace.

Learning Outcome:

At the end of this course the learner will have reliably demonstrated the ability to develop affirmative action programmes within a workplace environment.

What Differences can You See between these Statements?

Differences:

L.O. is a much broader performance statement

L.O. represents an end stage of performance

Learning outcomes are not written at the class level since they represent broad, statements which incorporate many areas of inter-related knowledge and skill that may be developed over time through a wide range of experiences. Class room or short learning sessions would *address* course learning outcomes, but not be considered sufficient opportunity for the student to achieve the outcome in a single episode of learning.

Evaluation of Curriculum Reform definition of **evaluation** as 'the determination of the worth of a thing', then the **evaluation** of educational curricula refers to determining the merit or worth of a part or thewhole of a curriculum. There are anumber of reasons why **evaluation** is important, first, according to Sanders, it informs and serves the needs of policy makers, administrators, and other members of the society. It also informs and helps in decision-making as it gives policy makers information. Secondly it serves as a reference to teachers, curriculum specialists, school administrators and others involved in curriculum development.

Different countries have different approaches to curriculum **evaluation**; an example from the Philippines shows what this country is doing in terms of curriculum **evaluation**:

- *Philippines:* The curriculum restructuring is being tried out in all public schools and we want to evaluate the following:

— The adequacy of support to the implementation of the curriculum (the context);

— How the curriculum is operationalized in schools, *i.e.* in terms of the input and the process; and

— To assess the initial learner behaviour change that may be attributed to the curriculum and the corresponding teacher behaviour change.

PART V: Evaluation of Curriculum Reform

1. *Diagnostic Evaluation:* This method of evaluation is carried out at the beginning of a programme or project, by first identifying aspects of a curriculum that have to be improved and then by making appropriate decisions to do so. Diagnostic evaluations provide essential information for designing appropriate programmes in curriculum development.

- *Thailand:* In order to develop the 2001 Basic Education Curriculum, Thailand used the following sources:

  — 'Studying Thai educational quality problems including social, cultural, economic, scientific and technological and political conditions and problems;

  — Studying and analysing the 1990 primary, lower and upper secondary curricula implementation;

  — Studying and analysing the national educational policies;

  — Collecting and studying theories and lines of thoughts about educational philosophy, curriculum development theories, learning theories, learning psychology and social and cultural information;

  — Collecting, studying and analysing and synthesizing the provision of educational management and national curricula of other countries; and

  — Studying and analysing standard-based education.

2. *Formative Evaluations:* An ongoing process where there is continual talking and planning, with educational personnel, on matters regarding the change of content in the curriculum or the student body. The evaluators who carry out formative evaluations are usually people who are already involved in the educational programme under **evaluation**. They are often individuals or groups who are internal to the educational system.
   - *Malaysia:* Research-based studies on the national curriculum: The Education Planning and Policy Research Division conducted a study on the implementation of the Integrated Curriculum for Secondary Schools. The findings of these Building the Capacities of Curriculum Specialists for Educational Reform studies provide input for **curricular** improvement. In general, the results of the formative **evaluation** are used by curriculum planners to revise and improve the implementation of a **curricular** programme.
3. *Summative Evaluations:* Occur mostly at the end of a project or programme. Summative evaluations are used to determine what has been achieved over a period of time, to summarize programme progress, and to report the findings to the stakeholders. The evaluators who conduct this type of evaluations are usually external evaluators, who according to Sanders are 'candidates independent of and unaffected by the object of the **evaluation**'.
   - *Indonesia:* Formulated the recommendation to 'Establish a collaborative process between curriculum teams and international consultants that work hand in hand to professionally share the process and outcomes of such curriculum development. There are numerous issues addressed to such projects that have the potential to assist and inform others in the field of curriculum development. The development of articles documenting and analysing such projects should be

submitted to international and Indonesian journals as a means of contributing to understanding and processes within this field of endeavour.

- *Malaysia:* The Education Planning and Policy Research Division conducted a study on the implementation of the Integrated Curriculum for Secondary Schools. Findings from summative **evaluation** concerned with the effectiveness of the whole **curricular** programme are used in making major decisions on whether to continue/expand/ modify or terminate certain **curricular** programmes.
- *Mongolia:* After 1990s Mongolia's curriculum reform went through different stages of development.

In 2001 the **evaluation** was made on the last stage of reform, which had started back in 1997. The outcome of the **evaluation** was that there is a need for changing the subject based standard and curriculum to the competence based standard and curriculum. The new standard has just been finalized.

Focus of Curricular Evaluation: Subject Content—Organisation and Mode of Transaction

The Importance of Evaluations

One of the methods used in evaluating curricula is by using external curriculum evaluations. This approach to **evaluation** mainly uses people from outside the system, those with the expertise. The factors that contribute to organizing external evaluations are: the need for independence, the span of control, legal requirements that are contractual and of course, the expertise involved in conducting the evaluations. Experts from different government bodies are asked to evaluate programmes as in the Mongolian example:

- *Mongolia:* The State Education Inspection Board, inspectors of local education with support from former parents, school governing board and local administration organize the external supervision. Inspection results are analysed and the processed information is submitted to relevant organizations and individuals, and used to effect changes in their policy and planning. The example from the Philippines shows that it is important to have external evaluators who are familiar with the type of evaluations they have to carry out:

- *Philippines:* 'The monitoring is done both at the national and local levels and a curriculum support desk has been organized to continue to receive feedback from the field and to respond to urgent concerns. External evaluators are also welcomed provided they have been oriented on the restructured curriculum.'

Another approach to **evaluation** is internal **evaluation**. This may be carried out either on a centralized or decentralized basis. A centralized system would require the formation of an **evaluation** unit within the system itself and one of the points mentioned in a decentralized system would be the use of existing, permanent groups within the system. 'Curriculum **evaluation** may be organized so that it is carried out by departments.'

- *Malaysia:* Monitoring and **evaluation** are normally carried out in every phase of curriculum implementation. In addition to supervision the school inspectors and subject supervisors at the State Education Departments, monitoring and supervision are also carried out by the various divisions within the Ministry of Education, *i.e.*, Curriculum Development Centre, Examination Syndicate, the School Division, Teacher Building the Capacities of Curriculum Specialists for Educational Reform

Sources That Initiate or Feed Change

Education Division and Education Planning and Policy Research Division. The area of **focus** differs for each division.

The example that follows illustrates monitoring of programmes to generate information to serve as a contribution to decisions about programme continuation.

- *Thailand:* Each Educational Institute is expected to design the monitoring system and **evaluation** scheme to provide relative feedback for the continuing revision of school-based learning contents along with implementation. The main purpose of **evaluation** is to facilitate or improve programmes or projects, by judging them. Judgements are made mainly on the basis of what has been observed, and this helps to modify or change a particular programme, project or curriculum. This trend can be observed in the following country examples:
- *China:* Regular assessment should also be undertaken at school level for principals, teachers, students, parents and community members to review the newly introduced curriculum and to take necessary initiatives to strengthen the effectiveness.
- *Malaysia:* In order to ensure smooth implementation of the national curriculum, several subject committees at the national level have been formed particularly for subjects like national language, English, mathematics and science. The role of such a committee is to review regularly the effectiveness of the teaching and learning of the subjects concerned. Changes in the curriculum contents are made based on the recommendations of the committees. Other subject committees are formed from time to time to review the subject curriculum and make recommendations for improvement.By using the opinions expressed by the general public, Mongolia has been able to revise its teaching content and the methods used in teaching and learning:

  "The main purpose of ***evaluation*** *is tofacilitate or improve programmes or projects, by judging them. Judgements are made mainly on the basis of what has been observed, and this helps to modify or change a particular programme, project or curriculum."*

Research-based Studies to Evaluate Success and Failure

- *Mongolia:* In the activities of the school-based content and in order to create an environment for application of the content, an opportunity was opened to broaden participation of the general public by implementing projects and programmes. At present this type of activity has a most important role in the revision of teaching and learning content and methodology.

- *Viet Nam:* To prepare for curriculum development, there is a lot of research on the theory and practice of curriculum renovation and methods of general education [...] Based on this research, the orientations and principles, procedures for developing curriculum are built to be a basis for the development of curriculum. The task of soliciting comments and **evaluation** play an important role in the finalization and institutionalization of the new curriculum. The following are country examples that indicate the results of the evaluations conducted at various levels of curriculum implementation. Based on the results, changes are brought about regarding the utility and appropriateness of the assessment, and this helps in decision-making concerning improvements or modifications to curricula. This is very clearly expressed in the example from China:
- *China:* 'Research-based studies on the state and effectiveness of various aspects of the national curriculum and its implementation, including the effectiveness of curriculum content, existing pedagogies and instructional approaches, teacher training, and of textbooks and instructional materials have been arranged. For example, MOE has organized the experts and professors of key education institutes or universities to collect and review all the senior high school entrance examination paper. The results and recommendations have been used for monitoring and improving examinations, and to guide the teaching reform.' From the presentation at the Seminar, an example from Indonesia shows that:
- The Curriculum Development Centre carried out an **evaluation** on the implementation of the 1994

curriculum. The findings show that there are still some unsolved Building the Capacities of Curriculum Specialists for Educational Reform problems, such as the existence of some disconnections, overlapping of content, and even misleading curriculum implementation, particularly for the subjects of Sports and Art. Therefore, these misconceptions were righted by providing a Curriculum Supplement Document for all subject matters and for all levels (...) for the purpose of selecting(reducing and adding) content. The example from Japan clearly elaborates the steps that the country has taken towards introducing revisions in the teaching methods, teaching objectives, and teaching content of particular curricula:

- *Japan:* The Ministry of Education has been conducting nation-wide surveys on students' achievement in some subject area. The purpose of this survey is to evaluate the effectiveness of implementation of the National Curriculum Standards. The results of this survey are to be used to improve the methods of teaching and learning in a nation-wide perspective and to design more effective Curriculum Standards in the near future (...) This implies that we should put more emphasis on developing children's number sense, as well as on introducing children's hands-on activities in mathematics classrooms. These survey results and analysis have been used in the process of revising the objectives and teaching content in the Curriculum Standards for mathematics. With the help of research conducted by the NRIES, Laos PDR has been able to take steps towards improving learner performance and quality education, enhancing mother-tongue use in schools with positive outcomes, and conducting action research in Science and Mathematics education. NRIES staff has led three evaluations:
- To study the situation of organization of teaching-learning, the effects of national teacher orientation workshops, the use of textbooks and teacher's guides

and to assess student learning outcomes. The **evaluation** findings indicated satisfactory achievements. The new curriculum was relevant to the student needs and the requirements of local and national development, and has contributed to the improvement of learning performance and the quality of education.

- A study of teaching Lao PDR for ethnic minority children and youth has been conducted in order to enhance language macro skills, such as listening, speaking, reading and writing. The research team has advanced the hypothesis that by possessing adequate language skills, the ethnic minority youth would be able to improve learning of other academic subjects: mathematics, sciences, social studies, technology, etc. The team decided to try out the concentrated language encounters techniques adapted to the learning environment in ethnic minority areas by taking into careful account the pecific features of ethnic languages and dialects. As a result, the student learning outcomes have considerably improved; both teachers and learners were also motivated to learn.
- Another aspect of enhancing learning achievements and teaching effectiveness at the secondary education level is related to action research conducted by NRIES Mathematics and Sciences Division, in cooperation with teachers of the Vientiane municipality secondary schools and professors of the National University. The research findings show that most of the students lack the **focus** in reading books and extracting useful information for using as the basic data for constructing or discovering knowledge. It is recommended to promote reading skills and introducing the reading techniques in school. In the Philippines, by using the information gleaned from reviews and studies, there was evidence to show that the curriculum needed to cut down on overcrowding:
- *Philippines:* A core group was organized to continue the study of the curriculum and to consolidate and study the results of the previous surveys, studies,

consultations and reviews. [...] All of the reviews and studies point to the low student performance. A number of factors are consistently identified as contributory to this problem, such as inadequacy of funds, prior preparation of teachers, high drop-out rate, high level of illiteracy, insufficiency of instructional support and facilities (*e.g.* laboratories, libraries, etc.) The major studies all recommend the need to decongest the curriculum. On the other hand, in the Philippines, studies also pointed out to the necessity for introducing analytical methodology in the curriculum:

- As regard secondary education, the Committee on Information Technology, Science, Mathematics Education and other Technologies states: 'The New Secondary Education Curriculum (NSEC) deserves a second look It must be vis-à-vis the NSAT (National Secondary Achievement Test) results of the last four years where the students achieved mean percentage scores of only about 50%. Building the Capacities of Curriculum Specialists for Educational Reform. The lowest scores were recorded in Science and Mathematics indicating that these are the most difficult subjects for the students, and for which additional contact time may be needed and innovative teaching techniques should be devised to make them interesting and less daunting to students. The basic education curriculum should be streamlined such that it will provide for greater concept understanding, mastery of skills (*e.g.* critical thinking and other scientific skills) and appreciation of science and technology as applied to daily life.'

As we have seen from the examples above curriculum quality is important to maintain, and standards of quality in education are achieved by constantly studying the worth and merit of educational curricula. The main **focus** of curriculum **evaluation** is looking at the policies that have been put into actionæthe structure and framework of curriculum development: curriculum design; the various instructional products and materials that are used; where the objectives of student outcomes can be analysed; checking/testing student progress; the effectiveness of teaching and teachers or instruction outcomes; the learning environment and finally the monetary resources available. Through educational evaluations, all these factors result in measuring the effectiveness of educational policies that are implemented in the curricula development process.

Subject Contents

ETDEWEB Access

The *ETDE Energy Database* contains a wealth of information on a variety of energy-related topics. While primarily considered a scientific and technical database, users will also find information targeted to policymakers and consumers. Thanks to the addition of subject-related categories and thesaurus terms (keywords) being added to records in the database, users can better target the information to get more precise results than are usually possible by just using Internet searching. The following pie chart represents the subject contents of the database for the last five years (2004-2008). These are very broad categories, but represent the diversity of coverage. The high percentages in the physics and materials area, although valid, are a bit higher than normal due to recent work with publishers to cover some older material.

Subject categories are used by ETDE to classify records. Typically, these fall into four general types:

(1) those representing energy sources, *e.g.*, COAL, LIGNITE, AND PEAT, SOLAR ENERGY, WIND ENERGY;

(2) those representing energy production, utilization, and management, *e.g.*, FOSSIL-FUELED POWER PLANTS and ENERGY CONSERVATION, CONSUMPTION, AND UTILIZATION;

(3) those representing energy conversion and storage, *e.g.*, DIRECT ENERGY CONVERSION and ENERGY STORAGE;

(4) those accommodating the basic information developed in support of energy production, conversion, and utilization, *e.g.*, CHEMISTRY and PHYSICS.

The table below shows a more in-depth look at the subject categories (category numbers are in parentheses) used for the database and provides users with a better idea of the breadth of what can be found. For even greater detail, users have access to both the full subject categories publication and subject thesaurus published jointly with the International Nuclear Information System (INIS) available in the reference aids section.

Tools, Techniques and Modes of Evaluation

There is no gainsaying that tools, techniques and modes of evaluation employed by the school and teachers leave much to be desired. It has been observed earlier that undue reliance has been placed on the paper pencil tests to measure the progress of the learners, even in the areas of learning where such a tool is found to be totally inadequate, if not altogether irrelevant or unsuitable. There is indeed a dire need to employ a fight technique or use an appropriate tool or a mode to assess the performance of the learner, making a judicious selection from among available tools and techniques such as observation schedules, rating scales, interviews, oral communications, interest inventories, anecdotal records etc. It is also necessary to deformalise both internal and external examinations. It is time that more and more informal means of evaluation are adopted in order to reduce the anxiety and fear experienced by the learners at all stages of school education. The principles of relevance and flexibility applicable to curriculum development need to be followed in evaluating the attainment of the learners.

The primary stage should be considered as a period of transition from learning through informal playway activities to learning with the help of organised and formal methods of teaching. Similar informal and relaxed me.

National Curriculum thods and modes should be adopted in evaluating the growth and development of the young learners. No rigid and/or formal testing should be introduced at this stage. More use of oral testing should be made to assess the development of basic skills in language, numeracy, and health, nutrition and sanitation. Periodical check-ups of physical, social and emotional growth and development should be made and carefully recorded. Similar efforts should be made to record evidence regarding psycho-motor skills related to non-scholastic areas such as Work Experience, An Education and Physical Education. In a nutshell, sufficient evidence should be collected with the help of informal and formal observations and other tools and techniques mentioned above in order to prepare a/ profile of the growth and development of every learner. From the middle stage onwards, written tests and examinations may be given more emphasis and importance, without discarding the good practices, modes, tools and techniques that are initiated at the primary stage.

What are Learning Outcomes?

- Learning outcomes are statements of what is expected that a student will be able to DO as a result of a learning activity (Jenkins and Unwin).
- Learning outcomes are explicit statements of what we want our students to know, understand or to be able to do as a result of completing our courses. (Univ. New South Wales, Australia)
- "Learning outcomes are statements that specify what learners will know or be able to do as a result of a learning activity. Outcomes are usually expressed as knowledge, skills or attitudes". (American Association of Law Libraries).
- Learning outcomes are an explicit description of what a learner should know, understand and be able to do as a result of learning. (Learning and Teaching Institute, Sheffield Hallam University)

Working Definition

Learning outcomes are statements of what a student should know, understand and/or be able to demonstrate after completion of a process of learning.

- The learning activity could be, for example, a lecture, a module or an entire programme.
- Learning outcomes must not simply be a "wish list" of what a student is capable of doing on completion of the learning activity.
- Learning outcomes must be simply and clearly described.
- Learning outcomes must be capable of being validly assessed.

From the definitions we see:

- Emphasis on the learner.
- Emphasis on the learner's ability to do something.

Focus on teaching – aims and objectives and use of terms like *know, understand, be familiar with.*

- Outcomes: Focus on what we want the student to be able to do-use of terms like define, list, name, recall, analyse, calculate, design, etc.
- Aims: Give broad purpose or general intention of the module.
- Objectives: Information about what the teaching of the module hopes to achieve.
- Learning outcomes are not designed to replace the traditional way of describing teaching and learning but to supplement it.

Outcome of Curriculum Evaluation : Change/ Refinement of Content, Organisation and Mode of Transaction

A well-designed curriculum is constantly evaluated:

- to find out the impact of provision, not simply the provision itself
- using a wide range of indicators, reflecting all aspects of the curriculum aims
- by learners, parents and carers, and the wider school community.

The results of this ongoing evaluation are used to decide how learning and assessment can be improved to allow all young people to make progress and achieve.

It is critical that schools reflect regularly on the changes they are making to their secondary curriculum. Are they helping more of their learners to achieve their aims? Not only will this reflection help them recognise success, it will also highlight areas that are less effective and that might need to be adapted. As learners and staff change, so the school curriculum will need to be reviewed. Some schools refer to this as a 'curriculum journey' – an ongoing development that uses information gathered through evaluations to keep the curriculum exciting, relevant and up to date.

Schools have found these activities useful in helping them to evaluate the impact of their curriculum provision.

If you really want to know that your curriculum development work is having the desired impact on your learners, you need to establish a clear baseline and then carry out regular, planned evaluations to check the progress of your work.

All schools are rich in information about what is working well and what is working less well. In particular, schools tend to be very good at analysing the information they have about student achievements in subjects that are tested externally, either through national curriculum tests or qualifications. However, your curriculum priorities are likely to be much broader than this. What other measures do you need to have in place to help you determine the progress your learners are making?

Considering a Range of Measures

Consider the curriculum as a plant and the ways you evaluate it as sources of light. If there is only one light source shining on the curriculum, it will grow towards that light. What other sources of light–as well as test results–would you like to have shining on your curriculum to help you determine that it is working? Bridge High School recognised that it needed to balance exam and test score data with information about their students' skilfulness and motivation. They used resource sheet D to note the torches they wanted to shine on their curriculum. You could use the blank version to do the same.

For each of the aims you have identified for curriculum development, consider what evidence you need to collect in order to show progress. Remember that you only need to collect evidence that is directly relevant to each aim. For example, if you want your learners to have enquiring minds and be independent thinkers, you might collect information on the number and type of questions they ask, their willingness to contribute and their ability to work independently.

When collecting evidence, try to translate qualitative information into quantitative, measurable data. If only a minority of your class can do something, is it less than 40 per cent? Less than 20 per cent? The more specific your measures of performance, the more likely it is that you will be able to demonstrate a link between your curriculum changes and their impact.

Collecting People's Views

The best way to demonstrate the progress you are making is to let the curriculum developments speak for themselves–to be self-advocating. The words of those directly involved, particularly learners, are often the most powerful evidence of the impact of change.

Does the learning experience have a built-in mechanism for reporting progress? This could come through the learners' work directly, through presentations, displays, websites or performances in a variety of contexts. You might want to enhance these measures with instrumental evaluation techniques such as using surveys, questionnaires, assessment tasks and personality profiles. You could use a student forum to gather information about learners' attitudes to school and their understanding of themselves as learners.

A range of stakeholders, including governors, parents, co-development partners and Ofsted, can also provide valuable views and information to help you evaluate your curriculum development. You could use resource sheet G to help you make notes on each group, including learners.

When and how often you collect evidence will depend on:

- the type of information you are collecting
- when you need information to make decisions about moving forward.

Evaluation should be an ongoing process and planning specific opportunities to gather, analyse and act on the information you collect needs to be part of your curriculum development journey.

As a team, consider when you need to evaluate your work over the next year. If you have not already done so, start putting together some baseline information about your learners that relates to your vision for what you want them to achieve. What are your learners like now? How do you know?

At this point it can also be helpful to think about trends in relation to your baseline. What will your learners be like in five years' time if you are really pleased with the way your new curriculum is working? What will they be like if you are satisfied? And what will they be like if you are unhappy with the outcomes you see? Some schools have found it helpful to ask different staff to complete resource sheet E, which addresses these three questions and can be a useful tool for discussion.

Who will Collect and Analyse the Evidence?

Talk with colleagues about the way you collect, record and analyse evidence at the moment. Can you tap into or develop systems already in place? How can you plan to measure success regularly by listening to your learners?

The voice and views of other professionals—for example colleagues, staff from other schools, the local authority or independent advisers—can make a valuable contribution to evaluating the success of curriculum development. Consider using:

- internal review–inviting others who work at your school to review a specific part of your curriculum development at one of its milestones
- external review–asking representatives from other schools to review aspects of your curriculum

- formal review–inviting an accrediting or approving agency to review your curriculum.

As a team, make sure that you're clear about who will be involved in and take responsibility for each aspect of evaluation. To make the most of the information you collect, you will need to build in opportunities to sit down together and look for trends, hypothesise, suggest and agree key messages, and change plans if necessary.

Completing an Evaluation Plan

Based on your discussions about what evidence to collect, how to collect it, when to evaluate and who will take responsibility, complete an evaluation plan to share with colleagues. Resource sheet H is a template for an evaluation plan that you could either complete as it stands or modify to meet the particular requirements of your curriculum development work.

Many curriculum innovations are well documented and reported by schools, but often the reports focus on activities rather than outcomes. One way to become a better self-advocate for your curriculum is to develop an evaluation portfolio from which you can extract the evidence you need to tell a convincing story.

Putting Together an Evaluation Portfolio

A good evaluation portfolio will:

- encourage you to collect evidence regularly
- focus on outcomes rather than activities
- include contributions from everyone involved
- be a good source of information for internal reviews, peer review and reporting, the self-evaluation framework (SEF) and external reviews and inspections
- become a permanent record of achievement.

Talk with colleagues about what to include in your evaluation portfolio.

- What are the key points in your curriculum development work? What evidence of achievement are you planning to collect at these points?

- What format will this evidence be in? How could you best present it in your portfolio?
- What type of portfolio are you going to create? A whole-school portfolio, capturing the complete story of your curriculum development? Separate portfolios for groups of learners? Or online portfolios for individual learners to demonstrate and record their learning?
- How can you draw on the ways that learners in your school already demonstrate their learning?

Make sure that your portfolio is brief, clear, persuasive and supported by evidence (including learners' work). It is a record of achievement rather than a formal report, although you will probably find it invaluable when you do need to report your findings to different audiences, such as governors, parents, staff and Ofsted. Many schools have found it useful to structure their evaluation portfolio around the three key questions shaping their curriculum thinking. Resource sheet I suggests the type of information you might include in your portfolio for each key question and offers a structure that you can use to start planning your own portfolio.

Sharing Your Success

It is important that you share information with learners and other key stakeholders about the progress of your curriculum development work, its successes and the difficulties faced. If you have put together an evaluation portfolio you will find this an invaluable source of information.

You could use resource sheet J to help you plan how and when to communicate your progress and success to others. Think about communicating appropriately for different audiences and situations – for example on the school website, at a governors' meeting, for a parents' evening display, on a self-evaluation form for Ofsted, or as part of the staff professional development programme.

I. The Nature and Purpose of ***Evaluation***

A. Anything in the schools can be evaluated in terms of its contribution to the students' overall learning and its cost.

B. **Evaluation** — gathering data to support a decision to accept, change, or eliminate something.

C. **Evaluation** serves to identify strengths and weakness of **curriculum** before implementation and the effectiveness of its delivery after implementation.

D. **Evaluation** Questions

1. Intrinsic Value-Is the planned **curriculum** "good" and "appropriate"? Assessments vary depending upon each person's philosophical and psychological orientation and the extent of agreement among "experts" in relevant subject areas.
2. Instrumental Value-Will what is planned to address the stated goals and objectives, and who is the intended audience (target population)?
3. Comparative Value-Is the new programme better than the old one? Comparative bases include student achievement, delivery cost, demand on resources, and responsiveness to community expectations. Most crucial question.
4. Idealization Value-How can the new programme be improved?
5. Decision Value-Will the **evaluation** process provide the evidence needed to determine whether it should be kept, changed, or eliminated. Same as 3.

E. Long-term assessment is important

1. Project Talent
   a. Initiated in 1960 with the testing of 400,000 secondary school students (interests, ability scores, and characteristics of schools, including course offerings)
   b. Fifteen years later (1975) a representative sample of the students were interviewed and reported their satisfaction with different aspects of their lives.
   c. Findings
   (1) In 1960 47% of the graduating boys and 38% of the graduating girls said their courses were

NOT helpful in preparing them for occupations. In 1971, 46% of the males and 40% of the females still felt that high school had been adequate at best.

(2) were that educational programmes should be modified to enable people to achieve greater satisfaction in intellectual development and personal understanding.

2. National Assessment of Educational Progress (NAEP)

   a. An information system which provides information regarding the educational achievements of children, youth, and young adults, and indicates both progress and problems.

   b. Reports test results by age and grade level.

   c. NAEP reported n 1982 that most improvements in mathematics achievement are limited to lower order skills—simple computation.

*II. Approaches to **Evaluation***

A. Scientific

1. Behaviorally oriented people tend to look at **evaluation** as a connection between what is and what all agree ought to be.
2. Ideal is a pretest-posttest, experimental-control group design
3. Focus is typically on learner outcomes as reflected in quantitative forms such as test scores that are amenable to statistical analysis.

B. Humanistic

1. Humanists tend to look at **evaluation** in terms of the different values of all programme participants and in terms of the perceived value of the processes and activities of the programme.

2. Data gathered is more qualitative than quantitative—descriptions of events rather than judgments of event.
3. Patterns observed from many observations form the basis for decisions.

C. Intrinsic and Pay-Off **Evaluation**

1. Intrinsic **evaluation** focuses on the **curriculum** design and development.
    a. Worth of goals and objectives
    b. Appropriateness of content
    c. Types of learning activities
2. Pay-off **evaluation** focuses on the usually short-term effects of the **curriculum**.
    a. Extent to which the objectives were achieved
    b. Effects on parents, teachers, administrators
    c. Often regarded as more important than intrinsic **evaluation**.
    d. Advocated goal-free **evaluation** in which evaluators look at all the results of the **curriculum** (unexpected side effects, overlooked achievement, new priorities), instead of looking only at those effects that were anticipated (such as higher tests scores).

D. Formative and Summative **Evaluation**

1. Formative **evaluation**
    a. Takes place at specified points during the development and pilot testing phases of **curriculum** building in order to identify and correct problems before the **curriculum** is put into full operation.
    b. Can be used during actual operation to fine tune the **curriculum**.
    c. Norman Grunlund advocates looking for and assessing unintended effects.

2. Summative **evaluation**
    a. Follows full implementation and focuses on overall effectiveness.
    b. May take place at designated end points throughout the curricular design such as at the end of the pilot testing stage and the end of the implementation stage.

*III. **Evaluation** Models*

A. The Eight-Year Study **Model**
    1. Establish broad goals or objectives
    2. Classify objectives (easier now with "Bloom's Taxonomy)
    3. Define objectives in behavioral terms
    4. Find situations in which achievement of objectives can be shown
    5. Develop or select measurement techniques
    6. Collect student performance data, and
    7. Compare data with behaviorally stated objectives.

B. The (Tyler)-Newton Metfessel-William Michael **Model**
    1. Involve everyone who is directly or indirectly affected.
    2. Develop goals and specific objectives and arrange them in hierarchical order.
    3. Translate goals and objectives into **curriculum** content and experiences.
    4. Select or create **evaluation** instruments to assess achievement of the objectives
    5. Conduct periodic observations
    6. Analyze data
    7. Interpret data
    8. Make decisions

C. Michael Provus's Discrepancy **Evaluation Model**
    1. Four components
        a. Determining programme standards
        b. Determining programme performance

c. Comparing standards with performance

d. Determining whether discrepancies exist between standards and performance.

2. Five stages at which programme performance is compared to programme standards

a. Design vs. Design Criteria

(1) Internal soundness—congruence with philosophical stance, adequacy of resources, etc.

(2) External soundness—comparison with similar programmes

(3) Identification and resolution of initial problems

b. Installation vs. Installation Criteria

(1) Is the programme operating as intended?

(2) Are all the parts (people, equipment, etc., in place?

c. Processes vs. Process Adjustment

(1) Are communication lines functioning as intended?

(2) Are planned activities functioning as intended?

d. Product vs. Product Assessment

(1) **Evaluation** of entire programme in terms of original goals.

(2) Effects on all affected.

e. Cost vs. Benefit

D. Robert Stake's Congruence-Contingency **Model** (1969)—also known as the Countenance **Model**

1. Data needs to be collected on the basis of:

a. Antecedents-Conditions existing before the treatment begins

(1) Student attitudes, achievement levels, attendance, etc.

(2) Teacher attitudes, years of experience, etc.

b. Transactions-The interactions among students, teachers, materials, and environment. The teaching-learning process.

c. Outcomes-The consequences of the programme—cognitive, affective, personal, community-wide, immediate, and long-term.

2. Evaluate data on the basis of what was intended and what was actually observed.

3. Ideal is to find that outcomes were contingent upon the antecedents and the transactions. The greater the congruence between the intended and the observed outcomes, the better.

E. Daniel Stufflebeam's Context, Input, Process, Product (CIPP) **Model** (1971)

1. Context **Evaluation**

a. "Its purpose is to provide a rationale for the determination of objectives."

b. Unmet needs are identified, reasons they are unmet hypothesized, and the **curriculum** environment defined (who, what, when, where, why)

2. Input **Evaluation**

a. The purpose is to "provide information for determining how to utilize resources to achieve project objectives."

b. Analysis of goals and objectives

c. Analysis of resources and experiences to be used to meet goals

d. Comparison with alternative programmes and strategies

3. Process **Evaluation**

a. Three main objectives:

1. To detect or predict defects in the procedural design or its implementation during the implementation stage,

2. provide information for programmed decisions, and
3. to maintain a record of the procedure as it occurs."

4. Product **Evaluation**
   a. Formative and summative data needed
   b. Rational interpretations needed on the basis of the recorded context, input, and process information.

F. Stufflebeam's Macro (Total) **Evaluation Model**
   1. Expansion of CIPP **model**
      a. Planning decisions made after context **evaluation**
      b. Structuring decisions made after input **evaluation**
      c. Implementation decisions made after process **evaluation**
      d. Recycling decisions made after product **evaluation**
   2. Four kinds of change
      a. Neomobilistic change-Large change, low information
      b. Incremental change-a series of small changes based on low information
      c. Homeostatic change-small change based on much information
      d. Metamorphic change-great change based on much information

G. Elliot Eisner's Connoisseurship **Evaluation Model** (1985)
   1. Focus is on the process itself.
      a. What took place?
      b. Who participated?
      c. What did they think of the experience?
   2. Follows the **model** of criticism and **evaluation** of art.

3. Requires upon "referential adequacy" and "structural corroboration" instead of scientific validity.
    a. Referential adequacy means that critical observations and interpretations must be empirically grounded (must be able to be replicated by independent observers).
    b. Structural corroboration means that there must be continuous inquiry about whether the various parts of the criticism fit together as a consistent whole.
4. The criticism should communicate to some public, what is going on in the school.

H. Robert Stake's Responsive **Evaluation Model** (1975)

1. As the Eisner Connoisseurship **Model**, the Responsive **Evaluation model** focuses on describing activities and processes rather than on test scores and outcomes. It seeks to "tell the story of the programme."
2. A formal **evaluation** plan consisting of ten steps is implemented. The ten steps are:
    a. Negotiate a framework for **evaluation** with the sponsors.
    b. Elicit topics, issues and/or questions of concern from the sponsors.
    c. Formulate questions for guiding the **evaluation.**
    d. Identify the scope and activities of the **curriculum**—the needs of clients and personnel.
    e. Observe, interview, prepare logs and case studies.
    f. Pare down information, identify the major issues or questions.
    g. Present initial findings in a tentative report.
    h. Analyze reactions and investigate predominate concerns more fully.

i. Look for conflicting evidence that would invalidate findings and corroborating evidence that would support findings.

j. Report the results.

IV. Practices of **Evaluation**

A. Six common **evaluation** phases

1. Focusing on the Curricular Phenomena to be Evaluated
   a. What are the objectives of the **evaluation** effort?
   b. Who and what will be evaluated? By who? When?
   c. What instruments and criteria will be used?
2. Collecting the information
   a. How will confidentiality be protected?
   b. Periodic collection of information important to see change over time.
3. Organizing the information-Coding, storing, and retrieving
4. Analyzing the information-Utilizing appropriate analysis techniques
5. Reporting the information-Report and interpret information either formally (written report) or informally (discussions)
6. Recycling the information-Using the information to continually improve the **curriculum**.

B. All phases should be planned during the development process.

V. Methodological Issues

A. Should objectives specify intents or realizations of those intents?

B. Should **evaluation** focus on the programme (the operation went according to accepted procedure) or on the students (the patient lived or died)?

C. Intended outcomes (achievement of specified objectives) or goal-free outcomes (Gee, look what we found).

D. Norm-Referenced or Criterion Referenced

1. Norm-referencing most useful in making decisions about people.
   a. Used to ascertain individual's relative position within the norming group.
   b. Criterion for mastery need not be stated.
   c. Test items constructed to discriminate among students of vary ability levels.
   d. Variability of scores is necessary for meaningful interpretation.
   e. Tests results amenable for reporting in the traditional A-F system.
2. Criterion-referencing can be used to make decisions about people and programmes.
   a. Used to ascertain whether a specific criterion or performance standard has been reached.
   b. Behavioral objectives stated, including criterion for mastery.
   c. Test items constructed to measure a predetermined level of proficiency.
   d. Variability is irrelevant.
   e. Test results are Pass-Fail

E. Standards

1. Absolute Maximum
2. Absolute Minimum (Criterion-referenced)
3. Relative (Norm-referenced)
4. Multiple (Pre-Post for each individual)

F. Technical Hazards

1. The use of grade-equivalent scores-A procedures typically used to obtain these scores makes them too low in the fall and to high in the spring. A second grader's grade-equivalent score of 3 on a reading test does not mean that the student can read at a third grade level. It means only that he has mastered some of the skills of third grade reading.

2. The use of gain scores. Students who initially have the lowest scores will have the greatest opportunity to show gain. P.E. teachers well aware of this.
3. The use of norm-group comparisons with inappropriate test dates. If the norming group was tested in May and the local students take the test in the fall, comparisons will be misleading.
4. The use of inappropriate test levels. Tests designated as appropriate for particular grade levels may, in fact, be too easy or too difficult for a particular group of students. To be most useful tests should reflect actual achievement level rather than grade level.
5. The lack of pre-and posttest scores for each student. If many low ability students dropout before the posttest, the posttest mean will be unrealistically high. Only matching pre-and posttest scores should be included in mean. Reason for dropouts should be noted.
6. Noncomparable treatment and comparison groups. Unless students are randomly assigned to treatment and control groups (something very difficult to accomplish in a typical school setting) initial difference between groups may influence outcomes.
7. Use of pretest scores to select programme participants. Lowest scoring students will appear to gain the most and highest scoring students will appear to gain the least (regression toward the mean).
8. Careless administration of tests. Students in treatment and control groups should complete pre- and posttests together. This helps avoid inconsistencies in test administration.
9. Assuming that an achievement gain is due to the treatment alone. Hawthorn effects such as novelty and extra attention may be at least partially accountable.

Outcomes Evaluation and its Impact on the Curricular Development and its Implementation

Regional Mechanism Implementation Process: The Mercosur accreditation mechanism has two phases on its implementation. First, the experimental phase, named MEXA, for which courses of agronomics, engineering and medicine were summoned.

On second phase, permanent, denominated ARCUSUR architecture, infirmary, odontology and veterinary medicine courses were summoned. In ten years of constant work this mechanism has made possible development of quality assurance processes in countries members and associates, and has also contributed to widespread concepts throughout all the actors of diverse university communities. On the other hand, it has contributed with incomes towards the harmonization of quality criteria in a more extended region, constituted by RIACES.

Bases for Agreement of Regional Quality Assurance: Agreement of quality assurance for Mercosur is based on mutual recognition of capacity of each country, through the designated agencies or official instances to the effect, to evaluate the quality of its own university programmes. In order to guarantee an even judgments emission, procedures and quality criteria have been agreed, including pairs from countries members and associates, participation in external **evaluation**. Thus, it is hoped to get a common format for **evaluation** reports and a regional speech in quality assurance terms.

1. Mercosur Experimental Quality Assurance Mechanism
2. Mercosur Quality Assurance Mechanism for University Programmes
3. Iberoamerican Network for Quality Assurance in Higher Education
4. *Members:* Argentina, Brazil, Paraguay and Uruguay. *Associates:* Chile and Bolivia

Also, it has been faced a process of actors qualification, as much as agencies and pairs, to make easier not only the proposal understanding, but also mechanism feedback after its application.

As a result, the application has provided useful data for revision and improvement of the process of quality assurance, and has also allowed the adjustment of national processes of quality assurance like a subsequent outcome.

Participation of the Multiple Actors: Process of designing quality criteria has been extended throughout ten years and has brought up permanent reflection as well as it has been widely spread in regional university community.

For quality criteria development, consultative commissions have been summoned for each degree programme. These commissions were initially integrated by two academic and a professional on the discipline into consideration, introducing vision of labor's environment into criteria's design.

It is also important to indicate, the interaction of Higher Education Institutions with Ministries of Education Authorities. This relationship has made possible building a joint work mechanism between the two institutions, in a frame of respect to university autonomy.

The Process of Validation of the Quality Criteria: Once it has been agreed the quality criteria for MEXA, they were put under a previous process of validation before application, to verify its applicability in a exercise named "pretest", in which higher education institutions from the region participated voluntarily. In this exercise it has not been assessed programmes quality, but feasibility of criteria's application and its validity like estimators of programmes quality.

Also, once the experimental phase has been finished, the mechanism was put under **evaluation** with the participation of institutions, pairs and agencies that have participated in the process. This **evaluation** process has allowed mechanism adjustment towards permanent quality assurance system, ARCUSUR.

Impacts

Educational Mercosur has advanced in a constant way, facing differences in rates of growth and development and in size and complexity of the educational systems of the diverse countries. It has also had to deal with differences in the educational qualifications of high school level. Furthermore, changes in countries educational policies have been occurred during the process. Languages difference has had to be handled, as well as progression in a common understanding of mechanism.

On national educational systems, it has also made possible the revision of normative referred to higher education, to allow the application of MERCOSUR accreditation mechanism. In addition, where previous experience in accreditation did not exist, like in Bolivia, Paraguay and Uruguay, it has facilitated process development and official instances for accreditation creation. In case of countries with prior experience, it has been an opportunity for reflection and learning and has contributed to legitimize the idea of higher education quality assurance.

On top of that, Mercosur accreditation mechanism evolves from an academic quality assurance mechanism, exclusively referring to programmes, to a proposal that gives quality guarantee of the individual graduate's certificates, making necessary a discussion about the normative for professional performance in the region.

In the specific field of the degree programmes themselves, which has entered the process, once the general quality criteria has been decided; consultative commissions have been concentrated in definition of two fundamental aspects: graduates proficiency and the curriculum that leads to professional title.

Fundamental agreements go around the minimum hours and contents, as well as the professional practices and the conditions for students to graduate. In each one of degree programmes called, it has resulted in curriculum revision, introducing compulsory fulfillment questions considered at the moment of the proposal as desirable aspects and conditions.

Thus, engineering programmes have been introduced students practical training and final work as aspects of obligatory fulfillment. In medicine, the medical internal school has been incorporated as obligatory inside degree level, and it has also been defined medical training practices throughout all the formation. It has also been included an instance for permanent **curricular** supervision, as well as **evaluation** of institutional management processes. In agronomics, criteria referred to research activities were adjusted to consider activities of research at degree level.

These conclusions of participant courses in the experimental phase have served as incomes to the new ones, working on this frame already developed. They are presently working at specific aspects, such as the hours dedicated to practical formation in dentistry and infirmary, definition of the subject of project in architecture and clinical practice in veterinary medicine. Another fundamental aspect for regional agreement is that courses must aims towards a person integral formation, not only as a professional, but also as a citizen and as a human being. This decision forces the inclusion of aspects referred to this issue in curriculum, not only as contents, but also as educational proficiency and allow the development of these skills throughout the whole learning process.

On the other hand, each individual programme faces or will face a particular situation when considering the introduction of these adjustments to its own curriculum and the consequences that these will have in students and teachers performance. Experiences of modification of curriculum have been registered during the process of self assessment for accreditation, in the attempt to satisfy the exigencies of Mercosur mechanism. This issue brings with itself the logical institutional tensions facing a change process, but also consequences in students, who are subjected to the curriculum transition.

UNIT-VI

Models of Curriculum Evaluation

Taylor's Model

Dr. T. Roger Taylor, in his 41 years as a classroom teacher, administrator, professor and internationally-known educational consultant, has authored/co-authored thousands of integrated, interdisciplinary thematic curriculum units. The units are written based on the **AHA!** (**Analyzing Human Activities**) Model, which is a differentiated curriculum model created by Dr. Taylor. This unique model includes specific application of the most recent brain research, multiple intelligences and constructivist hands-on project-centered learning in alignment with state defined benchmarks and standards.

Roger specializes in curriculum design of differentiated curriculum for the special needs learner as well as the highly gifted student. Both populations, special needs learners and gifted students, are highly "at-risk." With high stakes testing, the push has been to teach to the students that can attain the "proficient" level on standardized tests, ignoring the gifted (because they will "get it anyway") and the low achievers (they are not "worth" the extra effort numerically). Dr. Taylor's **AHA! Model** meets the needs of all the students in a very organized, easy to use manner. Good-bye to textbook driven education, and hello to relevant, higher-order thinking skills! Teachers who use Roger's model and teaching strategies are finding success in closing the achievement gap.

Americans are vitally concerned for the improvement of the quality of education. President Nixon rejected the notion of "more dollars for the same old programmes without making the urgent new reforms that are needed." He went on to propose "a new and searching look at our American school system."A critical aspect of the educational community's ability to meet the President's challenge is its ability to mount a viable programme evaluation effort. To date, educational evaluation has been most notable in its failure.

Speaking of evaluation in general, the American philosopher Clarence Irving Lewis points out that actions could not attain success except that there are evaluations, which are essentially predictions. "Whether the action is performed or not will depend upon evaluations made."In terms of general system theory, Lewis is emphasizing the necessity of feedback in any action scheme.

Action is an attempt to control the future, as far as is possible, for our own benefit. Action is based in the present, in the given situation; it is intentional behavior directed towards realizing desirable states-of-affairs and avoiding undesirable states-of-affairs.The movement is from the reality of the present to a chosen future. Lewis continues that "the principal function of empirical knowledge is that of an instrument enabling transition from the one to the other."

Feedback of evaluative reports to decision makers is a necessity in the rationally managed school system, if it is viewed as a system. On the revision of ongoing educational programmes, for instance, J. T. Hastings has stated that "without such feedback, either the decision to revise or the decision not to revise — and most certainly the decision of how to revise — must be based upon feeling tones and the arguments of personal preference." It has been frequently maintained that the demand for evaluative feedback is incompatible with the classical experimental design. For example, consider Dean Egon Guba s statement that "the application of conventional experimental design to evaluation situations. ..conflicts with the principle that evaluation should facilitate the continuous improvement of a programme."A requirement of invariance of treatment and control are sufficient on Guba's argument to preclude programme change. Thus, these conditions are sufficient to preclude evaluation feedback for managerial decision-making, because "treatments cannot be altered if the data about differences between treatments are to be unequivocal."

Guba considers this a problem of "evaluation methodology." As such, it is a problem of paramount importance to the development of evaluation theory. If the dissemination of evaluative findings is not permitted to preserve the experimental design, then evaluation loses its value to the decision-maker. On the other hand, if experimental design is to be abandoned, serious problems await evaluators in the development of alternatives. We find, however, that these contentions are not valid. It is not the case that treatment must remain invariant. Corrective action by programme managers, in light of evaluative feedback, can take place concurrent with an evaluation in the framework of an experimental design. Of crucial importance is what Guba intends by treatment alteration. Suppose that quantitative change is a change of the value of a given variable (whether an intensive or extensive measurement); then it is convenient to let qualitative change be a change of a variable or dimension itself. Could not the latter be Guba's intent? Let us, then, consider as a possible meaning of qualitative change that a variable or dimension is simply added or deleted from the analysis, as the programme manager adds or subtracts from the programme, and treatment alterations correspond to this.

The Principle of Dimensional Homogeneity states that for a given equation, all the dimensions or variables in the equation can be categorized in terms of a collection of fundamental measures. For example, if volume occurs in an equation, the dimensions of volume are categorized in terms of length. The principle also states that the dimensionality of the variables (the dimensionality of volume for instance is 3) on the right- and left-hand side of the equation, by fundamental measure, must be equal. This is known as the À Theorem. For example, velocity is distance per time. The fundamental measures for velocity are two, length and time. Dimensionality is 1 and-1, respectively. As this also is the case for distance divided by time, the formula is dimensionally homogeneous. If it were otherwise, the introduction or deletion of either fundamental measures or dimensionally across the equation would be a case of ad hoc theorizing, however subtle.

So it is not possible, as a methodological point, for there to be qualitative change in the sense of adding or deleting variables. Hence, we consider here only the case of treatment variance which is both a rational response to evaluative feedback and also treated as dimensionally homogeneous, and indicate how this is compatible with experimental design.

My colleague, Alfred Beradino and I have recently provided a proof that an experimental design and the feedback of action research findings are compatible. This provides sufficient conditions for the falsity of Guba's methodological argument. The question now can be raised whether a precedent exists in the literature for the use of experimental designs in this fashion. In the writings of Sir Ronald Fisher, we find sufficient conditions for the methodological (not practical) arguments for the use of experimental designs in evaluative research.

In his classic *Design of Experiments*, Fisher proposes to "examine the physical conditions of the experimental technique." After mentioning that matching of conditions across treatment levels in the experimental design is a formal condition for minimizing errors, Fisher argues it is impossible to realize this condition in fact, since "uncontrolled causes which may influence the result are always strictly jnnumerable."With regards matching of conditions, the assumption that "refinements constitute improvements to the experiment" is dismissed on the basis of cost considerations. Since matching is a sufficient but not a necessary condition, control of errors in the experiment can and must be realized by other means. The cost of complete matching across treatment levels would be (quite strictly) infinite, and since "an essential characteristic of experimentation is that it is carried out with limited resources," Fisher proposes randomization as an alternative. This is a procedure by which the experiment "may be guaranteed against corruption by the causes of disturbance which have not been eliminated." More precisely, random assignment of subjects to treatment levels permits a precise estimate of error. Thus there are two and only two sufficient conditions for experimental control; hence, one of the two is always necessary. Irrelevant variables are eliminated in effect either by matching of conditions, that is, "eliminated in the field," or by randomization. Fisher emphasizes the sufficiency of the latter technique when he argues that "it is apparent that the random choice of the objects to be/treated in different ways would be a complete guarantee of the validity of the test of significance, if these treatments were the last in time of the stages in the physical history of the objects which might affect their experimental reaction."

This is to say that randomization is sufficient in the absence of treatment variation, to which Guba would undoubtedly agree. In evaluation or action research, a new aspect is added. Because of the various institutional contingencies, it is usually an unacceptable policy to randomly choose subjects for treatment. It would be possible, for instance, to take the lower two-fifths of the students, as ranked by a standardized achievement test. This group could then have remedial treatment provided, by random assignment, to one half, which would amount to one-fifth of the total population. However, it is usually policy to take the lowest fifth, and administer treatment to them as a group. Thus no "control group" is available. This is, however, an institutional contingency, hence not a methodological problem per se. Randomization is still a possibility, hence Fisher's discussion of randomization is relevant to the methodology of evaluation.

Fisher generalizes his argument at this point by emphasizing that variance in treatment subsequent to randomization presents no "practical inconvenience." He states "subsequent causes of differentiation, if under the experimenter's control. .. can either be predetermined before the treatments have been randomized, or, if this has not been done, can be randomized on their own account." The first alternative here is merely the recognition that the rational decision maker's response to evaluative feedback is programme change. The second alternative is excluded from our discussion, as randomly distributed response by a programme manager is not conducive to systematic pursuit of policy.

At this point, we can discuss three possible sources of error: first, consequences of differences already randomized: these are accounted for by the initial randomization; second, natural consequences of the difference in treatment levels: since the null hypothesis argues there will be no treatment effect, there can be no consequences of this effect; and third, effects supervening by chance, independent of treatment levels: because of random assignment, estimates of deviance from a specified distribution across all treatment levels for these effects can be given. Any systematic variance will have been eliminated by the initial randomization.

The dissemination of evaluation findings to the rational programme manager will produce programme change. As a corollary of the Principle of Management by Exception, we know that if a defect in the programme is noted and reported, given adequate programme resources, the defect will be corrected by the rational manager. Thus both the corrective action of the manager, and the adequacy of resources are determinate. As such, the variance of treatment as a function of evaluative feedback can in Fisher's terms, be "predetermined."

Hence, we see that, contrary to the contentions of Guba, it is possible to implement a rigorous experimental design, and also provide feedback for managerial decision-making, in the context of action research. Whether practical concerns, such as the competence of the researcher, or the resources and administrative support available to him, do in fact militate against his ability to implement a rigorous design, is not a methodological issue, and not under consideration here.

On the other hand, if the manager is oblivious to feedback, or responds to feedback with random and affective behavior rather than systematic and rational action, this is a psychological issue, and not under consideration here. But the methodological "problem," posed by Guba, can be considered ill-conceived and non-existent

Stane's Model

Purpose

1. The Forestry Commission Education and Learning Strategy was discussed and approved by the Commissioners in September 2001.
2. This paper:
   - outlines the progress made throughout the FC since September 2001.
   - makes recommendations for implementing this strategy post FDR based on the progress made and on the strategy agreed in 2001.

Background

3. In January 2001 the Commissioners asked John James to establish the Education Steering Group to examine the FC's approach to education for young people and develop a strategy for learning. The members of this group represented each country and section of the organisation in order to reflect the fact that education is devolved and whatever we proposed had to be flexible to fit with a devolved structure. The group reported to the Commissioners on 13 September 2001.
4. The strategy built on the FC's existing expertise, empowered managers by confirming the mandate for education and learning and encouraged a flexible approach to delivery. The key components were:
   - the guiding principles that arose from our discussion of the strategy
   - a model that builds on our strengths and offers a flexible approach to delivery.
   - key elements for delivering the strategy. Progress
5. Commissioners requested a progress report on education and learning when the strategy was discussed. This paper summarises the progress and reflects the views of education staff in the countries.
6. The following general progress has been made over the last 18 months:

- the FC Child Protection Policy approved and in operation since autumn 2002, essential if we are to take our work with young people seriously.
- in the light of FDR a GB Learning Forum has not been established.

  However co-ordinating and sharing the good practice of FE education staff in England, Scotland and Wales continues to develop as the number of staff and level of activity in this work area increases although FDR means there will now no longer be overall co-ordination. As in other areas, formal mechanisms need to be established for this. The education newsletter will provide a stop gap method.
- two more Forest Education Initiative (FEI) co-ordinators, one for north Wales and one for Scotland, both supported by the Forestry Commission.
- the growth in activity and interest in Forest School in England and Wales has been facilitated by the Forestry Commission and presents us with opportunities for work with a wide range of user groups *e.g.* health and social inclusion.
- publications and materials are being developed and assessed by the FC learning website group. This small group has a representative from each country so that the development fits in with specific country requirements.

Country Progress

7. Wales
   - FC Wales are tying their education/learning delivery close to the Welsh Assembly Government (WAG) agendas including learning, social inclusion and health.
   - primary delivery mechanisms are FE Education Service, FEI and Forest Schools.
   - FE launched their education service at the end of October in the presence of the WAG Minister for Learning, Jane Davidson.

- the FC hosted a conference: 'Woodlands for Learning' on 2 December.
- this was chaired by Gareth Wardell and introduced by Jane Davidson. The two key outcomes from the conference was the establishment of a Learning Forum for Wales to help direct the 'Woodlands for Learning' programme and the delivery of a Children's Conference on Woodlands for June 2003.
- there is ongoing discussion with FC/FEI and FE to create an integrated education service to:
  - provide a more consistent delivery of learning opportunities.
  - strengthen the provision of learning for under 19's and those who work with them.
  - allocate resources more effectively according to agreed aims and objectives.
  - an ongoing evaluation of the education service has been initiated to ensure that achievements and experience are recorded.

8. England

- A Learning Seminar is planned for summer 2003. The seminar will look at: young people; skills acquisition & training; professional development.
- Delivery mechanisms are through FE and FEI.
- the FE Education Managers group is developing standards and materials to support FE education delivery.
- the Forest School movement is growing and a strong relationship with the FC and FEI is developing. The Welsh model is proving useful here.
- the Recreation and Health Advisor has discussed the possibility of using the Walkers Welcome package for 'educational access' in the South East and WIG for improving small patches of woodland for Forest School.
- no Learning Forum has been established.

9. Scotland
   - Treefest 2002 was the priority and all learning work was focused towards it. There were Treefest projects linked with FEI local groups eg the Treefest Woodland Bus in the Borders.
   - delivery mechanisms are FE and FEI. There is no Forest School presence at the moment.
   - presentation to the FC Conservators, autumn 2002.
   - small Learning Seminar is planned for March 2003 to explore the relationships between the evolving Scottish Executive education strategy, the forestry strategy and the FC learning strategy.
   - no Learning Forum has been established.
   - our major educational resource about forestry in Scotland ("Tree Trunk") has been developed so that lesson planning documents are now widely available in electronic format.
   - teacher in-service seminars are being held to promote Tree Trunk and other learning material for schools.
   - we are facilitating and supporting school visits (including special ones for teachers) to sawmills and other processing facilities. Related to this, we are developing teachers' resource material for use in conjunction with these visits.
10. To summarise, progress has been made since the introduction of the education strategy with much of the impetus stemming from the strategy itself. It is probably fair to say though that the rate of change has varied between the three countries and that some of the objectives we set in the strategy have not been met. In particular the formal mechanisms for involving others in our education work, the GB and country learning forums, have not been created. FDR gives countries further opportunities to develop these forums to involve external and internal learning expertise to guide their learning work to fit with both their forestry strategy and other government agendas.

Education and Learning in a Devolved FC–Wales as a Case Study

11. Education and Learning has always been devolved and those working in this area have always worked in a way to acknowledge this in each country. It is accepted, however, that the devolved FC will need to alter and strengthen its approach to learning. In this instance Wales provides a useful model to work with. They have taken the FC Strategy for Education and Learning and used it to guide their development to fit with the Welsh Strategy for Trees and Woodlands objective 'to maximise the use of woodlands for learning' and other WAG agendas.

12. Current education provision is through the FE Education Service and FEI. These were set up separately with distinct roles. FE Education Rangers aim to offer a woodland experience to every school in Wales and are delivering a service concentrating on Welsh Assembly Woodlands. FEI is a facilitator, which supports and encourages local partnerships in developing their own woodland learning provision. Through its extensive network, FEI can be a catalyst for new innovations such as Forest School.

13. Wales are currently discussing a 'FC Education Service'. They have evaluated existing and future provision according to the guiding principles in the FC Education and Learning Strategy paying particular attention to the principle of "Best Value". On the basis of this evaluation FC Wales are considering the development of an integrated education service which amalgamates the FE Education service with the FEI/Forest School service working to the same targets under a new line management structure.

14. This integrated education service will:
    - deliver quality learning experiences.
    - act as a key facilitator to enable others to use woodlands for learning.

- influence learning policy and practice both locally and nationally.

  It recognises the three delivery mechanisms for learning available to the FC: FE, FEI and Forests School. It also recognises and strengthens the partnerships involved with FEI and Forest School.

15. An integrated Education Service in Wales has the potential to: (brackets refer to the guiding principles in the Strategy):

    - strengthen our learning provision to under 19's but will enable great recognition of our work with families, youth groups and special needs groups for example (Audience).
    - have agreed aims, objectives and targets guided by a Learning Forum. (Consistency of Delivery and Partnership).
    - will ensure a more consistent delivery (Consistency of Delivery).
    - mean resources can be allocated more effectively according to the agreed aims and objectives. (Best Value).
    - will be better able to respond to local circumstances and educational opportunities (Diversity of Delivery mechanisms).
    - create better opportunities to share best practice internally and, with the increased level of partnership, across the external learning communities (Existing best practise and Partnership).

16. Special circumstances exist in Wales. Resources are available which has allowed this level of development to occur. But in some sense, resources have become available because of a focus on learning and a willingness to align this effort with the Assembly's priorities. We can all learn from the Welsh experience. An evaluative process has been established so that activities and achievements are recorded during the progress of the

initiative. This will give us a sound basis to bid for future support.

Recommendations for Education and Learning in a Devolved FC

17. Whilst there will always be a need for sharing good practice and guidance, the onus for taking education and learning forward will now rest with the countries However, the GB board might like to give the following pointers to the National Committees:
    a. education and learning for young people remains an important priority area in which the National Committees will want to ensure that progress is made.
    b. the FC Education and Learning strategy should be revisited and used to help progress work in this area. The strategy provides a cornerstone for countries to further develop their approach to lifelong learning.
    c. an integrated approach should be considered both in terms of mechanisms for service delivery (FE, FEI and Forest School) and effective management of resources.
    d. partnerships, internal and external, should be reflected in some kind of forum.
    e. good evidence of the educational value of forests, through evaluation that records activity and achievements as they happen, is the key to sustained public funding of forests for education.

FC Education and Learning Strategy

Mandate: The issue of the mandate for our involvement in education and learning arose in discussion. The group felt that managers were looking for reassurance that they had a mandate and confirmation that external partners would welcome our activities in this area. Clearly the FC does have a mandate for education and learning demonstrated by Ministerial and departmental statements and the 1967 Forestry Act.

The recent National Strategies strengthen this mandate for education and learning:

Woodlands for Wales: 'Priority for Action-Maximise the use of woodlands for learning'.

A New Focus for England's Woodlands: 'The government attaches great importance to education and we intend to build on work already done to use our woodlands as outdoor classrooms.'

Forests for Scotland: 'Education will have a major part to play in successful implementation of the Strategy.'

There is already evidence, as a result of these strategies, of our role in education and learning being recognised. The National Assembly for Wales has recognised the role the FC can play in delivering social objectives, including learning. FE Wales has received £1.1 million to expand on their work in this area and is currently recruiting seven additional education rangers. The education staff will be co-ordinated by the FE Wales Education and Health Manager.

FC Education and Learning Strategy

Guiding Principles

Audience: Resources are such that we are likely to focus our work initially with young people, under 19. However, education and learning is for everyone. Through engagement with children a large section of the community is reached, including parents, carers and professionals working with young people, and wider government agendas such as social inclusion can be addressed through mechanisms such as Forest School activities. This strategy will provide a cornerstone for the FC to further develop its approach to lifelong learning.

Partnership: To deliver the strategy, we need to consult and work very closely with others. We will need to build on existing partnerships, especially the FEI and Forest School, and establish new ones, particularly in the learning sectors. Our work needs to meet the requirements of learning professionals, including teachers, using our skills and assets to address national learning priorities. Partnerships will enable us to share our experiences and learn from others.

Existing Best Practice: The strategy recognises existing best learning practice in the FC has evolved from practitioners working at a local level. We should aim to share the results of this wide and varied experience and ensure that local initiatives can continue to thrive. Feedback confirms that current delivery is of a very high standard although the distribution of learning delivery, across the organisation, is inconsistent. This is dealt with in paragraph 18. Learning helps to reinforce links with people's local environment. This can strengthen communities, encourage care and a sense of ownership. Wherever possible we should deliver our learning programmes locally.

Diversity of Delivery Mechanisms: Education and learning takes place through many activities, in a variety of settings and circumstances. The strategy recognises this in the form of the menu of options.

Consistency of Delivery: After taking into account different local and regional circumstances, inconsistencies in FC provision of learning opportunities remain. By defining the policy, confirming the mandate, identifying delivery options and possible areas of new resources the organisation will achieve a more consistent delivery of learning.

Best Value: The resource implication of education provision should be assessed using a best value approach. This will take into account local opportunities, the quality of the learning experience and the other government agendas that can be delivered when selecting the delivery mechanisms for learning. The best value option may not necessarily be the cheapest.

The Value of Woodlands for Learning in Wales

Woodlands and their products offer unique opportunities for individuals to grow and develop through active learning about:

- aspects of Early Years Desirable Outcomes, National Curriculum Foundation subjects and elements of the Personal and Social Education curriculum.

- Welsh culture and natural heritage.
- sustainable Development.
- woodcraft skills.
- managing Risk where perceived risks are high and actual risk is minimised.
- healthy living.

Woodlands are the overall best outdoor environment for learning because they are:

- accessible for all communities.
- relatively robust.
- safer than most outdoor settings.
- suit different learning styles.

There are many different ways that woodlands can be used for learning. Client groups range from early years through compulsory schooling up to further and higher education. More informal family learning, therapy and out of school provision for young people are also involved in forest education. Practitioners using woodlands for learning include the voluntary sector, teachers, lecturers, early years professionals, health professional and therapists, parents, countryside rangers and youth workers.

Integrated FC Education Service for Wales

Guiding Principles

Audience: A combined structure will strengthen our provision to young people under 19. We will be able to complement our school-based focus with more informal learning opportunities with families, youth groups and special needs groups. Thus enabling us to access the whole learning community in Wales. A combined structure will reduce external and internal confusion about who is doing what.

Partnership: The Learning Forum will provide a structure for consulting with a representative group from the learning community. The combined structure will enable education rangers to engage with local partners to pass on their skills and expertise and learn from others.

Existing Best Practice: This structure develops the best practice currently provided. One integrated service will create more opportunities to share best practice internally. The increased level of partnership will enable sharing of best practice across the wide and diverse learning community.

Diversity of Delivery Mechanisms: By fully integrating the FE and FEI service, we will be in a better position to respond to local circumstances and educational opportunities rather than presenting learners with a set menu to choose from.

Consistency of Delivery: A combined service will have agreed aims, objectives and targets to be guided by the Learning Forum. This will result in a more consistent delivery of learning opportunities. Education Rangers will take on a local support role, which will ensure that the Forestry Commission can facilitate learning at a local level across the country.

Best Value: This scenario combines the FC resource for learning to create one learning service. Resources can be allocated more effectively according to agreed aims and objectives.

It will be easier to evaluate and review the quality of this service in response to the requirements of the learning community of Wales.

Provision will be sustainable as learning providers will be more engaged and more likely to use woodlands for learning independently.

Education staff will have more opportunities for professional development.

The CIPP Model

In the mid 1960s, Daniel L.Stufflebeam recognized the shortcomings of available evaluation approaches. Working to expand and systemized thinking about administrative studies and education decision making, he and others built on concepts only hinted at the much earlier work of educational leaders such as Henry Bernard, Horace Mann, William Tory Harris, and Carleton Washburne (Fitzpatrick, Sanders, & Worthen,

2004). Stufflebeam and his colleagues developed the CIPP Model in the 1960s. The CIPP Model is a comprehensive framework for guiding formative and summative evaluations of projects, programmes, personnel, products, institutions, and systems (Stufflebeam, 1968). The model is configured for use in internal evaluations conducted by an organization's evaluators; self-evaluations conducted by project teams or individual service providers, and contracted or mandated external evaluations. According to Stufflebeam (1999), the model has been employed throughout the United States and around the world in short-term and long-term investigations both small and large.

The CIPP framework was developed as a means of linking evaluation with programmed decision-making. It aims to provide an analytic and rational basis from programmed decision-making, based on a cycle of planning, structuring, implementing and reviewing and revising decisions, each examined through a different aspect of evaluation such as context, input, process and product evaluation. Stufflebeam (1999) viewed evaluation in terms of the types of decisions it served and categorized it according to its functional role within a system of planned social change. The CIPP model is an attempt to make evaluation directly relevant to the needs of decision-making during the different phases and activities of a programme.

In the CIPP approach, in order for an evaluation to be useful, it must address those questions which key decision-makers are asking, and must address the questions in ways and language that decision-makers will easily understand (Cronbach, 1982). The approach aims to involve the decision-makers in the evaluation planning process as a way of increasing the likelihood of the evaluation findings having relevance and being used. Stufflebeam thought that evaluation should be a process of delineating, obtaining and providing useful information to decision-makers, with the overall goal of programme or project improvement (Cronbach, 1982).

There are many different definitions of evaluation, but one which reflects the CIPP approach. Programme evaluation is the systematic collection of information about the activities, characteristics, and outcome of programmes for use by specific people to reduce uncertainties, improve effectiveness, and make decisions with regard to what those programmes are doing and affecting (Patton, 2004). Stufflebeam sees evaluation´s purposes as establishing and providing useful information for judging decision alternatives, assisting an audience to judge and improve the worth of some educational programme or object, and assisting the improvement of policies and programmes (Stufflebeam, 1983).

Based on Stufflebeam theory, there are four aspects of CIPP evaluation which assist decision-making. Context evaluations determines what needs are addressed by a programme and what programme already exist helps in defining objectives for the programme. Input evaluation determines what resources are available, what alternative strategies for the programme should be considered, and what plan seems to have the best potential for meeting needs facilitates design of programme procedures.

Process evaluation asses the implementation of plans to help staff carry out activities and later help the broad group of users judge programme performance and interpret outcomes. Product evaluations identify and asses outcomes (intended and unintended), short term and long term to help staff keep an enterprise focused on achieving important outcomes and ultimately to help the broader group of users gauge the effort´s success in meeting target needs (Stufflebeam, 1999).

One of the problems with evaluation in general is getting its findings used. Though its focus is on decision-making, CIPP aims to ensure that its findings are used by the decision-makers in a project. CIPP also takes a holistic approach to evaluation, aiming to paint a broad picture of understanding of a project and its context and the processes at work. It has potential to act in formative, as well as summative way, helping to shape improvements while the project is in process, as well as providing a summative or final evaluation overall. The formative aspect of it should also, in theory, be able to provide a well-established archive of data for a final or situations within the whole project (Stufflebeam, 2003).

Critics of CIPP have said that it hold an idealistic notion of what the process should be rather that its actuality and is too top-down or managerial in approach, depending on an ideal of rational management rather than recognizing its messy reality. In practice, the informative relationship between evaluation and decision-making has proved difficult to achieve and perhaps does not take into account sufficiently the politics of decision-making within and between organizations (Stufflebeam, 2003).

As a way of overcoming the top-down approaches to evaluation, those stakeholders and participative approaches have developed (for example, the approaches of Richard Stake and Lincoln and Guba). These argue that all stakeholders have a right to be consulted about concerns and issues and to receive reports which respond to their information needs, however in practice, it can be difficult to serve or prioritize the needs of a wide range of stakeholders (Worthen & Sanders, 1987). In stakeholder or participative approaches, evaluation is seen as a service to all involved in contrast to the administrative approach (such as CIPP), where the focus is on rational management and the linkage is between researchers and managers or decision-makers. In the stakeholders approach, decisions emerge through a process of accommodation (or democracy based on pluralism and the diffusion of power). So the shift in this type of approach is from decision-maker to audience. Cronbach (1982) argues that the evaluator´s mission is to facilitate a democratic, pluralist process by enlightening all the participants´. However, some of the commissioning agencies who receive the reports from participative evaluation say they do not always find then helpful in decision-making, because of the nature of the reports produced and lack of clear indications for decision-making or conflicting conclusions.

The CIPP Model treats evaluation as an essential concomitant of improvement and accountability within a framework of appropriate values and quest for clear, unambiguous answers. It responds to the reality that evaluations of innovative, evolving efforts typically cannot employ controlled, randomized experiments or work from publish evaluation instruments both which yield far too little information anyway. It cannot be overemphasized, however, that the model is and must be subject to continuing assessment and further development.

Goal-free Evaluation

Programme Evaluation

Educational programmes (and other publicly funded programmes) have continued to increase in size and expense. Not surprisingly, taxpayers and public officials have increasingly urged that these programmes be made more accountable to their publics. Indeed, "accountability" for expenditures of public funds has become the hue and cry of an ever-increasing number of economy-minded social reformers. In several countries, policy makers at both national and local levels now routinely authorize funds to be used for the express purpose of evaluating educational programmes to determine their effectiveness. Thus, "programme **evaluation**" has come into being as both a formal educational activity and as a frequently mandated instrument of public policy. Many private educational enterprises have similarly turned to programme **evaluation** as a means of answering questions about the benefits received from monies expended on various educational programmes. **Evaluation** if the curriculum is focused on change or improvement, as implied in the previous definition of "programme." Programme evaluations, however, often do not involve appraisal of curricula (*e.g.*, **evaluation** of a computerized student recordkeeping system or **evaluation** of the extent to which funds from a national programme for the hearing impaired are actually used to provide services to children with hearing impairments). For this reason, the closely related but more specialized topic of curriculum **evaluation** is not discussed further in this section.

1. *Purposes of Programme* ***Evaluation:*** Most programme evaluators agree that programme **evaluation** can play either a formative purpose (helping to improve the programme) or a summative purpose (deciding whether a pro-gram should be continued). Anderson and Ball

(1978) fur-ther describe the capabilities of programme **evaluation** in terms of six major purposes (which are not necessarily mutually exclusive). They are:

To define programme **evaluation**, it is necessary to define its component parts. In an educational context, a programme can be thought of as any educational enterprise aimed at the solution of a particular educational problem or the im-provement of some aspect of an educational system. Such a programme would typically be sponsored by public or private funds, possess specified goals, and exhibit some structure for managing the procedures, materials, facilities, and/or personnel involved in the programme.

(a) to contribute to decisions about programme installation;

(b) to contribute to decisions about programme continuation, expansion, or "certification";

(c) to contribute to decisions about programme modifications;

Evaluation can be defined most simply as the determination of the worth of a thing. In its simplest form, therefore, programme **evaluation** consists of those activities undertaken to judge the worth or utility of a programme (or alternative programmes) in improving some specified aspect of an educational system. Examples of programme evaluations might include **evaluation** of a national bilingual education programme, a university's preservice programme for training ur-ban administrators, a ministry of education's staff develop-ment programme, or a local parent education resource center. Evaluations may be conducted for programmes of any size or scope, ranging from an arithmetic programme in a particular school to an international consortium on metric education.

(d) to obtain evidence to rally support for a programme;

(e) to obtain evidence to rally opposition to a programme;

(f) to contribute to the understanding of basic psychological, social, and other processes (only rarely can this purpose be achieved in a programme **evaluation** without compromising more basic **evaluation** purposes).

2. *The History of Programme* ***Evaluation:*** The informal practice of programme **evaluation** is not new, dating back at least to 2000 *BC,* when Chinese officials were conducting civil-service examinations, and con a curriculum **evaluation** may qualify as a programme. *Programme* ***Evaluation*** more broadly accepted quantitative methods and the 1970s were marked by polemics as the two schools of thought struggled for ascendancy. The late 1970s and the early 1980s saw the dialogue begin to move beyond this debate as analysts accelerated their discussions of the benefits of integrating both types of methods within a programme **evaluation** (for instance see Cook and Reichardt 1979, Worthen 1981, and the especially useful summary by Madey 1982).

   Tinuing down through the centuries to the beginnings of school accreditation in the late 1800s. The first clear evidence of formal programme **evaluation**, however, a ppears to be Joseph Rice's 1897-1898 comparative study of spelling performance of 33,000 students in a large United States school system. Few formal evaluations of educational programmes were conducted in the next few decades, with Tyler and Smith's Eight-year Study of the 1930s being the next notable effort to evaluate the out-comes of an educational programme. During the late 1950s and early 1960s (the post-Sputnik years), cries for curriculum reform led to major new curriculum develop-ment programmes and to subsequent calls for their evaluation. The relatively few **evaluation** studies that resulted revealed the conceptual and methodological impoverishment of the field—or perhaps more accurately, the "nonfield"—of **evaluation** in that era. In many cases, the designs were inadequate, the data invalid, the analyses inaccurate, and the reports irrelevant to the important **evaluation** questions which should have been posed. Most of the studies depended on idiosyncratic combinations and applications of concepts and techniques from experimental design, psychometrics, curriculum devel-opment and, to a lesser extent, survey research. Theo-retical work related to educational **evaluation**, per se, was almost nonexistent. Few scholars had yet turned their attention to the development of generalizable **evaluation** plans which could be adopted or adapted spe-cifically to educational **evaluation** studies. In the absence of a "formal subject matter" or educational **evaluation**, evaluators of educational programmes were left to glean what they could from other fields to help them in their work.

Concurrent with programme evaluators' struggle to sort out the relative utility of quantitative and qualitative methods, a separate but closely related development was taking place. Beginning in the late 1960s, several evaluation writers began to develop and circulate their notions about how one should conduct educational evaluations; these efforts resulted in several new **evaluation** "models" being proposed to help the practicing programme evaluator. Although these seminal writings in educational evalua-tion (discussed in Sect. 3) were doubtlessly influenced by the quantitative-qualitative controversy and some proved more comfortable companions with one or the other methodological persuasion, several were broader in conceptualization, providing guidelines for conducting programme evaluations that could use either quantitative or qualitative data. As these frameworks for planning **evaluation** studies were applied and refined, programme evaluators began to turn to them as promising sources of guidance. Collectively, these writings, the so-called eval-uation models, represent the formal content of programme **evaluation** and are discussed in the following section.

3. *Alternative Approaches to Programme* ***Evaluation****:* Because of space restrictions, only some of the more popular current approaches used in conducting programme evaluations can be presented in this section.

Many of these (and other) approaches to programme **evaluation** are summarized in Worthen and Sanders (1987) and the work of authors mentioned but not referenced herein (and in other sections of this entry) can be found in that source. For convenience, these conceptual frameworks for **evaluation** are clustered into five categories, although some of the frameworks are sufficiently multifaceted that they could appear in more than one category. Most of these "models" have focused broadly on programme evalua-tion, although some are focused more specifically on curriculum **evaluation**. It should be noted that these frameworks deal with methods, not techniques: discussion of the many techniques which might be used in pro-gram evaluations is beyond the scope of this article.

Since a large number of persons serving in **evaluation** roles during the late 1950s and 1960s were educational and psychological researchers, it is not surprising that the experimental tradition quickly became the most generally accepted **evaluation** approach. The work of Campbell and Stanley gave enormous impetus to predominance of experimental or quasiexperimental ap-proaches to programme **evaluation**. Although some evaluators cautioned that correct use of the experimental model may not be feasible, the elegance and precision of this model led most programme evaluators to view the experimental method as the ideal model for programme evaluations.

Not all programme evaluators were enamored with the use of traditional quantitative methods for programme evaluations, however, and their dissatisfaction led to a search for alternatives. Qualitative and naturalistic methods, largely shunned by programme evaluators during the 1960s as unacceptably "soft," gained wider acceptance in the 1970s and thereafter as proposals for their application to programme evaluations were made by Parlett and Hamilton, Stake, Eisner, Guba and Lincoln, and others. Sharp disagreements developed between proponents of the newer qualitative approaches and adherents to the *Performance-Objectives Congruence Approaches* This approach to programme **evaluation** was originally formulated by Ralph Tyler, who conceived of evalua-tion as the process of determining the extent to which the educational objectives of a school programme or curriculum are actually being attained. He proposed a process in which broad goals or objectives would be established or identified, defined in behavioral terms, and relevant student behaviors would be measured against this yardstick, using either standardized or evaluator-constructed instruments. These outcome data were then to be compared with the behavioral objectives to determine the extent to which performance was congruent with expectations. Discrepancies between performance and objectives would lead to modifications intended to correct the deficiency, and the **evaluation** cycle would be repeated.

A judgment about which is best in terms of specified criteria. Thus, **evaluation** became an explicitly shared function dependent on good teamwork between evaluators and decision makers. This approach has proved appealing to many evaluators and programme managers, particularly those at home with the rational and orderly systems approach, to which it is clearly related. It was viewed by others, however, as failing to determine explicitly the program's worth and being dependent on somewhat unrealistic assumptions about the orderliness and predictability of the decision-making process.

Tyler's rationale was logical, scientifically acceptable, readily adoptable by programme evaluators (most of whose methodological upbringing was very compatible with the pretest—posttest measurement of student behaviors stressed by Tyler), and had great influence on subsequent **evaluation** theorists. Hammond's EPIC evaluation model followed Tyler's model closely, adding only a useful programme-description "cube" which elaborates instructional and institutional variables often overlooked in previous evaluations. Provus' discrepancy model of programme **evaluation** is clearly Tylerian and gains its name from the constant setting and juxtaposition of programme standards against programme performance to yield "discrepancy information" needed for programme improvements. Popham's instructional objectives approach also clearly stems from Tyler's earlier conceptions.

Judgment-oriented Approaches

This general approach to **evaluation**, which historically has been the most widely used **evaluation** approach, is dependent upon experts' application of professional expertise to yield judgments about a programme being observed. For example, the worth of a programme would be assessed by experts (in the view of the evaluation's sponsor) who would observe the programme in action, examine its products or, in some other way, glean sufficient information to render their considered judgment about the programme. Site visits initiated by funding agencies to evaluate programmes they support and visits by accrediting agencies to secondary schools and universities are examples of judgment-oriented programme evaluations.

Scriven, in his article *The Methodology of **Evaluation*** (Worthen and Sanders 1973), stressed judgment as the sine qua non of **evaluation** and, in his insightful examination of educational **evaluation**, did much to rescue this approach from the disrepute into which it had fallen in evaluation's headlong rush to gain respectability as a science. He stunned orthodox objectives-oriented evaluators by his suggestion that evaluators might go beyond measuring a program's performance to also evaluate the program's goals and later compounded the shock still further with his suggestion that evaluators should do **"goal-free"** evaluations, in which they not only ignore the program's goals but actually make every effort to avoid learning what those goals are. Thus, judgments about programmes were based on the actual outcomes of the programme, in-tended or not, rather than on the program's objectives oron decisions faced by programme managers.

Useful as this approach to **evaluation** is viewed by its many adherents, critics such as Guba and Lincoln (1981) have noted that it lacks a real evaluative component (facilitating measurement and assessment of objectives rather than resulting in explicit judgments of worth), lacks standards to judge the importance of observed discrepancies between objectives and performance levels, and depends on a highly utilitarian philosophy, promoting a linear, inflexible approach to **evaluation**.

Decision-Management Approaches

The most important contributions to a decision-oriented approach to programme **evaluation** are Stufflebeam's Context, Input, Process, and Product (app) **evaluation** model and Alkin's Center for the Study of **Evaluation** model, which follows a similar logic to the Context, Input, Process, and Product model but distinguishes between programme implementation and programme improvement, two subdivisions of what Stufflebeam terms process evaluation. In both models, objectives are eschewed as the organizer for the study and the decision to be made by pro-gram managers becomes pivotal. Stufflebeam has provided an analysis of types of decisions programme managers are required to make and proposes a different type of **evaluation** for each type of decision.

In both of these decision-oriented models, the evaluator, working closely with the programme manager, would identify the decisions the latter must make and collect sufficient information about the relative advantages and disadvantages of each decision alternative to enable the decision maker to make Another important judgement-oriented **evaluation** model is Robert Stake's Countenance Model, in which he suggests that the two major activities of formal evaluation studies are description and judgment (the "two countenances") of the programme being evaluated. Within the description phase, Stake follows Tyler's rationale ofcomparing intended and actual outcomes of the programme.

However, he argued that in the judgment phase standards and procedures for making judgmental statements must be explicated to ensure the publicness of evaluative statements, although he failed to provide any suggestions as to how to weight or combine individual standards into overall judgments about the programme.

Eisner's "connoisseurship model" casts programme evaluators as educational critics whose refined perceptual capabilities (based on knowledge of what to look for and a backlog of relevant experience) enable them to give a public rendering of the quality and significance of that which is evaluated. In this model, the evaluator is the "instrument," and the data collecting, analyzing, and judging that Stake tried to make more public are largely hidden within the evaluator's mind, analogous to the evaluative processes of art criticism or wine tasting. debate model in an adversary **evaluation** and have discussed pitfalls and potentials of the legal and other forensic paradigms in conducting programme evaluations. Despite the publicity given this approach to evaluation, as yet there is little beyond personal preference to determine whether programme evaluations will profit most from being patterned after jury trials, congressional hearings, debates, or other arrangements.

Pluralist-Intuitionist Approaches

Ernest House has used this descriptor to characterize several **evaluation** models, contrasting them with more "utilitarian" models. In this approach to **evaluation,** the evaluator is a portrayer of different values and needs of all the individuals and groups served by the programme, weighing and balancing this plurality of judgments and criteria in a largely intuitive fashion. Thus, the "best programme" is largely decided by the values and perspectives of whomever is judging (an obvious fact nonetheless ignored in most other **evaluation** approaches).

Examples of pluralist-intuitionist **evaluation** "models" are those proposed by Stake, Parlett and Hamilton, Rippey, and MacDonald's democratic **evaluation**. There are unique contributions of each of these proposals. Stake urges programme evaluators to respond to the audience's concerns and requirements for information, in terms of their value perspectives, and argues that the **evaluation** framework and focus should emerge only after considerable interaction with those audiences. Parlett and Hamilton draw on the social anthropology paradigm (and psychiatry and sociology participant observation research) in proposing progressive focusing of an **evaluation** whose purpose is to describe and interpret (not measure and predict) that which exists within an educational system.

Rippey focuses on the effects of programmes on the programme operators and views **evaluation** as a strategy for conflict management. MacDonald views **evaluation** as primarily a political activity whose only justification is the "right to know" of a broad range of audiences. Yet a common thread runs through all these **evaluation** approaches—value pluralism is recognized, accommodated, and protected, even though the effort to summarize the frequently disparate judgments and preferences of such groups is left as an intuitive process which depends heavily on the sagacity and impartiality of the evaluator.

Collectively, these judgment-oriented approaches to **evaluation** have emphasized the central role of judgment and human wisdom in the evaluative process and have focused attention on the important issues of whose stan-dards (and what degree of publicness) should be used in rendering judgments about educational programmes. Conversely, critics of this approach suggest that it often permits evaluators to render judgments that reflect little more than figments of fertile imaginations.

Others have noted that the presumed expertise of the evaluators is a potential weakness and worse, strong arguments can be made that serious disadvantages can accrue if a programme is evaluated only by content experts (Worthen and Sanders 1987). Finally, many programme evaluators are disinclined to play the single-handed role of educational judge (which they feel smacks of arrogance and elitism) proposed by some of these approaches.

Adversarial Approaches

Adversarial **evaluation** is a rubric that encompasses a collection of divergent **evaluation** practices which might loosely be referred to as adversarial in nature. In its broad sense, the term refers to all evaluations in which there is planned opposition in the points of view of different evaluators or **evaluation** teams—a planned effort to generate opposing points of view within the overall **evaluation**. One evaluator (or team) would serve as the program's advocate, presenting the most positive view of the programme possible from the data, while an-other evaluator (or team) would play an adversarial role, highlighting any extant deficiencies in the pro-gram. Incorporation of these opposing views within a single **evaluation** reflects a conscious effort to assume fairness and balance and illuminate both strengths and weaknesses of the programme.

Critics of this approach to programme **evaluation** discount it as hopelessly "soft headed" and argue that few if any programme evaluators are such paragons of virtue and wisdom as to be skillful in wielding the seductively simple, yet slippery and subtle tools this approach requires. Champions of pluralistic, responsive approaches reply that they can be readily used by any sensitive individual and that they are infinitely richer and more powerful than ocher approaches and, indeed, can subsume them, since they are flexible and do not preclude the use of other approaches within them, should that be desired by the evaluator's sponsor.

Several types of adversarial proceedings have been invoked as models for adversary evaluations in education, including judicial, congressional hearings, and debate models. Of these, most of the sparse literature in this area has focused on adaptations of the legal para-digm, providing insights into how concepts from the legal system (for instance, taking and cross-examination of human testimony) could be used in educational evaluations. Owens, Wolf, and others have adapted the legal model to educational evaluations, while Worthen and Rogers have described use of the.

An Appraisal of Current Programme Evaluation Models

Collectively, the writings reviewed briefly in Sect. 3, the so-called **evaluation** models, represent the formal content on which educational programme evaluators draw. It is, therefore, appropriate to ask how useful they are. The answer is "very useful, indeed," even though they collectively have not moved **evaluation** very far toward becoming a science or discipline in its own right (a dubi-ous aspiration, nonetheless sought by many evaluators). In a recent analysis, Worthen and Sanders (1987) sug-gested that (a) the so-called **evaluation** models fail to meet standard criteria for scientific models, or even less rigorous definitions of models, and (b) that which has come to be referred to as the theoretical underpinnings of **evaluation** lack important characteristics of most theories, being neither axiomatic nor deductive, having no real predictive power, and being untested and unvalidated in any empirical sense. That same analysis, however, suggested that these conceptions about how evaluations should be conducted—the accompanying sets of categories, lists of things to think about, descriptions of different **evaluation** strategies, and exhortations to which one might choose to attend—influence the practice of programme **evaluation** in sometimes subtle, sometimes direct, but always significant ways. Some programme evaluators design evaluations which adopt or adapt proposed models of **evaluation**. Many evaluators, however, conduct evaluations without strict adherence (or even intentional attention) to any "model" of **evaluation**, yet draw unconsciously in their **evaluation** philosophy, plans, and procedures on that which they have internalized through exposure to the literature of programme **evaluation**. So the value of the "models" lies in their ability to help us to think, to provide sources of new ideas and techniques, to serve as mental checklists of things we ought to con-sider, or remember, or worry about. Their value as pre-scriptive guidelines for doing **evaluation** studies seems much less.

Impediments to Improving Programme Evaluation

Despite the advances made in programme **evaluation**, there is obviously room for a great deal of improvement. In this section, four areas that need improvement for educational **evaluation** to reach its full potential are discussed briefly.

Evaluation Lacks an Adequate Knowledge Base

Since the early 1970s, Stufflebeam, Worthen and Sanders, Smith, and others have issued a call for **evaluation** to be researched to develop an adequate knowledge base to guide **evaluation** practice. That call is still largely unanswered, despite some promising research which has been launched on **evaluation** methods and techniques.

A programme of research aimed at drawing from other disciplines new methodological metaphors and techniques for use in educational **evaluation** existed at the Northwest Regional Educational Laboratory for nearly a decade and has introduced programme evaluators to promising new metaphors and techniques drawn from areas such as architecture, philosophic analysis, investigative journalism, and literary and film criticism. A second National Institute of Education-sponsored research effort at the University of California at Los Angeles focused largely on descriptive studies of **evaluation** practices in educational agencies. In addition, a few research studies aimed at generating knowledge about either particular **evaluation** strategies and procedures or factors affecting **evaluation** utilization have begun to appear.

These positive developments notwithstanding, there is still little empirical information about the relative efficacy of alternative **evaluation** plans or techniques or many **evaluation** components germane to almost any model. For example, virtually no empirical information exists about the most effective way to conduct a needs assessment or weight criteria in reaching a summative judgment.

Little is known about the extent to which various data collection techniques interfere with ongoing educational phenomena. Techniques for identifying goals are developed anew with every **evaluation**, since there is no evidence that any one way of conducting these activities is more effective than any other. Elaborate systems are developed for providing evaluative feedback, but there is little research evidence (as opposed to rhetoric and position statements) about the relative effectiveness of feedback under differing conditions and scheduling.

One could go on to create an exhaustive list of phenomena and procedures in **evaluation** which badly need to be systematically studied, but the above should suffice to make the point. Smith (1981) has summarized the needs for research on **evaluation** as requiring more knowledge about (a) the contexts within which **evaluation** is prac-ticed, (b) the nature of **evaluation** utility, and (c) the effectiveness of specific **evaluation** methods. Nearly a decade later those needs still remain largely unmet.

Evaluation Studies are Seldom Evaluated

The necessity of "meta-**evaluation**" has long been apparent to evaluators and completion of the *Standards for Evaluations of Educational Programmes, Projects, and Materials* (Joint Committee on Standards 1981) marked a welcome milestone. Although many **evaluation** writers had proposed their own sets of meta-**evaluation** criteria, none carried the profession-wide weight reflected in the comprehensive standards so carefully prepared by the Joint Committee. These standards include criteria within each of the following categories: utility standards; feasi-bility standards; propriety standards; and accuracy stan-dards.

Despite the wide acceptance and availability of these standards, however, there is no evidence that programme evaluations are being subjected to any closer scrutiny than was the case before their publication. Even casual inspection reveals that only a small proportion of evaluation studies are ever evaluated, even in the most perfunctory fashion. Of the few meta-evaluations which dooccur, most are internal evaluations done by the evaluator who produced the **evaluation** in the first place. It is rare indeed to see evaluators call in an outside expert to evaluate their **evaluation** efforts. Perhaps the reasons are many and complex why this is so, but one seems particularly compelling—evaluators are human and are no more ecstatic about having their work critiqued than are professionals in other areas of endeavor. Indeed, it can be a profoundly unnerving experience to swallow one's own prescriptions. Although the infrequency of good meta **evaluation** might thus be understandable, it is not easily forgivable, for it enables shoddy **evaluation** practices to go undetected and worse, to be repeated again and again, to the detriment of the profession.

Programme Evaluators Fail to Understand the Political Nature of Evaluation: Cronbach and co-workers (1980) have presented the view that **evaluation** is essentially a political activity. They describe **evaluation** as a "novel political institution" that is part of governance of social programmes. They assert that evaluators and their patrons pursue unrealistic goals of finding "truth" or facilitating "right" decisions, rather than the more pertinent task of simply enlightening all participants so as to facilitate a democratic, pluralist decision-making process.

While some may reject this view as overstated, it underscores the fact that programme **evaluation** is inextricably intertwined with public policy formulation and all of the political forces involved in that process. Evaluators who fail to understand this basic fact expend unacceptably large amounts of human and financial resources conducting evaluations that are largely irrelevant, however impeccably they aredesigned and conducted.

Approaches and Techniques: It may be that innocence about the political nature of the **evaluation** enterprise contributes to the naive hope that **evaluation** will one day grow into a scientific discipline. That day, if attainable, would seem far off. Education itself is not a discipline but rather a social process field which draws its content from several disciplines.

It seems unlikely that educational programme **evaluation**, which also borrows its methods and techniques from many disciplines will gain the coherence that would re-sult in it becoming a discipline in its own right. Perhaps that is just as well, for much of the richness and potential of educational programme **evaluation** lies in the depth and breadth of the strategies and tools it can employ and in the possibility of selectively combining them into stronger approaches than when used singly (Worthen 1981). Yet eclectic use of the evaluator's tools is a la-mentably infrequent occurrence in programme evaluations. Disciple-prone evaluators tend to cluster around their respective **evaluation** banners like vassals in a form of provincial bondage.

For programme **evaluation** to reach its potential, such intellectual bondage must give way to more mature and sophisticated approaches that draw appropriately on the richness and diversity of the many approaches, models, and techniques that characterize programme **evaluation** today.

Bibliography

Aggarwal, Santosh : *Three Language Formula: An Educational Problem*, New Delhi, Sian, 1991.

Allen, G. : *New Education: American Opinion*, May issue, 1971.

Altbach, Philip G. and Gail Kelly : *New Approaches to Comparative Education,* Chicago, The University of Chicago Press, 1986.

Anderson, L.W.: *International Encyclopedia of Teaching and Teacher Education,* Oxford, Pergammon Press, 1995.

Applebee, Arthur N.: *Curriculum as Conversation: Transforming Tradition of Teaching and Learning,* Chicago, University of Chicago Press, 1996.

Barnes, D.: *From Communication to Curriculum,* London, Pelican, 1990.

Beane, J. A.: *Toward a Coherent Curriculum*, Alexandria, VA: Association for Supervision and Curriculum Development, 1995.

Bentley, T. : *Learning beyond the Classroom: Education for a Changing World*, London, Routledge. 1998.

Borchardt, Frank L. & Eleanor M.T. Johnson: *Calico Resource Guide for Computing and Language Learning*, Durham, CALICO, 1995.

Bottery, M. : *The Ethics of Educational Management: Personal, Social and Political Perspectives on School Organization*, London, Cassell, 1992.

Brown, J. D.: *The Elements of Language Curriculum: A Systematic Approach to Program Development,* Boston, Heinle & Heinle, 1995

Buehl, D.: *Classroom Strategies for Interactive Learning*, Newark, International Reading Association, 2001.

Burke, Kay: *How to Assess Authentic Learning*, Palatine, IL: IRI/Skylight Publishing, Inc, 1994.

Burnaford, G.: *Teachers Doing Research,* Mahwah, Lawrence Erlbaum.

Caine, R.N. & G. Caine: *Making Connections: Teaching and the Human Brain*, Alexandria, Association for Supervision and Curriculum Development, 1991.

Carr, W. & Kemmis, S. : *Becoming Critical: Education, Knowledge and Action Research*, London, Falmer, 1986.

Chumbow, B.S. : *The Place of Mother Tongue in the National Policy of Education,* Port Harcourt, Nigeria, 1990.

Clifton, C., & Grant Haworth, J.: *Curriculum in Transition: Perspectives on the Undergraduate Experience,* Needham Heights, MT: Ginn Press, 1990.

Compton, Mary F. & Horace C. Hawn: *Exploration: The Total Curriculum*, Columbus, National Middle School Association, 1993.

Curtain, Helena A. & Carol Ann Pesola: *Languages and Children - Making the Match*, White Plains, Longman Publishing Group, 1994.

Diamond, R. M.: *Designing and Assessing Courses and Curricula: A Practical Guide,* San Francisco, Jossey Bass, 1998.

Diller, D.: *Literacy Work Stations: Making Centers Work,* Portland, Stenhouse, 2003.

Donaldson, Gordon A. : *Cultivating Leadership in Schools*, New York, College Press, 2001.

Donoghue, M.: *Foreign Language and the Elementary School Child*, Dubuque, William C. Brown, 1968.

Ehrman, M. E.: *Understanding Second Language Learning Difficulties,* Thousand Oaks, Sage, 1996.

Elliott, J. : *Action Research for Educational Change*, Milton Keynes, Open University, 1991.

Evers, C. & Lakomski, G. : *Knowing Educational Administration*, Oxford, Pergamon, 1991.

Finocchiaro, Mary & Michael Bonomo: *The Foreign Language Learner: A Guide for Teachers,* New York, Regents Publishing Company, 1973.

Fogarty, Robin: *How to Integrate the Curricula,* Palatine, IRI/ Skylight, 1991.

Forgarty, Robin, David Perkins, & John Barell: *How to Teach for Transfer,* Palatine, IRI/Skylight, 1992.

Galbraith, M.W. : *Education Through Community Organizations*, San Francisco, Jossey-Bass, 1990.

Gaudiani, Claire: *Teaching Writing in the FL Curriculum*, Washington, Center for Applied Linguistics, 1981.

Genesee, F. , & Upshur, J. A.: *Classroom-based Evaluation in Second Language Education,* New York, Cambridge, 1996.

Gibson, R. : *Critical Theory and Education*, London, Hodder & Stoughton, 1986.

Giroux, H. : *Critical Theory and Educational Practice*, Geelong, Australia, Deakin University, 1983.

Glatthorn, Allan: *Developing A Quality Curriculum*, Association for Supervision and Curriculum Development, Alexandria, VA, 1994.

Goodlad, John I. : *Educational Renewal: Better Teachers, Better Schools*, San Francisco, Jossey-Bass, 1994.

Grace, G. : *School Leadership: Beyond Educational Management*, London, Falmer, 1995.

Grittner, F.: *A Guide to Curriculum Planning in Foreign Languages*, Madison, Wisconsin Department of Public Instruction, 1985.

Hewitt, Paul G., City College of San Francisco, San Francisco: *Conceptual Physics*, Addison-Wesley Publishing Co., Menlo Park, CA, 1997.

Hirsch, Bette: *Languages of Thought: Thinking, Reading, and Foreign Languages,* New York, The College Board, 1989.

Jayasuriya, J.E. *Education in Korea: A Third World Success Story*, Colombo, Associated Educational Publishers, 1980.

John A. Upshur: *Classroom-Based Evaluation in Second Language Education*, New York, Cambridge University Press, 1996.

Johnson, R.K.: *The Second Language Curriculum,* New York, Cambridge University Press, 1989.

Jones, Beau Fly, Claudette M. Rasmussen and Mary C. Moffitt: *Real-Life Problem Solving. A Collaborative Approach to Interdisciplinary Learning*, American Psychological Association, Washington, DC, 1997.

Kennedy, K.J. : *Citizenship Education and the Modern State*, Washington, D.C: Falmer Press, 1997.

Kirkwood, G. and Kirkwood, C. : *Living Adult Education, Freire in Scotland*, Milton Keynes, Open University Press, 1989.

Krashen, S. & M. Long : *Child-Adult Differences in Second Language Acquisition*, Rowley, Newbury House, 1982.

LaFleur, R. A.: *The Teaching of Latin in American Schools*, Atlanta, Atlanta School Press, 1987.

Lovett, T. : *Adult Education, Community Development and the Working Class*, London, Ward Lock, 1975.

Mager, R.: *Preparing Instructional Objectives*, Belmont, David Lake Publishers, 1984.

Markee, N.: *Managing Curricular Innovation,* New York, Cambridge, 1997.

Marzano, Robert J.: *A Different Kind of Classroom: Teaching with Dimensions of Learning,* Alexandria, Association for Supervision and Curriculum Development, 1992.

McGivney, V. : *Informal Learning in the Community, A Trigger for Change and Development*, Leicester, NIACE, 1999.

Nadler, L.: *Designing Training Programs: The Critical Events Model*, Reading, PA: Addison-Wesley, 1982.

Nuna, S.C. : *Education and Development*, NIEPA, New Delhi, 1987.

Nunan, D., & Lamb, C.: *The Self-directed Teacher: Managing the Learning Process,* Cambridge, Cambridge University Press, 1996.

Okech, J.G.; Asiachi, A.J. : *Curriculum Development for Schools*, Nairobi, Educational Research Publications, 1992.

Omaggio, Alice C.: *Teaching Language in Context: Proficiency-Oriented Instruction,* Boston, Heinle and Heinle, 1993.

Paul, Richard: *Critical Thinking Handbook: High School, A Guide for Redesigning Instruction*, Foundation for Critical Thinking, Santa Rosa, CA, 1995.

Poster, C. and Kruger, A. : *Community Education in the Western World*, London, Routledge, 1990.

Potter D. : *Information Technology and Higher Education: A Twenty Year View*, Unpublished Paper, 1996.

Premi, M.K. : *Educational Planning in India*, New Delhi, Sterling, 1972.

Reimer, E. : *School is Dead, An Essay on Alternatives in Education*, Harmondsworth, Penguin, 1971.

Rogers, A. : *Adults Learning for Development*, London, Cassell, 1992.

Scott, C. : *Social Education*, Boston, Ginn and Co., 1908.

Short, Deborah J.: *How to Integrate Language and Content Instruction: A Training Manual*, Washington, Center for Applied Linguistics, 1991.

Simkins, T. : *Non-formal Education and Development*, Manchester, Manchester University, 1977.

Smith, M.K. : *Local Education, Community, Conversation, Action*, Buckingham, Open University Press, 1994.

Stark, J. S., & Lattuca, L. R.: *Shaping the College Curriculum: Academic Plans in Action*, Boston, Allyn and Bacon, 1997.

Stevenson, Chris & Judy F. Carr: *Integrated Studies in the Middle Grades: Dancing Through Walls*, New York, Teachers College Press, 1993.

Stoner, W.S. : *Natural Education*, Indianapolis, Bobbs Merrill, 1914.

Thomas, A. : *Educating Children at Home,* London, Cassell, 1998.

Wiggins, Grant : *Educative Assessment: Designing Assessments to inform and Improve Student Performance*, San Francisco, Jossey-Bass, 1998.

Williams G. : *Paying for Education beyond Eighteen: An Examination of Issues and Options,* Council for I0ndustry in Higher Education, London, 1996.

Index

A

Achievement, 19, 48, 50, 79, 90, 94, 97, 125, 132, 134, 135, 141, 155, 182, 183, 193, 195, 203, 204, 205, 206, 207, 208, 209, 213, 215, 220, 224.
Action Learning, 104, 105, 106, 107.
Administrators, 124, 142, 144, 186, 207, 241.
Agency, 162, 203.
Application, 6, 7, 8, 9, 10, 11, 12, 41, 54, 55, 58, 102, 103, 141, 157, 167, 191, 216, 217, 218, 220, 221, 244, 246.
Assessment Procedures, 20.
Authority, 67, 80, 81, 126, 168, 169, 202.

B

Behavioral Systems, 140.

C

Capacity Building, 132, 133.
Collaboration, 61, 78, 100, 148, 149, 173, 174.
Commission, 1, 2, 4, 76, 226, 227, 236.
Communication, 3, 18, 48, 54, 57, 61, 64, 68, 93, 100, 115, 152, 155, 164, 169, 171, 175, 176, 209.
Community, 1, 2, 13, 21, 22, 24, 27, 28, 29, 35, 42, 56, 57, 80, 87, 111, 131, 132, 151, 166, 191, 199, 205, 210, 217, 233, 235, 236.
Computer Skills, 60, 69.
Concept of Curriculum, 1, 13.
Construction, 1, 2, 3, 4, 5, 39, 40, 84, 139, 164, 177, 179, 185.
Construction Process, 1.
Consumer Education, 6, 7, 8, 9, 10, 11, 12.
Consumers, 6, 7, 8, 9, 10, 11, 12, 196.
Core Curriculum, 76, 77, 96.
Core Level, 116.
Corporate Value Systems, 29.
Culture, 10, 24, 26, 46, 61, 62, 75, 122, 235.
Curricular Development, 1, 3, 216.
Curricular Evaluation, 189.
Curriculum Concepts, 6.
Curriculum Cycle, 47, 177.
Curriculum Designing, 86.
Curriculum Determinants, 24.
Curriculum development, 19, 21, 87, 88, 112, 114, 117, 123, 124, 125, 126, 127, 128, 186, 187, 188, 192, 195, 197, 200, 201, 202, 203, 204.
Curriculum integration, 92, 99

Curriculum Organisation, 43, 47, 55, 58, 59, 60, 96.
Curriculum Tailoring, 93, 96, 99.
Curriculum Transaction, 45, 47, 129, 156.

D

Department, 6, 68, 120, 123, 143, 145, 149, 152, 153.
Development, 1, 2, 3, 4, 19, 21, 25, 27, 43, 44, 45, 46, 48, 50, 51, 53, 59, 60, 64, 66, 69, 70, 71, 73, 76, 80, 82, 85, 86, 87, 88, 91, 92, 95, 96, 98, 106, 108, 109, 110, 112, 114, 117, 121, 122, 123, 124, 125, 126, 127, 128, 132, 138, 140, 141, 146, 149, 152, 153, 154, 158, 168, 169, 174, 186, 187, 188, 189, 190, 192, 194, 195, 196, 197, 198, 200, 201, 202, 203, 204, 206, 207, 213, 216, 217, 218, 219, 222, 227, 228, 230, 231, 235, 236, 240, 243, 268.
Distribution, 7, 8, 126, 174, 225, 234.

E

Ecological Environment, 10.
Economic System, 7, 8.
Educational Institutions, 25.
Educational Objectives, 19, 43, 51, 52, 125, 134, 245.
Educational Programmes, 24, 206, 221, 240, 242, 243, 249, 253.
Employment, 12, 22, 95, 96, 97, 120.

F

File Sharing, 162, 174.
Foundations, 26, 32, 41, 125.

G

Government, 8, 9, 27, 36, 162, 169, 189, 227, 229, 233, 234.

H

Hierarchies, 101.
Hilda Taba, 109, 116, 118, 120, 121, 123, 125, 126.

I

Implement Team Teaching, 145.
Individual Improvement, 60, 67.
Institute, 6, 59, 68, 110, 191, 198, 252.
Institutions, 25, 27, 121, 126, 127, 134, 141, 217, 237.
Intelligences, 92, 96, 100, 220.
Internet, 57, 70, 78, 118, 156, 161, 162, 163, 164, 165, 166, 167, 168, 169, 170, 171, 172, 173, 174, 175, 176, 196.
Internet Protocols, 165, 166.
Internet Telephony, 175.

J

Joint Construction, 177, 179.
Judgment, 144, 245, 246, 247, 248, 249, 252.

L

Languages, 92, 169, 194, 218.
Leaders, 21, 22, 24, 59, 64, 67, 72, 153, 154, 180, 236.
Leadership, 24, 25, 60, 66, 67, 71, 72, 80, 104, 110.

Learning Experiences, 44, 45, 48, 55, 97, 101, 102, 107, 125, 126, 185, 240.
Learning Organisation, 103, 104, 105, 107.
Learning Strategy, 226, 129, 230, 232, 233.
Legislation, 8.
Library Skills, 71.
Literature, 2, 10, 75, 81, 82, 119, 141, 146, 149, 223, 250, 251.

M

Management, 57, 64, 66, 67, 68, 91, 94, 104, 105, 106, 108, 110, 111, 115, 134, 138, 147, 151, 155, 172, 187, 196, 219, 225, 230, 232, 239, 247, 249.
Mastery Learning, 97, 98, 140.
Material Development, 132.
Measurement, 27, 56, 60, 62, 63, 135, 208, 222, 245, 247.
Mechanisms, 63, 127, 227, 228, 229, 231, 232, 233, 234, 236.
Methodology, 4, 45, 53, 117, 192, 195, 222, 224, 246.
Model System, 31.
Modular Curriculum, 98.
Moral Rules, 33, 34.

N

National Agencies, 135.
National Aspirations, 25.
Networks, 56, 57, 162, 163, 164, 165, 167, 168, 169, 170, 174.

O

Opportunity, 58, 65, 71, 72, 102, 119, 150, 166, 184, 186, 192, 215, 218.
Organisation, 43, 46, 47, 55, 58, 59, 60, 96, 101, 103, 104, 105, 107, 108, 135, 142, 144, 148, 167, 174, 191, 201, 228, 236.

P

Performance, 19, 21, 42, 63, 64, 80, 94, 95, 106, 108, 114, 115, 134, 138, 143, 151, 182, 185, 186, 193, 194, 195, 197, 201, 208, 209, 214, 218, 219, 238, 242, 245, 246, 247.
Personal Development, 66, 87, 140.
Philosophical Foundations, 32.
Philosophy, 62, 72, 78, 104, 111, 117, 119, 187, 247, 251.
Policy, 8, 9, 24, 33, 41, 68, 80, 85, 114, 186, 188, 189, 190, 224, 225, 227, 231, 234, 240, 254.
Political System, 8.
Processing Approaches, 140.
Production, 7, 22, 54, 163, 174, 196, 197.
Programme Evaluations, 240, 241, 243, 244, 246, 248, 253, 255.
Programme Managers, 222, 245, 247.
Project, 16, 56, 57, 63, 68, 79, 89, 90, 102, 106, 107, 108, 120, 122, 130, 163, 165, 174, 180, 181, 183, 187, 188, 191, 205, 210, 219, 220, 237, 238.
Protection, 31, 43, 227.
Psychological Foundations, 26, 41.
Psychomotor, 52, 53.

R

Relationship, 1, 5, 8, 14, 17, 18, 19, 62, 65, 66, 74, 76, 78, 82, 83, 94, 112, 223, 235, 245.
Reporting, 63, 133, 135, 201, 203, 213, 214.
Research, 1, 6, 9, 24, 33, 36, 37, 44, 59, 75, 77, 98, 109, 110, 111, 112, 113, 114, 115, 118, 121, 123, 124, 126, 133, 134, 135, 141, 145, 150, 160, 162, 165, 168, 171, 174, 188, 189, 190, 191, 192, 193, 194, 219, 220, 223, 224, 225, 243, 249, 252, 253.

S

School Education, 44, 45, 46, 47, 91, 132, 133, 135, 197.
Scientific Ethics, 32, 33, 35, 36.
Social Development, 87, 91, 92, 95, 96, 98.
Social Interaction, 57, 141.
Social System, 9, 10.
Society, 1, 7, 8, 9, 11, 12, 24, 27, 29, 32, 35, 50, 75, 83, 86, 87, 89, 91, 98, 115, 169, 186.
Special Education, 91, 122.
Streaming Media, 174.
Subject Content, 189.
Subject Level, 115, 116.

T

Taxonomy, 6, 51, 52, 53, 55, 208.
Taylor, 109, 138, 220, 225.
Teacher Education Institutions, 134.
Team Teaching, 141, 142, 143, 144, 145, 146, 147, 148, 149, 151, 153, 154.
Technological Influence, 10.
Terminology, 53, 162, 182.
Treatment, 56, 129, 209, 215, 222, 223, 224, 225.

U

University, 1, 6, 14, 52, 59, 68, 69, 70, 83, 84, 85, 92, 110, 112, 113, 114, 116, 117, 118, 119, 120, 121, 122, 128, 137, 161, 163, 164, 165, 194, 198, 216, 217, 252.

V

Value Exceptions, 30.
Value System, 26, 28, 29, 30, 31, 32, 46.
Vocational Training, 96.

W

Welfare, 33, 35.
Wheeler, 109, 111, 113, 114.
Wisdom, 249, 250.
World Wide Web, 161, 162, 165, 168, 169, 171.

□□□